Corporate Finance

Corporate Finance

Aiden Preston

Larsen & Keller
www.larsen-keller.com

Corporate Finance
Aiden Preston
ISBN: 978-1-64172-103-5 (Hardback)

Larsen & Keller
Published by Larsen and Keller Education,
5 Penn Plaza,
19th Floor,
New York, NY 10001, USA

Cataloging-in-Publication Data

Corporate finance / Aiden Preston.
p. cm.
Includes bibliographical references and index.
ISBN 978-1-64172-103-5
1. Corporations--Finance. 2. Business enterprises-- Finance. I. Preston, Aiden.
HG4026 .C67 2019
658.15--dc23

Printed and bound in China.

For more information regarding Larsen and Keller Education and its products, please visit the publisher's website www.larsen-keller.com

Table of Contents

Preface

Corporate finance is an area of finance, which deals with an analysis of the sources of capital, the financial structure of a corporation, resource allocation and the strategies for increasing the value of the firm. The principal objective of corporate finance is to increase the value of the enterprise to shareholders. This is achieved by striking a balance between investments and payment of dividends to shareholders. Corporate finance comprises of the two sub-disciplines of capital budgeting and working capital management. This book is compiled in such a manner, that it will provide in-depth knowledge about the theory and practice of corporate finance. It outlines the processes and applications of corporate finance in detail. It is an essential guide for both academicians and those who wish to pursue this discipline further.

To facilitate a deeper understanding of the contents of this book a short introduction of every chapter is written below:

Chapter 1, Corporate finance is an area of finance that studies the capital structure of an organization and its sources of funding as well as strategizing ways to appreciate the value of the firm. This chapter has been carefully written to provide an introduction to corporate finance and includes topics like capital investments, capital financing and financial statement analysis. **Chapter 2**, The manner in which a corporation finances its assets through equity, debt or hybrid securities is termed its capital structure. The aim of this chapter is to explore the concept of capital structure and its theories for a holistic understanding of corporate finance. It elucidates the varied aspects like multiple capital structure, optimal capital structure, complex capital structure, Modigliani–Miller theorem, pecking order theory, etc. **Chapter 3**, A corporate bond is the bond that is issued by a corporation for raising finance/capital. A company may use different kinds of debts for financing its operations as part of its corporate finance strategy. The simplest corporate debt can be in the form of a term loan. The stock of a corporation is the capital that is raised by a corporation through the subscription and issuance of shares. The stock of a corporation refers to the equity stock of the owners of the corporation. The diverse aspects of corporate bond, debt and stock have been thoroughly discussed in this chapter, such as convertible bond, bearer bond, shares outstanding, common stock, preferred stock, etc. **Chapter 4**, An interest rate refers to the interest due per a specific period, for an amount of money lent, borrowed or deposited. The elements of time value of money and income analysis are also integral to the field of corporate finance. The topics elaborated in this chapter on nominal interest rate, real interest rate, time value of money, bond valuation, bond convexity and bond duration will help in developing a better perspective of interest rate, time and income analysis. **Chapter 5**, A dividend is the payment a corporation makes to its shareholders, usually in the form of a distribution of the profits earned or surplus achieved. This chapter discusses in detail the varied concepts and theories related to dividend and the distribution of profits, such as dividend policy, dividend yield and dividend payout ratio. **Chapter 6**, The management of a company's working capital for the sustainment of business operations is called working capital management. It involves the management of short-term assets and short-term liabilities. This chapter closely examines the key concepts of working capital management, such as working capital, accounting liquidity, financial ratio, economic value added, debtor finance, etc. for an extensive understanding of the subject.

I owe the completion of this book to the never-ending support of my family, who supported me throughout the project.

Aiden Preston

An Introduction to Corporate Finance

Corporate finance is an area of finance that studies the capital structure of an organization and its sources of funding as well as strategizing ways to appreciate the value of the firm. This chapter has been carefully written to provide an introduction to corporate finance and includes topics like capital investments, capital financing and financial statement analysis.

Finance is the life blood of business. It is required by all types of companies. It is required for starting a company. It is required for running a company. It is required for the survival, stability and growth of a company. It is required for expansion and diversification of a business. Finance is also required for closing down the company.

Corporate finance understands the financial problems of the organisation beforehand and prevents them. Capital investments become an important part of corporate financial decisions such as, if dividends should be offered to shareholders or not, if the proposed investment option should be rejected or accepted, managing short-term investment and liabilities.

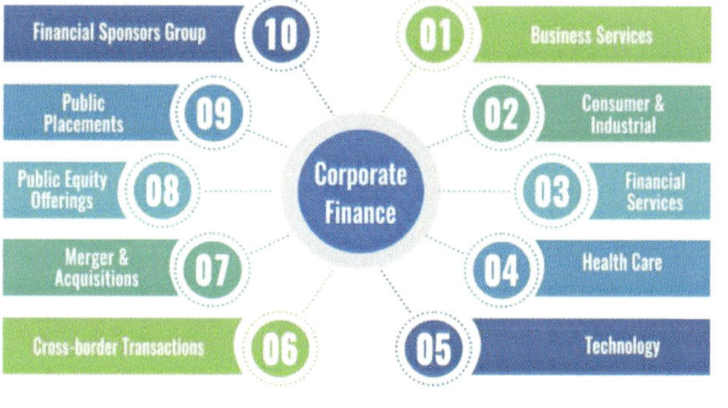

Corporate finance is different from business finance, while business finance refers to finance to all types of business such as partnership firms, joint stock companies, etc., corporate finance includes, planning, raising, investing and monitoring of finance in order to achieve the financial goals of the organization.

Finance Planning

In the planning phase, corporate finance needs to get a clear perspective on certain aspects, essentially the finance of the company has to be decided on questions like, what are the sources of finance, how much finance is required by the company and will it be profitable?

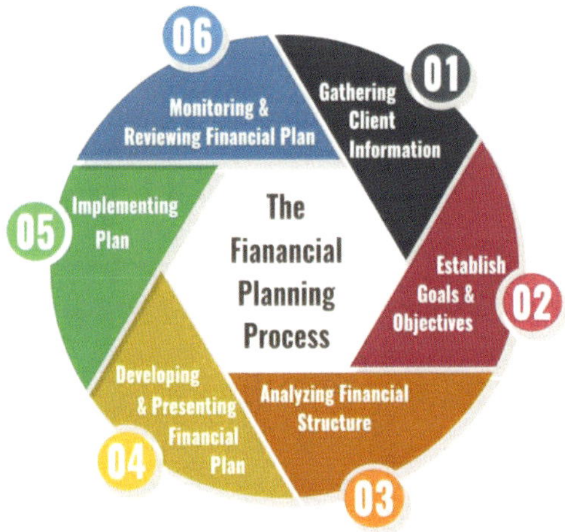

Raising Capital

Making capital investments is perhaps one of the most important tasks of corporate finance, which has serious business implications. To raise the finance, the corporate finance has to raise money from the company with the assistance of sources like shares, debentures, banks, financial institutions, creditors etc. A company may also choose to sell stocks to equity while raising long-term funds for business expansion. Capital financing is a very delicate balancing act. Corporate finance is also supposed to manage short-term financial management with a goal to have enough liquidity to carry out other operations of the organisation.

Investing Capital

There are two types of corporate finance, fixed capital and working capital. As the name suggests fixed capital is used to purchase fixed assets like land, building, property, machinery, etc.., while working capital is generally used to purchase raw material and manage day to day fixed expenses like overheads, salaries etc. Financing and investing decisions are like two sides to the same coin. The organisation raises finances only when they have suitable projects. In corporate finance there are various tools and techniques which help take appropriate informed investing decisions, hence it is very vital for the financial health of an organisation.

Monitoring the Finance/Managing Risks

Monitoring finance is a science, there is a method to it, it is a very complex job. It requires many tools and techniques. Corporate finance has to control and manage the finance of the company, they have to minimise the risk of investment and at the same time assure maximum returns on the invested capital.

The following points bring out the importance of corporate finance:

1. Research and Development: Corporate Finance is needed for Research and Development. Today, a company cannot survive without continuous research and development. The company has to go on making changes in its old products. It must also invent new products. If not, it will be get automatically thrown out of the market.

2. Motivating Employees: Manager and employees must be continuously motivated to improve their performance. They must be given financial incentives, such as bonus, higher salaries, etc. They must also be given non-financial incentives such as transport facilities, canteen facilities (eatery), etc. All this requires finance.

3. Promoting a Company: Finance is needed for promoting (starting) a company. It is needed for preparing Project Report, Memorandum of Association, Articles of Association, Prospectus, etc. It is needed for purchasing Land and Buildings, Plant and Machinery and other fixed assets. It is needed to purchase raw materials. It is also needed to pay wages, salaries and other expenses. In short, we cannot start a company without finance.

4. Smooth Conduct of Business: Finance is needed for conducting the business smoothly. It is needed as working capital. It is needed for paying day-to-day expenses. It is needed for advertising, sales promotion, distribution, etc. A company cannot run smoothly without finance.

5. Expansion and Diversification: Expansion means to increase the size of the company. Diversification means to produce and sell new products. Modern machines and modern techniques are needed for expansion and diversification. Finance is needed for purchasing modern machines and modem technology. So, finance becomes mandatory for expansion and diversification of a company.

6. Meeting Contingencies: The Company has to meet many contingencies. For e.g. sudden fall in sales, loss due to natural calamity, loss due to court case, loss due to strikes, etc. The company needs finance to meet these contingencies.

7. Government Agencies: There are many government agencies such as Income Tax authorities, Sales Tax authorities, Registrar of Companies, Excise authorities, etc. The company has to pay taxes and duties to these agencies. Finance is needed for paying these taxes and duties.
8. Dividend and Interest: The Company has to pay dividends to the shareholders. It has to pay interest to the debenture holders, banks, etc. It also has to repay the loans. Finance is needed to pay dividends and interest.
9. Replacement of Assets: Plant and Machinery are the main assets of the company. They are used for producing goods and services. However, after some years, these assets become old and outdated. They have to be replaced by new assets. Finance is needed for replacement of old assets. That is, finance is needed to buy new assets.

Stakeholder

A stakeholder is any individual or organisation that is affected by the activities of a business. They may have a direct or indirect interest in the business, and may be in contact with the business on a daily basis, or may just occasionally.

Stakeholders can be internal or external. Internal stakeholders are people whose interest in a company comes through a direct relationship, such as employment, ownership or investment. External stakeholders are those people who do not directly work with a company but are affected in some way by the actions and outcomes of said business. Suppliers, creditors and public groups are all considered external stakeholders.

An Example of an Internal Stakeholder

Investors are a common type of internal stakeholder and are greatly impacted by the outcome of a business. If, for example, a venture capital firm decides to invest $5 million into a technology startup in return for 10% equity and significant influence, the firm becomes an internal stakeholder of the startup. The return of the company's investment hinges on the success, or failure, of the startup, meaning it has a vested interest.

An Example of an External Stakeholder

External stakeholders are a little harder to identify, seeing as they do not have a direct relationship with the company. Instead, an external stakeholder is normally a person or organization affected by the operations of the business. When a company goes over the allowable limit of carbon emissions, for example, the town in which the company is located is considered an external stakeholder because it is affected by the increased pollution.

Conversely, external stakeholders may also sometimes have a direct effect on a company but are not directly tied to it. The government, for example, is an external stakeholder.

When it makes policy changes on carbon emissions, continuing from above, the decision affects the operations of any business with increased levels of carbon.

Types of Stakeholders

Any action taken by any organization or any group might affect those people who are linked with them in the private sector. For examples these are parents, children, customers, owners, employees, associates, partners, contractors, and suppliers, people that are related or located nearby.

Primary Stakeholders: Usually internal stakeholders, are those that engage in economic transactions with the business (for example stockholders, customers, suppliers, creditors, and employees).

Secondary Stakeholders: Usually external stakeholders, are those who – although they do not engage in direct economic exchange with the business – are affected by or can affect its actions (for example the general public, communities, activist groups, business support groups, and the media).

Excluded Stakeholders: Those such as children or the disinterested public, originally as they had no economic impact on business. Now as the concept takes an anthropocentric perspective, while some groups like the general public may be recognized as stakeholders others remain excluded. Such a perspective does not give plants, animals or even geology a voice as stakeholders, but only an instrumental value in relation to human groups or individuals.

The definition of corporate responsibilities through a classification of stakeholders to consider has been criticised as creating a false dichotomy between the "shareholder model" and the "stakeholders model" or a false analogy of the obligations towards shareholders and other interested parties.

Applications of the Term

Examples of a Company's Stakeholders

Stakeholders	Stakeholder's concerns
Government	taxation, VAT, legislation, employment, truthful reporting, legalities, externalities...
Employees	rates of pay, job security, compensation, respect, truthful communication, appreciation, acknowledgement, recognition.
Customers	value, quality, customer care, ethical products.
Suppliers	providers of products and services used in the end product for the customer, equitable business opportunities.
Creditors	credit score, new contracts, liquidity.
Community	jobs, involvement, environmental protection, shares, truthful communication.
Trade unions	quality, worker protection, jobs.

Owners	profitability, longevity, market share, market standing, succession planning, raising capital, growth, social goals.
Investors	return on investment, income.

Company Stakeholder Mapping

A narrow mapping of a company's stakeholders might identify the following stakeholders:

- Employees
- Communities
- Shareholders
- Creditors
- Investors
- Government
- Customers
- Owners
- Financiers
- Managers

A broader mapping of a company's stakeholders may also include:

- Suppliers
- Distributors
- Labor unions
- Government regulatory agencies
- Government legislative bodies
- Government tax-collecting agencies
- Industry trade groups
- Professional associations
- NGOs and other advocacy groups
- Prospective employees
- Prospective customers
- Local communities

- National communities
- Public at Large (Global Community)
- Competitors
- Schools
- Future generations
- Analysts and Media
- Research centres

In Management

In the last decades of the 20th century, the word "stakeholder" became more commonly used to mean a person or organization that has a legitimate interest in a project or entity. In discussing the decision-making process for institutions—including large business corporations, government agencies, and non-profit organizations—the concept has been broadened to include everyone with an interest (or "stake") in what the entity does. This includes not only vendors, employees, and customers, but even members of a community where its offices or factory may affect the local economy or environment. In this context, a "stakeholder" includes not only the directors or trustees on its governing board (who are stakeholders in the traditional sense of the word) but also all persons who paid into the figurative stake and the persons to whom it may be "paid out" (in the sense of a "payoff" in game theory, meaning the outcome of the transaction). Therefore, in order to effectively engage with a community of stakeholders, the organisation's management needs to be aware of the stakeholders, understand their wants and expectations, understand their attitude (supportive, neutral or opposed), and be able to prioritize the members of the overall community to focus the organisation's scarce resources on the most significant stakeholders.

Example

For example, in the case of a professional landlord undertaking the refurbishment of some rented housing that is occupied while the work is being carried out, key stakeholders would be the residents, neighbors (for whom the work is a nuisance), and the tenancy-management team and housing-maintenance team employed by the landlord. Other stakeholders would be funders and the design-and-construction team.

The holders of each separate kind of interest in the entity's affairs are called a constituency, so there may be a constituency of stockholders, a constituency of adjoining property owners, a constituency of banks the entity owes money to, and so on. In that usage, "constituent" is a synonym for "stakeholder".

In Corporate Responsibility

In the field of corporate governance and corporate responsibility, a debate is ongoing about whether the firm or company should be managed for stakeholders, stockholders (shareholders), or customers. Proponents in favour of stakeholders may base their arguments on the following four key assertions:

1) Value can best be created by trying to maximize joint outcomes. For example, according to this thinking, programs that satisfy both employees' needs and stockholders' wants are doubly valuable because they address two legitimate sets of stakeholders at the same time. There is evidence that the combined effects of such a policy are not only additive but even multiplicative. For instance, by simultaneously addressing customer wishes in addition to employee and stockholder interests, both of the latter two groups also benefit from increased sales.

2) Supporters also take issue with the preeminent role given to stockholders by many business thinkers, especially in the past. The argument is that debt holders, employees, and suppliers also make contributions and thus also take risks in creating a successful firm.

3) These normative arguments would matter little if stockholders (shareholders) had complete control in guiding the firm. However, many believe that due to certain kinds of board of directors structures, top managers like CEOs are mostly in control of the firm.

4) The greatest value of a company is its image and brand. By attempting to fulfill the needs and wants of many different people ranging from the local population and customers to their own employees and owners, companies can prevent damage to their image and brand, prevent losing large amounts of sales and disgruntled customers, and prevent costly legal expenses. While the stakeholder view has an increased cost, many firms have decided that the concept improves their image, increases sales, reduces the risks of liability for corporate negligence, and makes them less likely to be targeted by pressure groups, campaigning groups and NGOs.

Stakeholder Theory

Post, Preston, Sachs, use the following definition of the term "stakeholder": "A person, group or organization that has interest or concern in an organization. Stakeholders can affect or be affected by the organization's actions, objectives and policies. Some examples of key stakeholders are creditors, directors, employees, government (and its agencies), owners (shareholders), suppliers, unions, and the community from which the business draws its resources. Not all stakeholders are equal. A company's customers are entitled to fair trading practices but they are not entitled to the same consideration as the company's employees. The stakeholders in a corporation are the individuals and constituencies that contribute, either voluntarily or involuntarily, to its wealth-creating capacity and activities, and that are therefore its potential beneficiaries and/or risk bearers." This definition differs from the older definition of the term stakeholder in Stakeholder theory that also includes competitors as stakeholders of a corporation. Robert Allen Phillips provides a moral foundation for stakeholder theory in Stakeholder Theory and Organizational Ethics. There he defends a "principle of stakeholder fairness" based on the work of John Rawls, as well as a distinction between normatively and derivatively legitimate stakeholders. Real stakeholders, labelled stakeowners: genuine stakeholders with a legitimate stake, the loyal partners who strive for mutual benefits. Stakeowners own and deserve a stake in the firm. Stakeholder reciprocity could be an innovative criterion in the corporate governance debate as to who should be accorded representation on the board. Corporate social responsibility should imply a corporate stakeholder responsibility.

Problems with Stakeholders

A common problem that arises with having numerous stakeholders in an enterprise is their various self-interests may not all be aligned. In fact, they may be in direct conflict. The primary goal of a corporation, for example, from the viewpoint of its shareholders, is to maximize profits and enhance shareholder value. Since labor costs are a critical input cost for most companies, a company may seek to keep these costs under tight control. This might have the effect of making another important group of stakeholders, its employees, unhappy. The most efficient companies successfully manage the self-interests and expectations of their stakeholders.

Shareholder

A shareholder can be an individual person, a group of people, a partnership, another company, or any other kind of organisation or corporate body.

Shareholders are the owners of companies limited by shares. They are also called 'members' and they agree to become part of a company by taking a minimum of one share in it. The quantity of shares held by each person represents how much of the business they own. In turn, this determines their decision-making power, their profit entitlement, and the extent of their personal liability for debts.

As the beneficial owners of a limited company, they are not involved in day-to-day management or financial affairs. These duties are the responsibility of directors. Members can, however, appointed themselves as directors.

There may be only a small number of shareholders (as is common with a privately-held business), or there may be thousands, as is common for a publicly-held company whose shares trade on a major stock exchange.

Shareholders buy shares in a business with the intent of earning a profit either from dividend payments made by the company, or through an appreciation in the market price of the shares. They may also buy shares in order to gain control over a business.

In the event of the liquidation or sale of a business, shareholders have residual rights to any remaining assets. This means that all creditors are paid from the assets or proceeds of the business first, after which remaining funds (if any) are distributed to the shareholders based their relative proportions of ownership of the business. If there are no residual assets remaining after creditors have been paid, then the shareholders will have lost their investment in the business.

Conceptually, shareholders have the greatest risk of loss of any stakeholders in a business, but can also profit the most handsomely from an increase in the value of the business.

Types of Shareholders

Common Shareholders

Many companies only have one type of share, known as common stock. As such, most shareholders are common or "ordinary" stockholders and when you read about share valuations, this is usually what is meant. Common shareholders have an ownership stake in the company. This comes with various rights including:

- The right to vote on major company decisions such as board elections, or how to respond to a hostile takeover.
- The right to receive any common dividends the board declares.
- The right to participate in a distribution of assets when the company is liquidated.

Common shareholders also have the right to file a class action lawsuit against the company if there is an act of wrongdoing that potentially harms the company or negatively affects the value of its common shares. This enables them to exercise considerable control over how the company is managed and how it handles strategies for growth.

Preferred Shareholders

Preferred shareholders own a different type of share known as preferred stock. These shareholders have no voting right, which means they cannot influence management decision-making. What they do have, is a guaranteed right to be paid a fixed amount of dividend every year, and to receive this payment before the company pays a dividend to common shareholders. The amount of dividend is fixed or attaches to a specified interest rate; for example, a $10, 5-percent preference share would pay an annual dividend of 50 cents.

Both common stock and preferred stock can go up in value if the company is doing well. However, common stock is more volatile and tends to experience much larger capital gains – or losses – than preferred stock. The right to receive a fixed dividend means that preferred stock behaves more like debt than a common share. Investors who wish to generate a predictable investment income – rather than ride the volatility of the stock market – typically choose to own preferred shares.

Shareholder Rights

Shareholders enjoy certain rights, which are defined in the corporation's charter and by laws. Shareholders have the following rights:

- To inspect the company's books and records.
- To sue the corporation for misdeeds of the directors and officers.
- Common shareholders are entitled to vote on major corporate matters, such as who sits on the board of directors and whether a proposed merger should occur.
- If a company liquidates its assets, its shareholders have a right to a proportionate allocation of the proceeds. However, creditors, bondholders, and preferred stockholders have precedence over common stockholders.
- To receive a portion of any dividends the company declares.
- To attend, in person or via conference call, the corporation's annual meeting to learn about the company's performance.
- Common shareholders who do not attend the voting meeting have the right to vote by proxy through the mail or online.

The specific rights allocated to both common and preferred shareholders are outlined in each company's corporate governance policy.

Shareholder Loan

Shareholder loans, as the name implies, are funds that shareholders lend to the corporation in which they hold shares. To qualify as a shareholder loan under Internal Revenue Service code, the loan cannot be to start a corporation; it must be an established business. IRS regulations do allow loans from a shareholder who holds all of a corporation's shares.

Loan Contract

The Internal Revenue Service recommends that shareholder loan contracts include specifics that would be found in a loan between unrelated parties. Contracts should specify the loan amount, interest rate applied, repayment term, and the consequence for not repaying appropriately. If borrowers are providing collateral to secure the loan, the contract should state the collateral offered and the disposition in case of non-payment.

Below Market Loans

Shareholder loans charging no interest or an interest rate below the federal rate are known as below-market loans. The Internal Revenue Service publishes the federal rate monthly in the Internal Revenue Bulletin, available on the IRS website. Loans with advantageous interest rates have varied tax consequences for borrowers, depending on the details of the arrangement.

Tax Implication of Loans

The amount of interest not charged by below-market loans is considered income and is taxable to the borrower. Taxpayers determine this taxable amount by subtracting the amount of interest actually paid from the amount of interest that would be due if the shareholder loan was charged at the federal rate. Borrowers should compute this amount annually and report when filing their taxes.

Low-Balance Loans

The foregone interest may not be taxable on a below-market loan with a balance due of $10,000 or less. Corporations must have entered into the low-interest or interest-free loan with a principal purpose other than tax avoidance to qualify for this exception. Shareholder loans originating with a larger balance qualify for this exemption once the balance falls to $10,000 or less.

Shareholder loans impact an owner's basis in the company and any pass-through losses reported on the owner's tax return. At a minimum, loans must be made using the fair market value interest rate; otherwise, the transaction becomes complicated for financial-reporting and tax purposes. The interest on loans can be written off by a corporation, which is a benefit of using debt financing. If a company is already highly leveraged, additional debt may further reduce cash reserves through regular loan payments.

Applications

- This form of financing is quite common while funding young companies with positive cash flows because such firms are still not able to raise debt from banks but need debt anyway to create a tax shield.
- The contribution of shareholder loans to a corporation's capital structure generally relieves the corporation's debt load and is, therefore, used in leveraged buyouts to manage a degree of leverage.
- Shareholders can extend the loan in distressed or near-default situations to save the company.

Shareholder Loan Rule

Generally, when a shareholder takes a loan out of the corporation and does not repay it within a year, the loan will be included as income on shareholder's personal tax return in the year the loan was made. The "loan" here may not necessarily be cash withdrawn from the corporation. It can also be in the form of a payment made by the corporation on your behalf. Under the current tax rules, funds withdrawn from the corporation as a loan are not taxable in the hands of the shareholder. The shareholder could legitimately take funds out of the corporation indefinitely without incurring adverse tax consequences. To prevent this, the Canada Revenue Agency (CRA) imposed a rule to treat the loan as a benefit to the shareholder and tax the amount as income if it is not repaid within one year after the end of the taxation year of the lender in which the loan was made.

Shareholder Value

Shareholder value is that delivered to shareholders of a corporation because of management's ability to increase sales, earnings and free cash flow over time, leading to the ability for companies to increase dividends and encourage capital gains for its equity owners. A company's shareholder value depends on strategic decisions made by its board of directors and senior management, including the ability to make wise investments and generate a healthy return on invested capital. If this value is created over the long term, the share price increases and the company can pay larger cash dividends to shareholders.

Shareholder value involves managers giving priority to the interests of a single stakeholder, the investor, instead of seeking to balance the interests of multiple stakeholders, as in traditional theories of the firm, or to maximize managerial rewards, as in revisionist analyses.

Shareholder value has been linked with theories of investor engagement and therefore has similar objectives and ideas towards creating a single value for each shareholder. Shareholder value both encourages top management to focus on individual investors and it also creates a value system, whereas the top management have the possibility to monitor the performance and the effectiveness of the decisions.

Shareholder value as a single concept cannot function properly, however if it is tied with the corporate governance of the company. These two concepts works as support systems for the company.

Constructing the institutions of shareholder value forms of corporate governance involves four elements directly relevant to investor engagement. The first element is defining and determining the interests of principles and their agents. The second element is establishing the mechanisms for monitoring the performance of agents and disciplining perceived malfeasance. The third element is the process of molding the perceived interests of principals and agents, to establish congruence between them. The fourth element is providing incentives for agents to maximize performance in the pursuit of principals' interests.

Top 20 factors that maximise shareholder value:

1. Unique and sustainable market positioning – What do you do that others don't? Why will customers keep coming back to you? Have you ensured your proposition is continually developed ahead of the competition?
2. A revenue model that indicates that the company will become more profitable as it grows – So that revenues and the gross margins arising will outgrow the increase in cost of sales and fixed costs.
3. High proportion of contracted and recurring revenues – One off project revenue is valued lower that recurring revenue because of the repeated cost of customer acquisition and because it undermines the shareholder value that can be deduced from assured business going forward.
4. Simple story – A core product/service line that is performing well with no clutter such as significant (untested) new product lines draining EBITDA or expensive forays into new markets including new geographic territories.
5. Competent, successful, stable and motivated senior management team – Plus a plan for succession in each operational discipline. And/or the ability to be convincing that there can be continuity of key management if that's what the buyer wants.
6. Strong and sustained growth – Such that the acquirer can count on continued shareholder value growth and so that the NPV of that growth can be expressed in present sale price. The more this is evidenced by the forward order book the better.
7. Embedded upside or strategic advantage for buyer – Impressive, credible and content customer base with potential to increase their spend, management team with capabilities beyond current organisation, operating cost savings, intellectual property, geographic presence.
8. Operating in a hot sector – Like social networking or climate change/renewable energy but if not then find a link, however tenuous to those hot sectors.
9. Generating cash – Doing so from a good EBIT margin % at a sufficient level to be entirely self-funding for future growth from working capital for capex enhancements to product/service development.
10. Build barriers to entry – It could be your price point for services, your 'must have' technologies, your IP, your dominant market share, your exclusive agreements with leading suppliers or simply a locked in customer base, but

your value will increase if your future revenue is less threatened by new competition.

11. Maximise the number of 'Blue Chip' clients – Valuations can double if the bulk of your revenue is with recognized solid successful client organizations.

12. Gain an insight into the buyer's motivation and needs – The more you know about their business and which of their needs acquiring you solves, the more you can play up those attributes of your company the better. It could be you are 'in the way' of a buyer executing an industry roll-up strategy who wants to 'bulk up' fast.

13. High market profile – Already on the radar of potential buyers for some while. High profile so that its noticed and high profile in terms of being company that's obviously written or spoken about as a being successful and 'one to watch'. This can be enhanced by overt endorsements from major trusted branded partners or from awards.

14. A rival bidder – The more the better, and if they know each other better still. An auction conducted by advisers is best.

15. Get ready to sell – Who's taking the lead in negotiations, are all the 'actors' in the campaign fully briefed, do you have 'sales collateral' prepared (PPT and business plans plus all financials that make it easy to understand the business), are all the company secretarial docs up to date including monthly CEO reports etc. is there complete file of customer, supplier and staff contracts gathered together. Appoint an M&A adviser early in the process.

16. Credible reason why you want to sell – An answer to 'if you're growing that fast or doing that well why are you selling, and why now?' Show strength in purpose and don't give any sign of desperation – buyers detect weakness quickly.

17. No poison pills or factors that will cause transaction delays – Operating costs (particularly staff costs) out of line with market competition (either under or over paid), complex and over generous options agreements, high accumulated potential redundancy costs, spider web of personal guarantees or agreements that will be expensive/impossible to unwind quickly, litigation, lack of IP protection from URLs to registered trademarks to patents, weak or unsubstantiated data in the due diligence pack.

18. Impressive board and shareholder register with one or more high profile name NEDs – Gives buyer opportunity to retain the benefit of their contribution, and implicitly lends gravitas to the company by their presence on the board or investor list.

19. Commitment to sell – Be convincing that you are going to sell to the highest bidder and that you're not testing the market for a valuation.

20. Evidence of long term relationships with professional service providers – Banks, Lawyers, Accountants etc.

There is a linkage between value drivers and shareholder value, and therefore it is important for the management to be able to identify the specific value drivers.

The most common shareholder value drivers used for assessment in companies.

Table: Shareholder Value drivers.

Growth Rate	- Maintain competitive prices. - Pursue market-share opportunities to gain scale economies in production.
Operating profit margin	- Achieve relevant economies of scale for each of the value activities. - Introduce mechanisms to improve the rate of learning. - Search for cost-reducing linkages with suppliers product design, quality, packaging and order processing. - Search for cost-reducing linkages with channels. - Eliminate overhead that does not add value to product.
Working capital investment	- Minimize cash balance. - Manage accounts receivable to reduce average number of days outstanding. - Minimize inventory impairing required level of customer service.
Fixed capital investment	- Promote policies to increase utilization of fixed assets. - Obtain productivity-increasing assets. - Sell unused fixed assets. - Obtain assets at least cost.
Cost of capital	- Target an optimal capital structure. - Select least-cost debt and equity instruments. - Reduce business risk factors in manner consistent with strategy.

In table are the most common value drivers that companies are using when assessing the competiveness of the company. Many companies have different levels of management and therefore it is important to implement these strategic management decisions to focus on creating shareholder value.

Understanding the drivers of the business that are most critical to value creation enables management to focus its analysis more efficiently on key elements of a strategy.

The importance of strategically understand the different value drivers are the key aspects for the top management to evaluate the results more specifically.

To understand better what management need to consider when evaluating the shareholder value of the company is based on values. Value is abstract in its nature, managers need to know more concretely and clearly the target measures that derive the value of their business. In this model common financial variables and their variations are used as input variables to synthesize the market value added (MVA).

Shareholder Value and Effective Capital Market

The importance of shareholder value has a strong link to an efficient capital market. The capital market is the means to allocating resources from less to more profitable ones and therefore more socially productive uses in a more timely manner.

The shareholder value corporate governance regime provides the institutional framework for the effective operation of capital markets. The development of capital markets which efficiently maximize shareholder value depends on establishing the appropriate institutional, legal, and cultural preconditions which foster effective corporate governance systems and align the interests of senior managers with those shareholders.

The first precondition for an effective capital markets deals with the institutional conditions and it relates to the integrity of information, the ability of adequate information on corporate performance and the means of availability of evaluations.

The second precondition includes the rights of shareholders. It supports an effective evaluation process of the management performance.

The first one deals with the legal regulations of corporate procedures, exclusively the responsibilities and roles of the board of directors, including the oversight role of non-executive directors. The second aspect deals with the legal regulation of information intermediaries, including disclosure and conflicts of interests.

Thirdly, the cultural precondition is the creation of an environment of high trust, and especially the trust between economic relationships.

Trust may be personal, based on the knowledge of the character of the individual parties, or contractual, based on the acceptance of written commitments, underwritten by third parties and the legal system. Personal and contractual trust coexist.

The trust between economical relationships is linked to the effective capital market, and therefore have an importance for transparency of information over the capital market. Furthermore, the importance of shareholder value grown as a critical aspect for companies through the years.

There are six major sets of reasons for the growth of shareholder value as the driving force of capitalist development as is shown in table.

Table: Set of reasons of shareholder value growth

The first set of reasons	Financial development
Second set of reasons	Political development and changes in the environment
Third set of reasons	Economic and related to changes in the structure of the economy
Fourth set of reasons	Comparative international economic performance
Fifth set of reasons	Internationalization of capital flows
Sixth set of reasons	Academic specialism and growing the popularity of rational social choice theory

From table above it can been seen how shareholder value and effective capital market support each other. For a company to be successful in the capital market and maintain the market share, it is important to offer transparent economical information to gain trust among shareholders.

Most companies today relay on the amount of investments from the shareholders and that is how shareholder value needs to be created and maintained. Therefore, many companies have created investor engagement management to be able to maintain investor relationships currently and for the future funding aspects.

The goals of engagement vary, from advancing specific shareholder interests to achieving broad social objectives. So, too, do the forms of engagement, which range from simple requests for information to hostile targeting of company personnel or key practices. Some investors begin their intervention with behind-the scene influence and negotiation in private, at cooperative meetings with company management.

Maintaining the investor relationship can be done with many types of tools and techniques regarding contracts and constant monitoring. When the company has created investor engagement as part of handling investor relationships, and this gives investors a possibility to influence key management practices to ensure a growth in shareholder value.

There are a few types of investor engagement that involves different types of investor relationships. The first type of investor engagement deals with more traditional approach and it is more indirect, from this approach investor concede strategic and operational controls of the company management. The second type of investors engagement is more focused on the external management, in which the investors have possibilities to handle mechanisms to control the functioning of the capital market without being involved in the internal workings of the company.

The third type of investor engagement involving investors influencing internal governance of the company for the sole purpose at maximizing shareholder value. The fourth type deals with investors discussing strategic and operational matters with the corporate management as shown in table.

Table: Investor engagement in corporate governance

Type	Description	Action
Indirect/laissez-faire	Management-led/" let well alone"	Capital withdrawal; (threat of) exit
External	Exit protection	Shareholder resolutions
Internal	Influence board membership and independence	Non-executive Appointments
Negotiator	Face-to-face dialogue	Persuasion; relational financing
Direct	Investor-led	Executive appointments

Managing investor relationships deals with different aspects of the relationship, since it a two-way, both investors and managers try to control their end of the relationship.

In seeking to manage investors, senior managers possess four major types of resources: material, legal, cultural and intellectual. The first major type of resource is material, the direct control of corporate assets, including financial assets, subject to auditor oversight. The second major resource is the legal protection of managerial authority. Thirdly, both state authorities and the broader culture, which endorse corporate managerial authority, support this legal protection. Lastly the fourth major resource is knowledge and understanding. Managers generally have deeper knowledge and understanding of corporate affairs than investors or their agents, and are able to deploy than greater knowledge in cases of disagreement.

There are many arguments from the perspective of shareholder value and how it is linked to investor management, and also therefore the importance of handling the relationships between investors and managers.

There are two types of arguments for shareholder value. The first is economic and concerns the relationship between shareholder value and economic performance, evaluating the expectation that shareholder value maximizes corporate performance and therefore collective welfare. The second is social and political, claiming that shareholder value is necessary to compensate investors for their acceptance of unsecured risks.

It has been argued that shareholder value when done correctly contributes to the higher capital returns, however, the efficiency of using shareholder value as part of the strategic decision-making requires a more fundamental analysis.

There are five main justifications for the view that shareholder value is the most efficient form of corporate governance. The first justification deals with the internal means of management control. The second justification includes the efficient of capital market and how the resources are flowing in the market to ensure that investments flow from low areas of production to high production. The third justification handles the role of the capital market when introducing new capital. The fourth justification handles high risk investments. The last justification deals with corporate managers.

These justifications support shareholder value and its importance in creating and keeping up a strong relationship between investors and corporate managers. Investors are expecting high returns on the investments and therefore seek support from managers to keep a stable platform between investments and the capital market. For an effective capital market to be successful, it needs to be possible to find parts of the market where funds are being used ineffectively and it is up to managers to be able to transfer the funds to be used more effectively.

The corporate control that handles the mechanism of transferring resources from less profitable to high profit. Other ways of monitoring performance and preventing entrenchment of company interests, and therefore, include political regulations and production. One of the main reasons of arguing for shareholder value means that markets are acting more efficiently.

It has been shown that shareholder value has a natural preference for profit distribution rather than earnings retention, and therefore the process of innovation is less positive.

There are shown to be more benefits of using this type of innovations, however, it is getting harder to identify these particular innovations.

For that reason, shareholder value must be aligned with the incentives of senior managers and investors. Without external monitoring and alignment between investors and corporate management interests, what can affect managers' incentives and be distorted.

Distribution of the financial means has been one of the main concerns, when it comes to efficient control and equal share of assets and income. When companies are not focusing on equal distribution, it can have a negative effect on the company. The company has to put high focus on minimizing risks by developing strategies in production.

The fluidity of capital markets can foster a rapid development of new technology and development of technology sectors and revitalize existing sectors, and therefore, the importance of implementing shareholder value as part of the objective of the company strategies do affect the capital market and its transparency. Shareholder value is strongly linked to investor engagement and maximizing profit returns.

There are three major categories of justifications for investor engagement. The first major category deals with shareholder value as its primary function as increasing shareholder wealth. The second category is ensuring company conformity. The third major category deals with achieving both economic and social objectives.

These conditions are crucial for a working investor engagement between investors and corporate managers. The balance between transparency and goals for both investors and managers keep the relationship open among the company and capital market. In shareholder value thinking, the corporation is considered as a unity, seeking to maximize shareholder value; a plurality of interests leads to conflict and reduces corporate efficiency.

Measuring Shareholder Value

Measuring shareholder value has been subjected to much criticism when it comes to the traditional financial measurements that have been used in evaluating company performance. For that reason, new financial measurements have merged and there has been an attempt to give a broader perspective of the performance rather than using the traditional measurements, which only measure the specific part of the company performance.

In simple terms, shareholder value is about putting the needs of shareholders at the heart of management decisions. It is argued that shareholders invest in a business with a view to maximizing their financial returns in relation to the risks that they are prepared to take. As managers are appointed by the shareholders to act on their behalf, management decisions and actions should therefore reflect a concern for maximizing shareholder returns.

For understanding of shareholder value measurement, is it important to evaluate the stages of creating shareholder value. Creating shareholder value for the company is a four-stage process.

The first stage is to set objectives for the business that recognize the central importance of maximizing shareholder returns. This will set a clear direction for the business. The second stage is to establish an appropriate means of measuring the returns, or value, that have been generated for shareholders. The third stage is to manage the business in such a manner as to ensure that shareholder returns are maximized. This means setting demanding targets and then achieving them through the best possible use of resources, the use of incentives systems and the embedding of a shareholder value culture throughout the business. The final stage is to measure the shareholder returns over a period of time to see whether the objectives have actually been achieved.

Table: The four-stage process for creating shareholder value

Set objectives that recognize the supremacy of shareholders.
Select an appropriate measure of shareholder return.
Generate shareholder returns through focused management.
Measure shareholder returns to see whether the objectives are being achieved.

As it can be shown in table below, the traditional measurements used in the evaluating business is too narrow and do not take into consideration the whole perspective of the business. The traditional measurements do not consider the shareholder value and therefore should not be used to measure shareholder returns.

Table: Four broadly problems with using accounting profit, or a ratio based on profit, to assess shareholder returns

Profit is measured over a relatively short period of time (usually one year).	When measuring shareholder returns, are we considered with maximizing shareholder returns for long term.
Risk is ignored.	A fundamental business reality is that there is a clear relationship between the level of returns achieved and the level of risk that must be taken to achieve those returns.
Accounting profit does not take account of all of the costs of the capital invested by the business.	The conventional approach to measuring profit will deduct the cost of borrowing in arriving at profit for the period, but there is no similar deduction for the cost of shareholder funds.
Accounting profit reported by a business can vary according to the particular accounting policies that have been adopted.	The way that accounting profit is measured can vary from one business to another. Some businesses adopt a very conservative approach, which would be reflected in particular accounting policies.

The traditional measurements that have been used for evaluating the company's financial and performance position in the capital market do not consider all the important aspects of shareholder value to be able to get an overall image if shareholder has increased or decreased.

The most common traditional measurement that has been used for business evaluation is Net Present Value (NPV Analysis).

The Net Present Value analysis covers the long-term aspects when evaluating shareholder value of a business, however, this measurement lacks the account of risk and acknowledge of the cost of shareholders' funds. Another problematic aspect deals with the company's possibilities to affect the measurement by choosing different accounting policy choices.

The Net Present Value Formula

$$NPV = -C_0 + \frac{C_1}{1+r} + \frac{C_2}{(1+r)^2} + \ldots + \frac{Cr}{(1+r)^T}$$

$$-C_0 = Initial\ Investment$$

$$C = Cash\ Flow$$

$$r = Discount\ Rate$$

$$T = Time$$

Net Present Value is more easily understood, when using the formula in practice, and to do so the cash flows must be discounted for the desired rate of return.

Shareholders have a required rate of return. Managers must strive to generate long-term cash flows for shares (in the form of dividends or proceeds from the sale of the shares) that meet this rate of return. The expectation that the managers will, in the future, fail to generate the minimum required cash flows will have the effect of reducing the value of the business as a whole and, therefore, of the individual shares in it.

The NPV approach is considered the most important criterion when assessing shareholder value changes; however, when extending the NPV analysis to Shareholder Value Analysis (SVA), it considers the maximization of shareholder value and how it affects the NPV approach of evaluation of the overall business.

When evaluating an investment project, shareholder wealth will maximize the net present value of the cash flows generated from the project. Leading on this, the business as a whole can be viewed as simply a portfolio of investment projects and so to maximize the wealth of shareholders the same principles should apply. The SVA approach involves evaluating strategic decisions according to their ability to maximize value, or wealth, for shareholders.

Part of evaluating businesses using NPV and SVA approaches is to measure free cash flow, which are the available funds generated from business actions and given to shareholders for long-term purposes.

This shortened approach leads us to identify the key variables in determining free cash flows as being: sales revenue, operating profit margin, tax rate, additional investment in working capital and additional investment in non-current assets. These are value drivers of the business that reflect key business decisions. These decisions convert into free cash flow and finally into shareholder value. The managers can take actions which includes as follows: Boost sales revenue, increase operating profit margin, reduce the effective tax rate, reduce the investment in working capital and reduce the investment in non-current assets.

Implentation of Shareholder Value in Decision-making

Shareholder value can be implemented in the decision-making process, is it important for the top management to decide what value drivers are implemented in the process.

The first step is to achieve consensus among senior management about the overall goal of the organization- what constitutes success? It takes time to achieve consensus, and the implications of accepting shareholder value as the governing objective are far-searching.

For this to be possible, the company needs to have a stable and growing revenue base, and these are a result of satisfied customers and motivated staff. Successful organizations do not underestimate the time challenge that it takes for adjusting and bringing new performance measurements.

Implementing a new performance measurement measure such as economic profit or a new incentive scheme may be necessary, but will certainly not be sufficient to maximizing value. While concepts such as economic profit are relatively simple, their implications for management behavior can be wide-ranging.

When improvements are done to the strategic decision-making process, is it important for the top management to have the right tools and information to discourage fear of new decisions and also to have a damage control plan.

Fear can result in attempts to discredit the approach. All manner of justifications will be made to protect the status quo and retain businesses that are destroying value. The most important tools that top management can use to dissolve the fear among their staff, is train both top management and all the staff members. Training gives the staff a chance to understand the importance of change and how it is implemented into their daily work. For the training to work sufficiently, the top management needs to build so called know-how, a value capability, inside the company and these principles needs to be set up with the right type of tools and supported by appropriate techniques such as returns, risk and growth.

Important aspects of implementing shareholder value need to be understood by the management. A part of shareholder value approach deals with heavy focus on returns, risk and growth, and therefore, is it important to fully manage all of these aspects.

In the beginning, after changes have been made by implementing shareholder value into the decision-making process, the company must use more of the equity. When this is done correctly, the returns will increase as an effect from implementing shareholder value principles.

The trick in managing shareholder value is to select those growth opportunities that will deliver returns above the cost of equity. The top management has to choose strategies that promote shareholder value, but also provide the operating management with tools and techniques to assess risk and evaluate the shareholder returns.

For the transparency of the capital market to be successfully communicated, the company must have open communication. This open communication will reflect on the share price as well as play a big role for investors, since this creates trust between investors and the company for future investments.

Those who support this approach argue that SVA can be a powerful tool for strategic planning. SVA can be extremely useful when considering major shifts of direction such as acquiring new businesses, selling existing businesses, developing new products or markets and reorganizing or restructuring the business, because it takes account of all the elements that determine shareholder value.

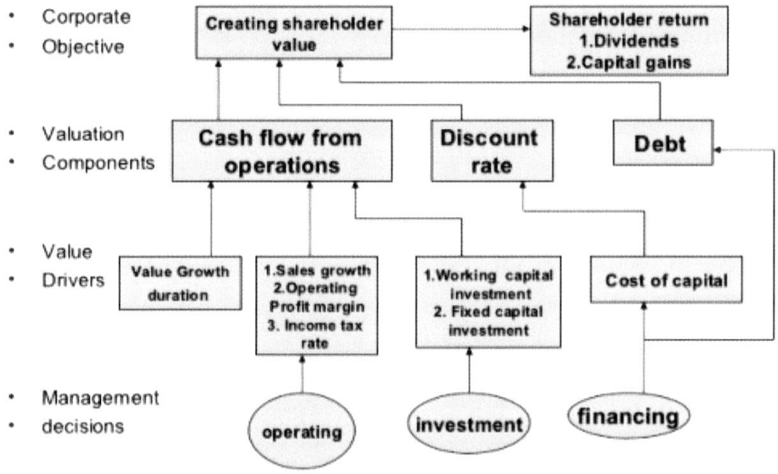

Figure: Shareholder value creation network

Sensitivity analysis can be used in identifying the most effective variables of shareholder value. Furthermore, with each value driver, which has a direct effect on free cash flow, can the management emphasize performance of the company's shareholder and value targets. The supporters of SVA approach believes that this measurement should replace all the traditional measurements used when evaluating value creation such as profit, earnings per share and return on ordinary shareholders' funds.

We can see that SVA is really a radical departure from the conventional approach to managing a business. It will require different performance indicators, different financial reporting systems and different management incentive methods. If SVA is implemented, it can provide the basis of targets for managers to work towards, on a day-to-day basis, which should promote maximization of shareholder value.

Another traditional measurement that has been evaluated as being used rather than SVA approach is Economic Value Added (EVA) approach.

Economic Value Added Formula;

$$\text{EVA} = \begin{matrix}\text{Net Operating} \\ \text{Profit after Taxes}\end{matrix} - \left(\text{Capital} * \begin{matrix}\text{The Cost} \\ \text{of capital}\end{matrix} \right)$$

Only when EVA is positive it can be said that the business is increasing shareholder wealth. To maximize shareholder wealth, managers must increase EVA by as much as possible. EVA relies on conventional financial statements (income statement and statement of financial position) to measure the wealth created for shareholders.

One of the benefits of EVA is that managers are subjected to discipline as a result of the charge for capital that has been invested. EVA approach encourages managers to use the business resources effectively.

When comparing EVA with the SVA approach, both approaches in fact are quite close to each other. Both approaches calculate the shareholder wealth in the same way, since EVA approach calculates shareholder value by adding to the capital invested to the present value of future EVA flows and then deducts the market value of any borrowings.

Table: Two approaches to determining shareholder value

SVA Approach: Discounted free cash flows	EVA Approach: Capital Invested + Discounted future EVA flows
Total Business value: Less	Total Business value: Less
Market value of borrowings: Equals	Market value of borrowings: Equals
Shareholder value	Shareholder value

Although both EVA and SVA are consistent with the objective of maximizing shareholder wealth and, in theory, should produce the same decisions and results, the supporters of EVA claim that this measure has a number of practical advantages over SVA. One such advantage is that EVA sits more comfortably with the conventional financial reporting systems and financial reports. There is no need to develop entirely new systems to implement EVA as it can be calculated by making a few adjustments to the conventional income statement and statement of financial position.

It is also claimed that EVA is more useful as a basis for rewarding managers. Both EVA and SVA support the idea that management rewards should be linked to increases in shareholder value. This should ensure that the interests of managers are closely aligned to the interests of shareholders. Under SVA approach, management rewards will be determined on the basis of the contribution made to the generation of long-term cash flows. However, there are practical problems in using SVA for this purpose.

Economic value added is committed to maximizing shareholder wealth, however, using EVA methods, the results will reflect on long-term goals. The company needs to have stable level of revenue, operating assets and borrowings before drastic changes to the shareholder value can be made.

Another traditional measurement that has been widely used in calculating shareholder value. Return on Investment (ROI) as shown in Figure 12, which is used in identifying business operating divisions on profitability and it works well alongside with other approaches when assessing shareholder value.

Return on Investment Formula;

$$ROI = \frac{(\text{Investment Gain} - \text{Investment Cost})}{(\text{Investment Cost})} \times 100$$

When defining divisional profit for this ratio, the purpose for which the ratio is to be used must be considered. For evaluating the performance of a divisional manager, the controllable profit is likely to be the most appropriate, whereas for evaluating the performance of a division, the divisional profit for the period is likely to be more appropriate.

ROI is a measure of profitability, as it relates profits to the size of the investment made in the division. This relative measure allows comparison between divisions of different sizes. However, ROI has its drawbacks. Where it is used as the primary measure of performance for divisional managers, there is a danger that it will lead to behavior that is not really consistent with the interests of the business overall.

When measuring performance of the business, ROI is mostly used as primary measurement. However, ROI only measures performance short-term, and therefore, important investments can be rejected even though the investments can have a positive NPV long-term wise.

Shareholder Value Creation

When the company is maximizing shareholder returns for its shareholders, it is important for the company to be able to create value by understanding the strong linkage between shareholders and the value created.

Shareholder value creation should be the ultimate goal of strategy- the primary measurement guiding corporate decisions and the myriad day-to-day choices of any business units.

When implementing value-based planning as another objective for creating shareholder value, is it possible for the company to maximize company profits and ensure a stable growth in the future.

Shareholder value has become the key metric that allows the company to measure in dollar values the long-term impact of management decisions and business strategies. This shift in the way the company keeps score has been driven by significant regulatory and competitive changes over the past ten years.

Part of the value creation deals with identifying its market share by evaluating financial performance by using Economic Value Added (EVA) as well as other traditional measurements.

Economic value added is a period measure of shareholder value that focuses on both after tax income and asset utilization. One of the features of the shareholder value system that makes it attractive for companies was the correlation between economic value added and the market premium, or market value added. Market value added tracks economic value added much more closely than more popular measures such as earnings per share, operating margins or return on equity.

When managers are evaluating the company performance as well as the its competitiveness, the measurement of economic value added will encourage managers to become more entrepreneurial, and therefore, they are able to identify successful strategies.

Measuring economic value added encourages managers to develop an entrepreneurial spirit. It does this by identifying the winners – those units creating returns beyond the average that shareholders could expect to earn by investing in companies of similar risk. It also provides a powerful decision-making tool for operations managers by identifying factors that aid in creating an excess over minimum required returns. Over time, this is how shareholder value is created.

One aspect of shareholder value creation is implementing a value-based management system, which can be used as an important tool in the decision-making process.

Value-based management is a multi-period system for measuring economic value added that can be used for planning and resource allocation, including decisions on investments and acquisitions. New tools were put in place to enhance communications and institutionalize the adoption of VBM. However, the most important part of the process was obtaining strong top management support and involvement. VBM has fundamentally changed the way managers think about their businesses. It enables them to consider both short-and long-term impact their decisions will have on the value of the corporation by helping them identify and quantify the sources of value creation – key value drivers for their business. In order to optimize shareholder value, they must evaluate the effect all their decisions have on their value drivers.

Value-based management has been proven to be an effective tool when analysing financial performance for a company, and how these financial decisions affect the decision-making process from top management. By reevaluating these financial units has companies been able to make critical decisions according to their strategic and financial fit.

By focusing on shareholder value, companies will discover opportunities to achieve significance growth with profitability that will be rewarding to all – employees, customers, and shareholders.

When it comes to adopting a new approach that affects an extremely important part of the company regarding the future of investments and compensation, the overall attitude is filled with skepticism. Therefore, the role of the company's top management is to show a supporting attitude towards new ideas and approaches.

Economic value added is a one-period, accounting-based measure of value creation. It is defined as the spread between your return on invested capital minus your weighted average cost of capital, multiplied by the amount of capital invested.

The discounted cash flow value of your company – the basis of shareholder value management – is a multi-period measure where forecasted free cash flow is discounted at the weighted average cost of capital. Both measures accurately reflect careful management of the balance sheet as well as the income statement.

For compensation purposes, however, economic value added is better.

Using value-based management as one of the yardsticks of company's financial targets has created a positive perspective that has influenced the long-term goals of companies. However, the type of perspective requires a balanced top management with great focus on the task at hand.

When top management becomes convinced that value based performance measures results in better decisions because they are linked more directly to the creation of shareholder value in the marketplace, then the company is ready to consider implementing value-based management. Top management's responsibility is to prepare the ground for its wholehearted adoption.

As part of using shareholder value implemented into the decision-making process, is it important to understand how value is created? When value has been successfully created for the shareholders, this in return will create a higher amount of future investments for the company.

Table: Implementation of shareholder value management.

A strong focus on strategic planning at both the business unit and corporate levels with corporate strategy evolving from business unit strategies.
Integrated performance measurement driven down to grass roots level of the front line management.
Planning led by those responsible for implementation.
Excellent flow of information and facts used to provide benchmarking and facebased decision making.
Genuine dialogue – two –way communication between layers of management.
Planning ingrained in the culture of the organization.

Capital Investments

The term capital investment has two usages in business. First, capital investment refers to money used by a business to purchase fixed assets, such as land, machinery, or buildings.

Secondly, capital investment refers to money invested in a business with the understanding that the money will be used to purchase fixed assets, rather than used to cover the business's day-to-day operating expenses. For example, to purchase additional capital assets a growing business may need to seek a capital investment in the form of debt financing from a financial institution or equity financing from angel investors or venture capitalists.

Objectives of Capital Investment

There are various investment avenues in the market today. Nevertheless, the main objectives behind any kind of capital investment remains more or less the same – growth, income and safety. Investors can have more than one of these objectives in mind while investing but success usually comes with the expense of one of these objectives.

Safety: Safety of our capital investment depends largely on the type of investment. Even though there is no hundred percent safe investment, government issued securities, corporate bonds etc. are some that fall in the relatively safe categories. These securities can usually preserve your capital and at the same time provide you with a specific return rate.

Income: A certain amount of safety would have to be sacrificed if income from capital investment is the main aim. Increase in yields is associated with a certain degree of risk, thus as yield increases, safety decreases. Safest investments in the markets are usually the ones that have the lowest income returns. It is generally seen that all investors look for income generation too in their portfolios.

Growth: Capital gain on the capital investment comprises growth of capital and this is different from yield. Capital gains occur when security bought is sold at a higher price than its original purchase price. On similar lines, if security is sold at a lower price, capital loss occurs. Thus, long term growth occurs at the expense of ongoing investment returns.

Apart from these three main objectives, there can be secondary objectives too while considering capital investment. These usually include tax minimizations and a certain degree of liquidity. Capital investment that give tax exemptions can reduce overall income tax burden. Likewise, liquidity of investment is highly desired by investors. Many investments are illiquid and cannot be converted to cash immediately. Shares are relatively the most liquid investment since they can be sold in a day or two.

Thus capital investment with any of the above mentioned five objectives usually becomes a success when one of two of the objectives are sacrificed for the benefits of the others. Mostly, income and safety have to be shown the way out if growth is desired, thus most of the investment portfolios should be guided by one predominant objective. Other objectives would occupy less significant positions in the investment scheme of things.

Hence investments must be planned accordingly, with appropriate weightings assigned to each objective. The choice of objective should largely depend on factors like:

- Temperament of investor
- Stage of life
- Family situation
- Marital status
- Income etc.

Capital investment is spending that has long term value to a business. This is often contrasted with expenses that have value to the business today. The following are common types of capital investment.

Land and Buildings

The purchase of land and buildings for your business.

Construction

Any costs that go into constructing a building or structure is a capital investment.

Landscaping

Productive changes to land such as an irrigation system for a farm.

Improvements

Maintenance is expensed. Significant improvements to capital that significantly extend its lifespan are capital investments.

Furniture and Fixtures

Anything that goes into the interior of a building such as a couch or painting that is part of the decor.

Infrastructure

Infrastructure such as networking equipment for a data centre.

Machines

Machines such as an industrial robot.

Computing

Computing equipment and devices.

Vehicles

Vehicles used in your business.

Software Development

Software development can often be capitalized for software that is successfully operationalized. A failed project is expensed. As such, a project needs to be finalized before it can be capitalized.

Software

Software you buy from other firms is typically considered a capital investment. Recurring as-you-go license fees are expensed.

Acquisitions

Acquiring another company that adds value to your business.

Branding

A brand purchased from another company is a capital investment. Developing your own brand is typically viewed as an expense.

Intellectual Property

Intellectual property purchased from another company such as a patent. Your own research and development is typically viewed as an expense with some exceptions.

There are five ways you can break down how to approach finding capital for your business. Each has pros and cons. Depending on how much you need, weigh the options of what you are giving for what you are getting.

1. Personal Assets
2. Family and Friends
3. Banks and SBA Lenders
4. Crowdfunding Resources
5. Professional Investors

Personal Assets are exactly as they sound. These are the business owners' personal savings, home equity, investment and retirement portfolios. If a business owner deems that $100,000 in capital investment is required to establish the business and also to then get the required equipment and launch, he might use his own resources to accomplish this, so he would retain 100 percent of his company's ownership. To do this properly, the owner loans his business the money and pays himself back over time.

Family and Friends as a capital investment category is probably one of the riskiest places to seek capital investment. The reason is that this category is made up not of business associates; this category is made up of the people you will have in your life, even if the business fails. Family gatherings and holidays can become tense, if your business is not performing and your family investor wants to see results. The investment might come by way of a loan or by taking an ownership interest in the company.

Banks and SBA Lenders have small business programs for capital investment. These are loans. A business might qualify for an SBA loan that includes the real property purchase, along with capital for machinery. Many businesses don't realize that the SBA has funding programs valued for millions of dollars depending on the project, industry and size of the company.

Crowdfunding Resources have become more and more relevant in the digital-savvy entrepreneurs' toolbox. Once upon a time, a business had to hold an official stock offering to get hundreds, if not thousands of investors, to each invest a small amount. These stock offerings are highly regulated and complicated, but crowdfunding resources such as Kickstarter have simplified the way a business can raise funds and launch a new company or product.

Professional Investors generally hold the title of a venture capitalist or an angel investor. Venture capitalists usually work with large financial institutions and raise very large amounts of money. Angel investors tend to focus on younger businesses in their first, most vulnerable years. Professional investors scrutinize the deals, and may take on a managerial role instead of only a silent investor's role, to ensure that the company grows to the capacity it needs, to turn a profit for the investor.

Types of Business Funding

There are three basic ways to look at funding, and an infinite number of ways to mix and match financing options. Funding methods include debt financing, equity financing and lease financing.

Debt Financing involves getting a loan. This form of financing can be seen as less risky to some investors, who understand that if a company experiences financial hardship, the order of repayments are payroll, taxes, loans and then equity investors are paid the remaining amount, if any. Since debt is higher on the repayment platform than equity, some investors will look to structure the capital investment as a debt instrument.

Equity Financing is when someone gets some level of ownership in the company for the investment. This is like a stock bought on the NASDAQ stock exchange. A company might have one million outstanding shares. If someone invests $500,000 for $1 per share, they now have a 50-percent ownership of the company. Business owners risk losing the company to a takeover, if an equity owner is able to get the majority of shares through investment. When a business owner starts his company, he might own it for the minimal initial investment and his sweat equity (meaning his time and energy to grow the business). Investors will seek an owner who has some actual cash invested in the business. This is called "having skin in the game."

Lease Financing is often used to obtain large equipment, machinery or vehicles needed for business operations. Often, these items are expensive, with massive depreciation and potentially becoming quickly outdated. By leasing, the business owner is able to obtain things with less capital investment over time, and to switch out machinery for updated models in shorter periods of time, while keeping the most updated operating equipment, thereby moving the company forward. Usually, this type of leasing is offered by a bank or financial institution via the distributor that's offering the equipment for lease. For example, a tractor-trailer might be leased with terms offered through the tractor company partnering with the financial institution.

Using Capital Investment Funds

Although a business owner can seek funds for both long- and short-term capital needs, capital investment tends to be for long-term needs. The reason is that a company requiring capital to maintain operations suggests that a company isn't sustainable or is already at potential risk of financial hardship. Capital investment is designed to grow a business. The way an investor looks at capital investment is to consider how the business revenues will grow, based on the funds.

Thus, a business could use the capital investment to open a second location in a busier location that could triple the overall revenues of the company. The purchase of a centralized warehouse could make fulfillment easier for the company and reduce transit costs by 30 percent, allowing the company to become more efficient, and thus, more profitable. As a business owner seeking capital investment, consider the bigger items required for growth. A new trucking line, real property for office space, mechanic bays or even large computer hardware and software networks, could be funded with capital investment.

Capital Investment vs. Working Capital

As already mentioned, most investors don't want a business to use any capital investment for working capital. Even though the terms sound similar, they refer to two very different things. Working capital is your money used for operating expenses and operations. An investor would like to see a minimum of one year's worth of working capital before even talking about capital investment. Capital investment is often an equity position that seeks to provide the funds for the long-term growth strategies, not to sustain the immediate operating costs.

There is one period in which an investor is more likely to include working capital into the investment capital. This is at the start of the company, before anything has been launched. However, even in a situation like this, most venture capitalists or angel investors want to see that the business owner has some ability to put some capital investment into his own company. Rarely will professional investors risk money strictly on the experience and sweat equity of a business owner. Working capital should be well-managed, with business owners maintaining strict standards. Expenditures should match budget expectations and the company revenues should be consistent. This is the scenario in which a company seeking growth funds is attractive to investors. Investors like to see that working capital is being used wisely and the company is being intelligently managed for growth. This gives owners credibility when seeking investment capital.

Importance of Capital Investment Decisions

Investment decision otherwise known as capital budgeting decision is perhaps the most important decision taken by a Finance Manager. Whatever is the objective of the firm, whether profit maximization or wealth maximization, capital budgeting decision affects performance of the firm decisively. These investment decisions have the following implications for the firm.

They define the strategic focus and direction of the business. The capital expenditure made in new investments may result in entry into new products, services or new markets.

Capital budgeting decisions require large funds and generally have long repayment periods. The results of capital budgeting continue to impact the finances of the firm for many years. Due to long project life, assessment involves number of years of future events leading to difficulty and uncertainty regarding the accuracy of assessment.

Capital budgeting decisions are mostly irreversible. They involve investment in plant and machinery or new soft wares or technology etc. They are normally industry or user specific. If the project does not proceed ahead, it may be difficult to find buyers for the assets and the only alternative would be scar the assets at a huge loss.

An under investment will result in inefficient operations like inadequate capacity and, increased expenditure, non competitive production and pricing resulting in poor market share and have serious financial implications. On the other hand an over investment would result in higher depreciation and increased operating costs and result in liquidity crisis.

Therefore Finance Managers carefully align capital investments with the short term and long-term company goals, analyze impact of such investments over a period of time and scrutinize capital budgeting decisions both technically and financially. While the capital investment decisions of the firm are very important, Finance Managers face certain difficulties in fully appraising the decisions. These difficulties are inevitable and are due to the very nature of the investment, which relies on future events for achieving the objects of the investment. The major difficulties are:

- Measurement of the costs and benefits: Measuring the costs and benefits of the proposal is difficult particularly when involves intangibles like benefits of employment, improvement in quality of life etc.
- Uncertainty associated with future: The precise value of cost and benefit is difficult to quantify as benefits are spread over a period in future which is characterized by uncertainty.
- Difficulty of comparison: As the costs and benefits of an investment proposal is spread over period of time occurring at different points of time, comparing the values on a commons basis is difficult due to the changes in value of money over a time horizon.

Type of Capital Investment Decesions

A. On the Basis of Firm's Existence

1. Buying New and Replacement of Fixed Asset

If company or firm is newly incorporated, it will take which new fixed asset should be purchased but an existing form will take capital investment decisions relating to replacement of any old fixed asset due to modernization. Company will take decision which fixed asset should be replaced and which new fixed asset should be purchased after replacement.

2. Expansion of Fixed Asset

In these decision, company may take decision to extend fixed asset for improving efficiency. Suppose, we have one plant but due to increase of demand, we can take decision for expansion it.

3. Diversification Decision

For reducing risk of business, company may take decision to diversify its business or market. Suppose, one company is doing online business of selling laptop, it may take decision for selling of ipad or mobile. But for this, it need to invest big amount.

B. On the Basis of Decision Situation

1. Mutually Exclusive Decision

Mutually exclusive decision are those capital decision in which we accept one proposal and other will not include in it. For example, we can buy semi automatic machine or highly automatic machine. If we have taken decision for buying semi automatic, it means, we will not use highly automatic machine. Cost of major factor for taking such decision. Cheap investment may be our best option. Following example may explain it more.

Example EVALUATING LEASE VERSUS PURCHASE ALTERNATIVES

Laven and Co., Certified General Accountants, are considering whether to buy or lease a photocopy machine. A five-year lease requires payments of \$550 at the beginning of every three months. The same machine can be purchased for \$9000 and would have a trade-in value of \$1500 after five years. If the accounting firm can borrow funds at 11% compounded quarterly, should it buy or lease a photocopy machine?

Solution

The preferred alternative is the one having the lower present value of expenditures (net of any amounts recovered from resale, salvage, or trade-in).

As discussed in Section 13.2, leasing is usually regarded as an alternative to borrowing the funds to purchase the asset. Therefore, the appropriate discount rate to use in the present-value calculation is the firm's cost of borrowing. The lease payments form a simple annuity due with

$$PMT = \$550 \qquad n = 4(5) = 20 \qquad \text{and} \qquad i = \frac{11\%}{4} = 2.75\%$$

The present value of the lease payments is

$$\begin{aligned} PV(\text{lease}) &= PMT\left[\frac{1-(1+i)^{-n}}{i}\right] \times (1+i) \\ &= \$550\left(\frac{1-1.0275^{-20}}{0.0275}\right)(1.0275) \\ &= \$8605 \end{aligned}$$

BGN mode
20 N
11 I/Y
550 +/− PMT
0 FV
P/Y 4 ENTER
Same C/Y
CPT PV
Ans: 8605

If the photocopy machine is purchased, there will be an initial expenditure of \$9000 and a \$1500 recovery from trading it in five years later. The present value of these payments is

$$\begin{aligned} PV(\text{purchase}) &= \$9000 - FV(1+i)^{-n} \\ &= \$9000 - \$1500(1.0275^{-20}) \\ &= \$9000 - \$872 \\ &= \$8128 \end{aligned}$$

Same *N*, *I/Y*, *P/Y*, *C/Y*,
0 PMT
1500 FV
CPT PV
Ans: −872
\+ 9000 =
Ans: 8128

Hence, purchasing of the photocopy machine is the lower cost alternative. The current economic value of the difference in net costs over the five-year lifetime is \$8605 − 8128 = \$477.

2. Accept and Reject Decision

If we take decision of accept and reject of project on its return basis, then these type of decision will be accept and reject decisions.

3. Contingent Decision

These are the decisions in which one decision requires other decision. Suppose, we have to take decision to make plant, for making plant, we also have to take decision for making building and buying of machinery.

Capital Financing

Capital financing refers to any capital that is the outcome of a business decision. In other words, a company's current assets and liabilities, but it is more complicated than that. Capital financing is a term used to describe four distinct forms of capital: working capital, debt capital, equity capital and venture capital. These designations refer to the source of the capital financing.

Working Capital Financing

Working capital financing is financing that comes from the net profits a company earns; it is the revenue that remains after the company's current debts or obligations are paid. Examples include cash, receivables, inventory and assets. Working capital has important uses in meeting the daily expenses of the company, as well as funding unexpected costs like low profits or equipment repair, recurring costs like insurance and business licenses, inventory for raw materials, cyclical costs such as seasonal increases in sales, or operating costs until payment is received from customers and costs related to process and operational improvements. These functions are largely the domain of working capital financing.

Debt Capital Financing

Debt capital financing is financing that comes from debt, usually in the form of a loan, line of credit, lease or some other such method. Debt capital can be used to finance working capital needs but it is more commonly used to finance growth, acquisitions, expansion, product development, share repurchasing and other such investments that generate income directly, over an extended period of time.

Equity Capital Financing

Equity capital financing is used similarly to debt capital financing, but instead of coming from debt like a loan, the extra capital comes from a company issuing stock or equity. Issuing stock has a benefit of allowing the company to avoid the interest and fees associated with taking on debt, but it carries with it a large potential negative in that issuing equity dilutes the company, its holdings and its ability to make decisions.

Venture Capital Financing

Venture capital can take the form of debt capital financing or equity capital financing, only instead of the company pursuing this directly, it sells an interest in the company, either via a stake in the company or a promise of future earnings, and generates capital in this way. Aside from working capital financing, venture capital financing has the least cost of any financing types. However, this type of financing is usually only a possibility for companies that are extremely high growth and early in its lifecycle.

Financial Statement Analysis

Financial statement analysis involves gaining an understanding of an organization's financial situation by reviewing its financial statements. This review involves identifying the following items for a company's financial statements over a series of reporting periods:

- Trends: Create trend lines for key items in the financial statements over multiple time periods, to see how the company is performing. Typical trend lines are for revenues, the gross margin, net profits, cash, accounts receivable, and debt.
- Proportion analysis: An array of ratios are available for discerning the relationship between the size of various accounts in the financial statements. For example, one can calculate a company's quick ratio to estimate its ability to pay its immediate liabilities, or its debt to equity ratio to see if it has taken on too much debt. These analyses are frequently between the revenues and expenses listed on the income statement and the assets, liabilities, and equity accounts listed on the balance sheet.

Financial statement analysis is an exceptionally powerful tool for a variety of users of financial statements, each having different objectives in learning about the financial circumstances of the entity.

Users of Financial Statement Analysis

There are a number of users of financial statement analysis. They are:

- Creditors: Anyone who has lent funds to a company is interested in its ability to pay back the debt, and so will focus on various cash flow measures.
- Investors: Both current and prospective investors examine financial statements to learn about a company's ability to continue issuing dividends, or to generate cash flow, or to continue growing at its historical rate (depending upon their investment philosophies).
- Management: The company controller prepares an ongoing analysis of the company's financial results, particularly in relation to a number of operational metrics that are not seen by outside entities (such as the cost per delivery, cost per distribution channel, profit by product, and so forth).

- Regulatory authorities: If a company is publicly held, its financial statements are examined by the Securities and Exchange Commission (if the company files in the United States) to see if its statements conform to the various accounting standards and the rules of the SEC.

Methods of Financial Statement Analysis

There are two key methods for analyzing financial statements. The first method is the use of horizontal and vertical analysis. Horizontal analysis is the comparison of financial information over a series of reporting periods, while vertical analysis is the proportional analysis of a financial statement, where each line item on a financial statement is listed as a percentage of another item. Typically, this means that every line item on an income statement is stated as a percentage of gross sales, while every line item on a balance sheet is stated as a percentage of total assets. Thus, horizontal analysis is the review of the results of multiplc time periods, while vertical analysis is the review of the proportion of accounts to each other within a single period.

The second method for analyzing financial statements is the use of many kinds of ratios. Ratios are used to calculate the relative size of one number in relation to another. After a ratio is calculated, you can then compare it to the same ratio calculated for a prior period, or that is based on an industry average, to see if the company is performing in accordance with expectations. In a typical financial statement analysis, most ratios will be within expectations, while a small number will flag potential problems that will attract the attention of the reviewer.

There are several general categories of ratios, each designed to examine a different aspect of a company's performance. The general groups of ratios are:

1. Liquidity ratios: This is the most fundamentally important set of ratios, because they measure the ability of a company to remain in business. Click the following links for a thorough review of each ratio.

- Cash coverage ratio: Shows the amount of cash available to pay interest.
- Current ratio: Measures the amount of liquidity available to pay for current liabilities.
- Quick ratio: The same as the current ratio, but does not include inventory.
- Liquidity index: Measures the amount of time required to convert assets into cash.

2. Activity ratios: These ratios are a strong indicator of the quality of management, since they reveal how well management is utilizing company resources. Click the following links for a thorough review of each ratio.

- Accounts payable turnover ratio: Measures the speed with which a company pays its suppliers.
- Accounts receivable turnover ratio: Measures a company's ability to collect accounts receivable.
- Fixed asset turnover ratio: Measures a company's ability to generate sales from a certain base of fixed assets.
- Inventory turnover ratio: Measures the amount of inventory needed to support a given level of sales.
- Sales to working capital ratio. Shows the amount of working capital required to support a given amount of sales.
- Working capital turnover ratio: Measures a company's ability to generate sales from a certain base of working capital.

3. Leverage ratios: These ratios reveal the extent to which a company is relying upon debt to fund its operations, and its ability to pay back the debt. Click the following links for a thorough review of each ratio.

- Debt to equity ratio: Shows the extent to which management is willing to fund operations with debt, rather than equity.
- Debt service coverage ratio: Reveals the ability of a company to pay its debt obligations.
- Fixed charge coverage: Shows the ability of a company to pay for its fixed costs.

4. Profitability ratios: These ratios measure how well a company performs in generating a profit. Click the following links for a thorough review of each ratio.

- Breakeven point: Reveals the sales level at which a company breaks even.
- Contribution margin ratio. Shows the profits left after variable costs are subtracted from sales.
- Gross profit ratio: Shows revenues minus the cost of goods sold, as a proportion of sales.
- Margin of safety: Calculates the amount by which sales must drop before a company reaches its break even point.
- Net profit ratio: Calculates the amount of profit after taxes and all expenses have been deducted from net sales.
- Return on equity: Shows company profit as a percentage of equity.
- Return on net assets: Shows company profits as a percentage of fixed assets and working capital.

- Return on operating assets: Shows company profit as percentage of assets utilized.

Understanding the different types of financial analysis is crucial in making informed business decisions. People who analyze the financial statements of a company include company executives, competitors, creditors, managers and potential investors. Three of the most common types of financial statement analysis are horizontal, vertical and ratio analysis.

Horizontal Analysis

A horizontal analysis compares two or more years of a company's financial statements. The analyst can find the same information from different years by reading across the page. In comparing dollar figures and percentages in this way, differences from year to year are easy to find. A variation of the horizontal analysis is called the trend analysis. The trend analysis starts with the first year a company is in business, also known as the base year. The base year percentages are shown as 100 percent, and the increase or decline in percentages can be easily shown.

Vertical Analysis

Vertical analysis is called such because the corporation's financial figures are listed vertically on the financial statement. This type of analysis involves the calculation of percentages of a single financial statement. The figures on this financial statement are taken from the company's income statement and balance sheet. Vertical financial statement analysis is also known as component percentages.

Ratio Analysis

There are several types of ratio analysis that can be used in interpreting financial statements. Ratios may be computed for each year's financial data and the analyst examines the relationship between the findings, finding the business trends over a number of years.

Balance sheet ratio analysis determines a company's ability to pay its debts and how much the company relies on creditors to pay its bills. This is an important indicator of the financial health of the corporation.

Liquidity ratios show how well the company is able to turn assets into cash. When evaluating the liquidity ratio, an analyst looks at the working capital, current ratio and quick ratio.

Working capital is a measure of cash flow. The difference between total current assets and total current liabilities equals the working capital. The working capital calculation is always a positive number.

The current ratio is a popular measure of financial strength. The current ratio is figured by dividing total current assets by total current liabilities. A favorable current ratio would be 2 to 1. If a company's current ratio is low, it may consider ways of improving this figure by decreasing the amount of financial indebtedness or putting more of the company's profits back into the working capital.

The quick ratio measures liquidity, or the ability to pay back debts in a timely manner. To figure the quick ratio, you add government securities, cash and receivables. You then divide this number by total current liabilities. A company's quick ratio is an important measure of its survivability should the sales revenues drastically decrease.

There are generally six steps to developed an effective analysis of financial statements.

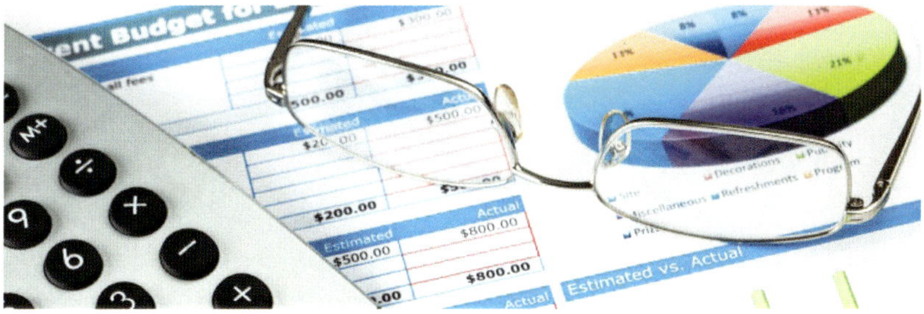

1. Identify the industry economic characteristics.

First, determine a value chain analysis for the industry—the chain of activities involved in the creation, manufacture and distribution of the firm's products and/or services. Techniques such as Porter's Five Forces or analysis of economic attributes are typically used in this step.

2. Identify company strategies.

Next, look at the nature of the product/service being offered by the firm, including the uniqueness of product, level of profit margins, creation of brand loyalty and control of costs. Additionally, factors such as supply chain integration, geographic diversification and industry diversification should be considered.

3. Assess the quality of the firm's financial statements.

Review the key financial statements within the context of the relevant accounting standards. In examining balance sheet accounts, issues such as recognition, valuation and classification are keys to proper evaluation. The main question should be whether this balance sheet is a complete representation of the firm's economic position. When evaluating the income statement, the main point is to properly assess the quality of earnings as a complete representation of the firm's economic performance. Evaluation of the statement of cash flows helps in understanding the impact of the firm's liquidity position from its operations, investments and financial activities over the period—in essence, where funds came from, where they went, and how the overall liquidity of the firm was affected.

4. Analyze current profitability and risk.

This is the step where financial professionals can really add value in the evaluation of the firm and its financial statements. The most common analysis tools are key financial statement ratios relating to liquidity, asset management, profitability, debt management/coverage and risk/market valuation. With respect to profitability, there are two broad questions to be asked: how profitable are the operations of the firm relative to its assets—independent of how the firm finances those assets—and how profitable is the firm from the perspective of the equity shareholders. It is also important to learn how to disaggregate return measures into primary impact factors. Lastly, it is critical to analyze any financial statement ratios in a comparative manner, looking at the current ratios in relation to those from earlier periods or relative to other firms or industry averages.

5. Prepare forecasted financial statements.

Although often challenging, financial professionals must make reasonable assumptions about the future of the firm (and its industry) and determine how these assumptions will impact both the cash flows and the funding. This often takes the form of pro-forma financial statements, based on techniques such as the percent of sales approach.

6. Value the firm.

While there are many valuation approaches, the most common is a type of discounted cash flow methodology. These cash flows could be in the form of projected dividends, or more detailed techniques such as free cash flows to either the equity holders or on enterprise basis. Other approaches may include using relative valuation or accounting-based measures such as economic value added.

The Next Steps

Once the analysis of the firm and its financial statements are completed, there are further questions that must be answered. One of the most critical is: "Can we really trust the numbers that are being provided?" There are many reported instances of accounting irregularities. Whether it is called aggressive accounting, earnings management, or outright fraudulent financial reporting, it is important for the financial professional to understand how these types of manipulations are perpetrated and more importantly, how to detect them.

Problems with Financial Statement Analysis

While financial statement analysis is an excellent tool, there are several issues to be aware of that can interfere with your interpretation of the analysis results. These issues are:

- Comparability between periods. The company preparing the financial statements may have changed the accounts in which it stores financial information, so that results may differ from period to period. For example, an expense may appear in the cost of goods sold in one period, and in administrative expenses in another period.
- Comparability between companies. An analyst frequently compares the financial ratios of different companies in order to see how they match up against each other. However, each company may aggregate financial information differently, so that the results of their ratios are not really comparable. This can lead an analyst to draw incorrect conclusions about the results of a company in comparison to its competitors.
- Operational information. Financial analysis only reviews a company's financial information, not its operational information, so you cannot see a variety of key indicators of future performance, such as the size of the order backlog, or changes in warranty claims. Thus, financial analysis only presents part of the total picture.

References

- Freeman, R. Edward; Moutchnik, Alexander (2013). "Stakeholder management and CSR: questions and answers". UmweltWirtschaftsForum. 21 (1): 5–9. doi:10.1007/s00550-013-0266-3
- Shareholder-loan-vs-equity-investment-78974: smallbusiness.chron.com, Retrieved 11 June 2018
- Capital-investment-2948114: thebalancesmb.com, Retrieved 19 July 2018
- Post, James (2002). "Redefining the Corporation: Stakeholder Management and Organizational Wealth". Stanford University Press. Retrieved 2009-01-29
- Examples-capital-investment-54295: smallbusiness.chron.com, Retrieved 09 July 2018
- Importance-of-capital-investment-decisions, financial-management: mbaknol.com, Retrieved 25 May 2018
- Gelter, Martin and Jurg Roth (2007). "SUBORDINATION OF SHAREHOLDER LOANS FROM A LEGAL AND ECONOMIC PERSPECTIVE" (PDF). cesifo-group.de. Retrieved 2014-02-04
- Financial-statement-analysis: accountingtools.com, Retrieved 19 April 2018
- Financial-statement-analysis: accountingtools.com, Retrieved 10 June 2018

2

Capital Structure

The manner in which a corporation finances its assets through equity, debt or hybrid securities is termed its capital structure. The aim of this chapter is to explore the concept of capital structure and its theories for a holistic understanding of corporate finance. It elucidates the varied aspects like multiple capital structure, optimal capital structure, complex capital structure, Modigliani–Miller theorem, pecking order theory, etc.

The term capital structure refers to the percentage of capital (money) at work in a busi-ness by type. Broadly speaking, there are two forms of capital: equity capital and debt capital. Each type of capital has its benefits and drawbacks, and a substantial part of wise corporate stewardship and management is attempting to find the perfect capital structure regarding risk/reward payoff for shareholders. This is true for Fortune 500 companies and for small business owners trying to determine how much of their start-up money should come from a bank loan without endangering the business.

Components

Senior Debt: A class of loans with priority on the repayment list if a company goes bankrupt. Holders of this form of financing have first dibs on a company's assets. This means that in a liquidation event, lenders holding subordinated notes are not paid out until senior creditors are paid in full. Because of the minimal risk that accompanies this block of the capital structure, senior lenders loan money at lower rates (i.e., lower interest payments and less restrictive debt covenants) relative to more junior tiers.

Subordinated Debt: A class of loans that ranks below senior debt with regard to claims on assets. For this reason, this block of the capital structure is more risky than senior borrowings. However it also comes with commensurately higher returns, usually in the form of higher interest payments.

Mezzanine Debt: A class of subordinated debt that blends equity and debt features. It therefore receives liquidation after senior capital and is generally used when traditional funding is insufficient or unavailable. Correspondingly, mezzanine firms lend at higher interest rates than traditional debt providers, and usually reserve the right to trade some of their debt for equity. Though mezzanine financing exhibits both equity- and debt-like characteristics, it's usually classified as a category within subordinated debt. For more details.

Hybrid Financing: A class of the capital structure in publicly-traded companies that also blends equity and debt features. By definition, hybrid securities are bought and sold through brokers on an exchange. Hybrid financing can come with fixed or floating returns, and can pay interest or dividends.

Convertible Debt: A class of hybrid financing. Convertible bonds are the most common type of hybrid financing, and usually take the form of a bonds that can be converted to equity. The conversion can only happen at certain points in the firm's life, the equity amount is usually predetermined, and the act of converting is almost always up to the discretion of the debt holder.

Convertible Equity: A class of hybrid financing. Convertible equity usually takes the form of convertible preferred shares, which is preferred equity that can be converted to common equity. Like convertible debt, convertible preferred shares convert into common shares at a predetermined fixed rate, and the decision to convert is typically at the owner's discretion. Importantly, the value of a firm's convertible preferred shares is usually dependent on the market performance of its common shares.

Preferred Equity: A class of financing representing ownership interest in a company. As opposed to fixed income assets (e.g., debt), equity is a variable return asset. However, preferred equity has both debt and equity characteristics in the form of fixed dividends (debt) and future earnings potential (equity). Correspondingly, it gives the holder upside and downside exposure. Its claims on the company's assets and profits come behind those of debt holders and ahead those of common stock holders. Generally, preferred equity obligates management to pay its holders a predetermined dividend before paying dividends to common shareholders. On the flipside, preferred equity typically comes without voting rights.

Common Equity: Also a class of financing representing ownership interest. Common equity is the junior-most block of the capital structure and therefore represents ownership in an business after all other obligations have been paid off. For this reason, it comes with the highest risk and the highest potential returns of any tier in the capital structure.

Importance of Capital Structure

The importance or significance of Capital Structure:

1. Increase in value of the firm:

A sound capital structure of a company helps to increase the market price of shares and securities which, in turn, lead to increase in the value of the firm.

2. Utilisation of available funds:

A good capital structure enables a business enterprise to utilise the available funds fully. A properly designed capital structure ensures the determination of the financial requirements of the firm and raise the funds in such proportions from various sources for their best possible utilisation. A sound capital structure protects the business enterprise from over-capitalisation and under-capitalisation.

3. Maximisation of return:

A sound capital structure enables management to increase the profits of a company in the form of higher return to the equity shareholders i.e., increase in earnings per share. This can be done by the mechanism of trading on equity i.e., it refers to increase in the proportion of debt capital in the capital structure which is the cheapest source of capital. If the rate of return on capital employed (i.e., shareholders' fund + long- term borrowings) exceeds the fixed rate of interest paid to debt-holders, the company is said to be trading on equity.

4. Minimisation of cost of capital:

A sound capital structure of any business enterprise maximises shareholders' wealth through minimisation of the overall cost of capital. This can also be done by incorporating long-term debt capital in the capital structure as the cost of debt capital is lower than the cost of equity or preference share capital since the interest on debt is tax deductible.

5. Solvency or liquidity position:

A sound capital structure never allows a business enterprise to go for too much raising of debt capital because, at the time of poor earning, the solvency is disturbed for compulsory payment of interest to .the debt-supplier.

6. Flexibility:

A sound capital structure provides a room for expansion or reduction of debt capital so that, according to changing conditions, adjustment of capital can be made.

7. Undisturbed controlling:

A good capital structure does not allow the equity shareholders control on business to be diluted.

8. Minimisation of financial risk:

If debt component increases in the capital structure of a company, the financial risk (i.e., payment of fixed interest charges and repayment of principal amount of debt in time) will also increase. A sound capital structure protects a business enterprise from such financial risk through a judicious mix of debt and equity in the capital structure.

Factors Determining Capital Structure

Risk of Cash Insolvency

Risk of cash insolvency arises due to failure to pay fixed interest liabilities. Generally, the higher proportion of debt in capital structure compels the company to pay higher rate of interest on debt irrespective of the fact that the fund is available or not. The non-payment of interest charges and principal amount in time call for liquidation of the company.

The sudden withdrawal of debt funds from the company can cause cash insolvency. This risk factor has an important bearing in determining the capital structure of a company and it can be avoided if the project is financed by issues equity share capital.

Risk in Variation of Earnings

The higher the debt content in the capital structure of a company, the higher will be the risk of variation in the expected earnings available to equity shareholders. If return on investment on total capital employed (i.e., shareholders' fund plus long-term debt) exceeds the interest rate, the shareholders get a higher return.

On the other hand, if interest rate exceeds return on investment, the shareholders may not get any return at all.

Cost of Capital

Cost of capital means cost of raising the capital from different sources of funds. It is the price paid for using the capital. A business enterprise should generate enough revenue to meet its cost of capital and finance its future growth. The finance manager should consider the cost of each source of fund while designing the capital structure of a company.

Control

The consideration of retaining control of the business is an important factor in capital structure decisions. If the existing equity shareholders do not like to dilute the control, they may prefer debt capital to equity capital, as former has no voting rights.

Trading on Equity

The use of fixed interest bearing securities along with owner's equity as sources of finance is known as trading on equity. It is an arrangement by which the company aims at increasing the return on equity shares by the use of fixed interest bearing securities (i.e., debenture, preference shares etc.).

If the existing capital structure of the company consists mainly of the equity shares, the return on equity shares can be increased by using borrowed capital. This is so because the interest paid on debentures is a deductible expenditure for income tax assessment and the after-tax cost of debenture becomes very low.

Any excess earnings over cost of debt will be added up to the equity shareholders. If the rate of return on total capital employed exceeds the rate of interest on debt capital or rate of dividend on preference share capital, the company is said to be trading on equity.

Government Policies

Capital structure is influenced by Government policies, rules and regulations of SEBI and lending policies of financial institutions which change the financial pattern of the company totally. Monetary and fiscal policies of the Government will also affect the capital structure decisions.

Size of the Company

Availability of funds is greatly influenced by the size of company. A small company finds it difficult to raise debt capital. The terms of debentures and long-term loans are less favourable to such enterprises. Small companies have to depend more on the equity shares and retained earnings.

On the other hand, large companies issue various types of securities despite the fact that they pay less interest because investors consider large companies less risky.

Needs of the Investors

While deciding capital structure the financial conditions and psychology of different types of investors will have to be kept in mind. For example, a poor or middle class investor may only be able to invest in equity or preference shares which are usually of small denominations, only a financially sound investor can afford to invest in debentures of higher denominations.

A cautious investor who wants his capital to grow will prefer equity shares.

Flexibility

The capital structures of a company should be such that it can raise funds as and when required. Flexibility provides room for expansion, both in terms of lower impact on cost and with no significant rise in risk profile.

Period of Finance

The period for which finance is needed also influences the capital structure. When funds are needed for long-term (say 10 years), it should be raised by issuing debentures or preference shares. Funds should be raised by the issue of equity shares when it is needed permanently.

Nature of Business

It has great influence in the capital structure of the business, companies having stable and certain earnings prefer debentures or preference shares and companies having no assured income depends on internal resources.

Legal Requirements

The finance manager should comply with the legal provisions while designing the capital structure of a company.

Purpose of Financing

Capital structure of a company is also affected by the purpose of financing. If the funds are required for manufacturing purposes, the company may procure it from the issue of long- term sources. When the funds are required for non-manufacturing purposes i.e., welfare facilities to workers, like school, hospital etc. the company may procure it from internal sources.

Corporate Taxation

When corporate income is subject to taxes, debt financing is favourable. This is so because the dividend payable on equity share capital and preference share capital are not deductible for tax purposes, whereas interest paid on debt is deductible from income and reduces a firm's tax liabilities. The tax saving on interest charges reduces the cost of debt funds.

Moreover, a company has to pay tax on the amount distributed as dividend to the equity shareholders. Due to this, total earnings available for both debt holders and stockholders is more when debt capital is used in capital structure. Therefore, if the corporate tax rate is high enough, it is prudent to raise capital by issuing debentures or taking long-term loans from financial institutions.

Cash Inflows

The selection of capital structure is also affected by the capacity of the business to generate cash inflows. It analyses solvency position and the ability of the company to meet its charges.

Provision for Future

The provision for future requirement of capital is also to be considered while planning the capital structure of a company.

EBIT-EPS Analysis

If the level of EBIT is low from HPS point of view, equity is preferable to debt. If the

EBIT is high from EPS point of view, debt financing is preferable to equity. If ROI is less than the interest on debt, debt financing decreases ROE. When the ROI is more than the interest on debt, debt financing increases ROE.

Ways to Determine your Capital Structure

Determining your corporation's capital structure is done by calculating the percentage of the total funding that each component represents. By analyzing a corporation's financial statements, we are able to compile a list of all the capital components on the books. Taking into account all capital components that contribute to the overall capital structure, we are able to calculate the percentage of the total capitalization represented by each capital component. And digging deeper, we will uncover the corporation's leverage which is described by the ratio of debt financing to equity financing.

Understanding a corporation's capital structure is necessary to determine which of the many available options is the most fiscally responsible to pursue. Financing with equity versus debt has different capital costs and, as such, will have significantly different long-term effects on the health of a corporation's finances.

The steps to determining your Capital Structure are as follows:

1. Identify all of the corporation's capital components by examining the most recent financial statements. Compile a list of all debt and equity, including retained earnings, common shares, debt financing and contributions.
2. Calculate the sum total of all debt and equity you have identified. This figure should equal the sum total of all the corporation's assets.
3. Take each component of the corporate structure and divide it by the sum total of all components, as calculated in step 2. These calculated figures represent what each source of capital's percentage is relative to the sum total of the corporate structure.
4. These percentages, if calculated on a regular base, can be used to monitor what mix of debt versus equity a corporation currently holds on its books.

Debt financing is the most costly source of capital versus equity. By monitoring a corporate structure over time and incorporating mezzanine debt into the structure, an effective and fiscally responsible capital structure can be planned and achieved.

Multiple Capital Structure

Multiple capital structure is the classification of a company's stock and bond offerings into different classes. Each class has distinct characteristics in order to meet the needs of a range of investors. For example, bonds offer steadier, fixed-income investments, while stocks present more potential for capital gains. A multiple capital structure creates more possibilities than issuing just one class of stock. Individual components have varying required rates of return that affect the weighted average cost of capital (WACC).

For example, Berkshire Hathaway's common stock is divided into class A and class B shares. Class A shares (BRK.A) have more voting rights and can be converted to class B shares. Class B shares (BRK.B) have fewer voting rights and cannot be converted to class A shares. Class B shareholders have one two-hundredth of the per-share voting rights that class A shareholders have.

Another major difference between BRK-A and BRK-B is the share price. As of June 27, 2018, at market close, Berkshire Hathaway class A stock traded at $281,600.00 per share, compared with $184.91 for class B shares.

In his 1996 annual letter to shareholders, Berkshire Hathaway Chairman Warren Buffett said: "As I have told you before, we made this sale (of a new class of shares) in response to the threatened creation of unit trusts that would have marketed themselves as Berkshire look-alikes. In the process, they would have used our past, and definitely non-repeatable, record to entice naive small investors and would have charged these innocents high fees and commissions." If the stock was left in the hands of unit trusts, "Berkshire would have been burdened with both hundreds of thousands of unhappy, indirect owners and a stained reputation."

Buffet introduced class B shares to allow investors the ability to purchase the stock directly instead of having to go through unit trusts, or mutual funds that mirror Berkshire Hathaway's holdings.

A second example is Google. Two tickers represent class A (GOOGL) and class C (GOOG) shares. Company insiders own Google's B shares, which don't trade on the public markets. As of market close on June 27, 2018, GOOGL closed at $1,112.39, while GOOG closed at $1,102.09.

Recent Trends with Multiple Capital Structures

Multi-class structures have been out of favor in recent years, largely due to the trend toward multi-class high-vote/low-vote and, sometimes, no-vote equity structures. For example, in 2017, both Snap and Blue Apron offered shares to the public for the first time that had little or no voting rights. In 2016, a coalition of investors and pension funds lobbied against multi-class structures. Following this, in 2017, the Council for Institutional Investors (CII) also announced its belief that a single vote per share is important to good corporate governance. The S&P Dow Jones and MSCI recently banned Snap and other companies with multiple share-class structures from inclusion in several of its indices.

Optimal Capital Structure

The optimal capital structure indicates the best debt-to-equity ratio for a firm that maximizes its value. Putting it simple, the optimal capital structure for a company is the one which proffers a balance between the idyllic debt-to-equity ranges thus minimizing the firm's cost of capital. Theoretically, debt financing usually proffers the lowest cost of capital because of its tax deductibility. However, it is seldom the optimal structure for as debt increases, it increases the company's risk.

The short and long term debt ratio of a company should also be considered while examining the capital structure. Capital structure is most commonly referred as a firm's debt-to-equity ratio, which gives an insight into the level of risk of a company for the potential investors. Estimating an optimal capital is a key requirement of a company's corporate finance department.

Estimating the Optimal Capital Structure

There are numerous ways in which a company's optimal capital structure can be estimated. The most commonly used ones are:

Method 1

One method of estimating a company's optimal capital structure is utilizing the average or median capital structure of the principle companies engaged in the market approach. This approach is helpful as the appraiser is well aware about which companies are included in the analysis and the degree to which they are related to the subject company. However, this method features a limitation that fluctuations in market prices and the spread out nature of debt offerings and retirements might cause the actual capital structure of a principle company to be significantly different from the target capital structure.

Method 2

This method is applied if the risk of a company did not change because of the nature of its capital structure, and a company would wish as much debt as possible, as the interest payments are tax deductible and debt financing is always cheaper than equity financing. The main objective of this method is determining the debt level at which the benefits of increased debt does not overshadow the increased risks and potential costs associated with a economically distressed company.

Example

Jenny works as a financial analyst at Morgan Stanley. She is asked to create an optimal capital structure spreadsheet that contains different leverage, interest expenses, tax expenses with a tax rate 35%, the cost of debt, and the cost of equity. Based on the inputs, Jenny calculates the market value of the firm and the book value of the firm, as follows:

Optimal Capital Structure						
Leverage	**0%**	**10%**	**20%**	**30%**	**40%**	**50%**
EBIT	$92,400	$92,400	$92,400	$92,400	$92,400	$92,400
Interest	$0	$3,176	$6,738	$11,261	$16,940	$24,063
Profit before taxes	$92,400	$89,224	$85,663	$81,139	$75,460	$68,338
Taxes (35%)	$32,340	$31,228	$29,982	$28,399	$26,411	$23,918
Profit after taxes	$60,060	$57,995	$55,681	$52,740	$49,049	$44,419
Cost of debt (Kd)	**8.00%**	**8.75%**	**9.00%**	**9.50%**	**11.00%**	**13.00%**
Cost of equity (Ke)	**11.00%**	**11.50%**	**12.00%**	**12.50%**	**14.00%**	**16.00%**
Market value of debt	$0	$36,300	$74,861	$118,539	$154,000	$185,096
Market value of equity	$546,000	$504,308	$464,005	$421,922	$350,350	$277,621
Market value of the firm	**$546,000**	**$540,608**	**$538,866**	**$540,461**	**$504,350**	**$462,717**
Book value of debt	$0	$50,000	$100,000	$150,000	$200,000	$250,000
Book value of equity	$500,000	$450,000	$400,000	$350,000	$300,000	$250,000
Book value of the firm	**$500,000**	**$500,000**	**$500,000**	**$500,000**	**$500,000**	**$500,000**
Book value debt ratio	0.0%	10.0%	20.0%	30.0%	40.0%	50.0%
Market value debt ratio	0.0%	6.7%	13.9%	21.9%	30.5%	40.0%
ROA	12.01%	12.01%	12.01%	12.01%	12.01%	12.01%
ROE	12.01%	12.89%	13.92%	15.07%	16.35%	17.77%
Shares outstanding	5,000	4,850	4,550	4,300	4,000	3,800
Stock price	**109.20**	103.98	101.98	98.12	87.59	73.06
WACC	**11.00%**	15.09%	19.36%	24.01%	29.57%	35.60%

The different leverage does not have an impact on the company's EBIT. However, as the cost of debt increases from 8.00% to 13.00% and the market value of debt increases from $36,300 to $185,096, the interest expenses increase and the profits after tax decline.

The cost of debt and the cost of equity indicate the required return on debt and on equity so that investors buy the company's stock. As the leverage increases from 0% to 50%, the cost of debt and the cost of equity increase, respectively, suggesting that investors require a higher return to undertake a higher risk.

Jamie concludes that a WACC of 11.00% maximizes the firm's value ($546,000), and the stock price (109.20) at the lowest cost of capital.

Concept of Optimal Capital Structure

Every firm should aim at achieving the optimal capital structure and try to maintain it. Optimal capital structure refers to the combination of debt and equity in total capital that maximizes the value of the company. An optimal capital structure is designated as one at which the average cost of capital is the lowest which produces an income that leads to maximization of the market value of the securities at that income.

Optimal capital structure may be defined as that relationship of debt and equity which maximizes the value of company's share in the stock exchange.

Optimum capital structure is defined as 'the one in which the marginal real cost of each available method of financing is the same' and it includes both the explicit and implicit cost under the term real cost.

According to Prof Ezra Solomon, 'Optimal capital structure is that mix of debt and equity which will maximize the market value of a company'. Hence there should be a judicious combination of the various sources of long-term funds which provides a lower overall cost of capital and so a higher total market value for the capital structure. Optimal capital structure may thus be defined as, the mixing of the permanent sources of funds used by the firm in a manner that will maximize the company's common stock price by minimizing the firm's composite cost of capital.

Features of Optimal Capital Structure

The salient features of an optimal capital structure are described below:

a) The relationship of debt and equity in an optimal capital structure is made in such a manner that the market value per equity share becomes maximum.

b) Optimal capital structure maintains the financial stability of the firm.

c) Under optimal capital structure the finance manager determines the proportion of debt and equity in such a manner that the financial risk remains low.

d) The advantage of the leverage offered by corporate taxes is taken into account in achieving the optimal capital structure.

e) Borrowings help in increasing the value of company leading towards optimal capital structure.

f) The cost of capital reaches at its minimum and market price of share becomes maximum at optimal capital structure.

Constraints in Designing Optimal Capital Structure

The capital structure of a firm is designed in such a manner that the cost of capital is kept at its lowest and the value of the firm reaches its maximum. The firm manoeuvers its debt-equity proportion to reach the optimum level. However in practice, reaching the level of optimum capital structure is a difficult task due to several constraints that appear on the way of implementing that structure.

The main constraints in designing the optimum capital structure are:

1. The optimum debt-equity mix is difficult to ascertain in true sense.

2. The concept of appropriate capital structure is more realistic than the concept of optimum capital structure.

3. It is difficult to find an optimum capital structure as the extent to which the market value of an equity share will fall due to increase in risk of high debt content in capital structure, is very difficult to measure.

4. The market price of equity share rarely changes due to changes in debt-equity mix, so there cannot be any optimum capital structure.

5. It is impossible to predict exactly the amount of decrease in the market value of an equity share because market factors that influence market value of equity share are highly complex.

Complex Capital Structure

A complex capital structure refers to corporation that has outstanding dilutive securities including rights or options to purchase stock and convertible preferred stock or bonds. In other words, the capital structure is made up of common stock along with many different securities that can increase the amount of common shares outstanding.

This organization is considered a complex structure because the total number of common shares outstanding can be increased at any time without the direction of the board of directors. The most common example of dilutive securities is stock options paid to executives. Corporations traditionally compensate their executives with a combination of wages, bonuses, and options. Stock options allow the executive to purchase newly issued common shares for a set price during a set period of time. The executive officer can choose to exercise his options whenever he wants during the time period or not exercise them altogether.

Now assume the company has multiple employees paid with options as well as numerous convertible preferred shares and bonds outstanding. All of these dilutive securities can be cashed in and increase the outstanding common shares at any point without direction from the company itself.

Example

These securities allow the holders to increase their ownership percentage and decrease the average common shareholders' ownership percentage at will. The larger the option or series of convertible bonds, the greater the fluctuation in the common shares will be when they are exercised. Since most large corporations have millions of shares, these securities rarely affect the ownership percentages in a material degree, but they can for smaller entities.

As you can see, this is much more complex of an organization than a corporation with a simple capital structure and no dilutive securities outstanding. The only way a corporation with a simple capital structure can increase common shares is to issue new ones to investors.

The valuation of different layers of ownership securities in companies with complex capital structures has been gaining popularity among those looking to raise capital, as well as with investors willing to provide such capital in exchange for securities that are senior to common stock while still providing greater returns than debt. In addition, many companies see stock-based compensation grants, commonly referred as "cheap stock," as a way to align their goals with the goals of their employees. As these securities continue gaining popularity among investors, employees and companies, the Internal Revenue service ("IRS") and Security and Exchange Commission ("SEC") have increased the scrutiny, and frequently targeted valuations, of these securities to insure compliance with financial reporting (ASC 718) and Internal Revenue Code Section 409A (IRC 409A).

For financial specialists who provide valuation services, the valuation and allocation of the total value of a company among its different classes of securities can be a difficult and daunting task. Fortunately, the American Institute of Certificate Public Accountants ("AICPA") has recognized the need for guidance in this area. In 2004, the AICPA issued a practice aid to assist in the valuation and disclosure related to the issuance of privately held company equity securities issued as compensation. In 2013, the AICPA replaced the 2004 edition when it published Valuation of Privately-Held-Company Equity Securities Issued as Compensation, (the Practice Aid). This publication, often referred to as the "Cheap Stock Guide," presented various methodologies for allocating the enterprise value (EV) of an entity across its different classes of securities.

Allocation of Value Techniques for Complex Capital Structures

In order for us to allocate the EV of a company among its different classes of securities, we need to understand the total EV of a company. This includes all classes of securities such as debt, preferred and common stock. Common shareholders are considered to have the residual claim on the value of the company after senior securities, such as debt and preferred equity, have received their returns. The AICPA Practice Aid introduces several methodologies to allocate EV among the different classes of securities, including the Current Value Method (CVM), Option Pricing Method (OPM), and Probability Weighted Expected Returns Method (PWERM).

The Current Value Method, also referred to as the "Waterfall Method," is the most straightforward and simplest method. It is based on allocating the EV across the various classes of securities, in conformance with liquidation preferences and conversion values. The residual value is then allocated to common shareholders. The CVM of allocation is based on initially estimating EV on a controlling basis and assuming an immediate sale of the enterprise. This method calls for allocating that value to the various series of preferred stock based on liquidation preferences or conversion values, whichever would be greater. Although fairly easy to implement, this method's usefulness is limited to situations in which a liquidity event (e.g. acquisition, IPO, or dissolution) is imminent or expectations about the business continuing as a going concern is not applicable.

The Practice Aid includes other methodologies to address the allocation of EV under different circumstances. These methods assume the value of each security is based on the timing and uncertainty of future economic benefits. For instance, Option Pricing Method is considered most appropriate when specific liquidity events are difficult to forecast. It considers each class of stock a call option with a claim on the EV of the company, and allocates EV based on a breakpoint or on payoff scenarios, in accordance with liquidity preferences, conversion features and other attributes. This method is fairly complex, particularly when multiple classes of convertible preferred shares, stock options and warrants are present.

The Probability Weighted Expected Returns Method is based on assigning probabilities to possible future scenarios such as an IPO, merger, acquisition, liquidation or continued operations. The future values are then allocated among the different classes of securities according to its rights and the probabilities assigned to each future event. The allocated EVs are then discounted to present value using a risk-adjusted discount rate. This method incorporates expectations about forward looking events. It can be complex to implement and is sensitive to subjective assumptions.

An additional technique, the Backsolve Method, is a form of the market approach that relies on previous transactions involving other classes of securities (e.g. preferred shares) to estimate the value of one class of security (e.g. common shares). Using the pricing of recent transactions as a known value for a specific security, the Backsolve Method can also be used in conjunction with the OPM and PWERM to value multiple classes of securities. Further, this method involves an iterative process inferring an EV for the total company equal the price of the recent transaction.

Modigliani–Miller Theorem

The Modigliani-Miller theorem forms the basis of modern day thought in the corporate financial structure in which a firm can replicate or undo its financial actions and maintain market value based on the profit generated by its assets.

The theorem proposes that:

- The market value of a leveraged firm versus an unleveraged firm is not affected if the profits and future returns are the same. The weighted average cost of capital (WACC) is not affected by the firm's leverage.
- The market value is not dependent on a firm's dividend policy; therefore, the value is unaffected whether a firm chooses to pay dividends or reinvest its profits.
- The value of the firm is independent of the financial policy of the company. The

firm will still have good performance whether it is financed by equity, debt or a combination of the two. Therefore, regardless of the risk associated with investment, the method of financing does not determine the market value.

- The market value is not affected by a firm's debt-equity ratio.

The theorem assumes that:

- The financial market operates without taxes.
- Information is symmetrical; therefore, a private investor will have access to the same market information as a corporation would and that the borrowing rates would be the same for both.
- Market frictions, such as transactional costs and bankruptcy costs, are excluded.
- Financial policy does not divulge any information.

Lastly, the theorem explores the idea of "even footed-ness" among firms, which questions the types of friction, such as transaction costs and legal constraints, that would allow some firms to have access to different market opportunities or information. This idea has been used to aid in global economics research in order to resolve economic problems, such as monetary and international economics and public finance.

Without Taxes

Proposition I

$$V_u = V_L$$

where

V_u *is the value of an unlevered firm* = price of buying a firm composed only of equity, and V_L *is the value of a levered firm* = price of buying a firm that is composed of some mix of debt and equity. Another word for levered is *geared*, which has the same meaning.

To see why this should be true, suppose an investor is considering buying one of the two firms, U or L. Instead of purchasing the shares of the levered firm L, he could purchase the shares of firm U and borrow the same amount of money B that firm L does. The eventual returns to either of these investments would be the same. Therefore the price of L must be the same as the price of U minus the money borrowed B, which is the value of L's debt.

This discussion also clarifies the role of some of the theorem's assumptions. We have implicitly assumed that the investor's cost of borrowing money is the same as that of the firm, which need not be true in the presence of asymmetric information, in the absence of efficient markets, or if the investor has a different risk profile than the firm.

Proposition II

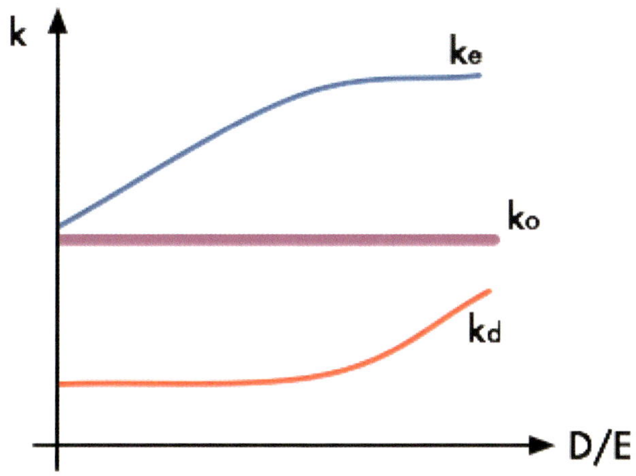

Proposition II with risky debt. As leverage (D/E) increases, the WACC (ko) stays constant.

$$r_E(Levered) = r_E(Unlevered) + \frac{D}{E}(r_E(Unlevered - r_D)$$

Here

- r_E *is the expected rate of return on equity, or cost of equity.*
- r_D *is the expected rate of return on borrowings, or cost of debt.*
- $\frac{D}{E}$ *is the debt-to-equity ratio.*

A higher debt-to-equity ratio leads to a higher required return on equity, because of the higher risk involved for equity-holders in a company with debt. The formula is derived from the theory of weighted average cost of capital(WACC).

These propositions are true under the following assumptions:

- No transaction costs exist, and
- Individuals and corporations borrow at the same rates.

These results might seem irrelevant (after all, none of the conditions are met in the real world), but the theorem is still taught and studied because it tells something very important. That is, capital structure matters precisely because one or more of these assumptions is violated. It tells where to look for determinants of optimal capital structure and how those factors might affect optimal capital structure.

With Taxes

Proposition I

$$V_L = V_U + T_C D$$

where

- V_L is the value of a levered firm.
- V_U is the value of an unlevered firm.
- $T_C D$ is the tax rate T_C x the value of debt *(D)*
- the term $T_C D$ assumes debt is perpetual

This means that there are advantages for firms to be levered, since corporations can deduct interest payments. Therefore leverage lowers tax payments. Dividend payments are non-deductible.

Proposition II

$$r_E = r_0 + \frac{D}{E}(r_0 - r_D)(1 - T_C)$$

where:

- r_E is the required rate of return on equity, or cost of levered equity = unlevered equity + financing premium.
- r_0 is the company cost of equity capital with no leverage (unlevered cost of equity, or return on assets with D/E = 0).
- r_D is the required rate of return on borrowings, or cost of debt.
- D / E is the debt-to-equity ratio.
- T_c is the tax rate.

The same relationship as earlier described stating that the cost of equity rises with leverage, because the risk to equity rises, still holds. The formula, however, has implications for the difference with the WACC. Their second attempt on capital structure included taxes has identified that as the level of gearing increases by replacing equity with cheap debt the level of the WACC drops and an optimal capital structure does indeed exist at a point where debt is 100%.

The following assumptions are made in the propositions with taxes:

- Corporations are taxed at the rate T_c on earnings after interest,

- No Transaction costs exist, and
- Individuals and corporations borrow at the same rate.

Pecking Order Theory

Pecking order theory of capital structure states that firms have a preferred hierarchy for financing decisions. The highest preference is to use internal financing before resorting to any form of external funds. Internal funds incur no flotation costs and require no additional disclosure of proprietary financial information that could lead to more severe market discipline and a possible loss of competitive advantage. If a firm must use external funds, the preference is to use the following order of financing sources: debt, convertible securities, preferred stock, and common stock. This order reflects the motivations of the financial manager to retain control of the firm (since only common stock has a "voice" in management), reduce the agency costs of equity, and avoid the seemingly inevitable negative market reaction to an announcement of a new equity issue.

Implicit in pecking order theory are two key assumptions about financial managers. The first of these is asymmetric information, or the likelihood that a firm's managers know more about the company's current earnings and future growth opportunities than do outside investors. There is a strong desire to keep such information proprietary. The use of internal funds precludes managers from having to make public disclosures about the company's investment opportunities and potential profits to be realized from investing in them. The second assumption is that managers will act in the best interests of the company's existing shareholders. The managers may even forgo a positive-NPV project if it would require the issue of new equity, since this would give much of the project's value to new shareholders at the expense of the old.

The pecking order theory is more towards the behavioural consideration on the continuum of economic – behavioural thesis of financing organizational activities probably to meet the behavioral aspect of agency theory. The primary aim was not of capital structure construction but description of how managers select and make use of the different sources of funds to finance their operations. This makes pecking order more meaningful to existing firms. Although at the end of the exercise a capital structure emerges which is altered as new investment opportunities emerge. The pecking order theory of capital structure on its part gives less weight to tax considerations and predicts that companies make financing choices according to the cash available to them and the degree of external financing constraints. This is working on the endogenous and exogenous constraints in raising capital for firm expansion. Security issue decision is done in the context of information sensitivities of different securities. Thus companies in the same industry may have quite varied gearing ratios depending for example on their profitability, pattern of cash flow and degree of information asymmetry being faced.

The pecking order theory contrasts the traditional position on capital structure construction both in terms of underlying assumptions and method. Myers and Majluf devised the pecking order theory of capital structure to explain several aspects of corporate financing behaviour. Myers and Majluf espoused the security issue decision in the context of the effects of information asymmetry on different securities. This includes the tendency of firms to rely on internal sources of funds, and to prefer debt to equity if external financing is required. Condition precedent here is that an organization must have been in existence and is profitable before pecking order can be introduced. The basic assumptions in the pecking order theory as put forward by Myers and Majluf and expanded by us are that;

1. New shares must be issued to outsiders. The assumption is that a placing takes place directly to outsiders or that if a rights issue is used the existing shareholders sell their rights. A corollary is that the model's force may be reduced to the extent that shares are issued using the rights issue mechanism and shareholders elect to take up their rights. The model collapses if all rights are taken up by existing shareholders.

2. Even where rights issue is employed, the firm will incur costs which do not have the same treatment as costs on debt source. In the same vein, equity is more subject to undervaluation than debt.

3. Under (1) and (2) above, the assumption is that at the end of new issues, ownership structure is altered.

4. Managers know more about the true value of the company's existing assets than shareholders (information asymmetry).

5. Managers know more about the true value of the company's potential investment project.

Pecking order, as argued by Myers, is one way of avoiding wealth transfer to outsiders and negative effect of adverse selection by avoiding equity issues. The argument of pecking order is that due to information asymmetry between investors and managers, adverse selection considerations make equity issues the least desirable source of financing. Since adverse selection costs are present in all external funding sources in different degrees, managers of firms rely on internal sources of funds before they consider issuing any securities. Accessing external capital markets arises only when financing needs exceed internally available funds with the inherent adverse selections costs in respect of external sources of finance, informational sensitivity of a security is correlated with its risk.

The pecking order involves a financing hierarchy where firms first exhaust their internal funds, followed by issuance of short-term securities. In that instance, companies will prefer to fund projects with internally generated cash flows and internal equity. If external funds are required, debt will be chosen before equity since it is less subject to undervaluation. External equity will be issued as a last resort. Pecking order therefore aims at substantially maintaining existing ownership structure, improving the returns to the existing shareholders of the firm and by extension making managers of firms to enjoy the confidence of shareholders. Consequently the self interests of firm managers are also served in this process. Management of organizations in essence follows a preference ordering when it comes to financing new investments in the attempt to manage adverse selection costs and moral hazard;

1. Internal financing of investment opportunities is preferred, in part because it avoids the outside scrutiny of suppliers of capital. In addition, there is no floatation costs associated with the use of retained earnings. In this circumstance, a target dividend payout ratio that ensures some level of retained earnings is set in keeping with long-run investment opportunities.

2. When cash flows are insufficient to fund all desirable investment opportunities, and a "sticky" dividend policy precludes a dividend cut, resort must be made to external financing and here straight debt is preferred. Debt results in less intrusion into management by suppliers of capital and floatation costs are less than other types of external financing. Also, asymmetric information and financial signalling consideration come into play – for example debt issues are regarded as "good news" by investors. If debt is issued, this means management believes the stock is undervalued and the debt either overvalued or valued fairly by the market.

3. Next in order is preference stock financing, which has some of the features of debt.

4. Where funds from the above sources are inadequate, stocks are issued as last resort.

Van Horne opines that management of organizations makes use of pecking order in financing their investments because the method affords management the following advantages;

(a) Using retained earnings first makes management to avoid the scrutiny of suppliers of capital and as well floatation costs,

(b) Using debt next ensures less intrusion into management by suppliers of capital and floatation costs are less than other type of external financing,

(c) Playing on asymmetric information and signaling effects, raising debt issues is regarded as "good news" by investors,

(d) Debt issues signify that management believes the equity stock is undervalued and the debt whether overvalued or valued fairly by the market.

Rational for Pecking Order

As argued by Myers, pecking order theory of capital structure is one way of avoiding wealth transfer to outsiders and managing the negative effect of adverse selection by avoiding equity issues. This implies that it is the result of these actions of managers that is seen as capital structure. Behind the expressly stated reasons of adverse selection and moral hazard for pecking order theory of capital structure, are implicit rationales. These implicit rationales ordinarily serve as the bedrock of what the body of literature has shown. Pecking order therefore has as primary objective maintenance of existing ownership structure and ensuring that managers of firms enjoy the confidence of shareholders. Pecking order is a behavioural explanation of why management follows a financing order even though the method is consistent with some rational economic arguments such as asymmetric information and signaling effect. It is also explained by the urge on the part of managers to manage floatation costs.

This is consistent with the observation that the most profitable companies within an industry tend to have the least leverage. The pecking order method of financing suggests that corporations do not have a well-thought-out capital structure, but rather that management follows route of least resistance that manages the adverse selection costs in financing their operations. Capital structure that results is a by-product of managerial actions and changes whenever there is an imbalance between internal cash flows and capital investment requirement.

Trade-off Theory of Capital Structure

The Trade-off theory of capital structure refers to the idea that a company chooses how much debt finance and how much equity finance to use by balancing the costs and benefits. Trade-off theory of capital structure basically entails offsetting the costs of debt against the benefits of debt.

The Trade-off theory of capital structure discusses the various corporate finance choices that a corporation experiences. The theory is an important one while studying the Financial Economics concepts. The theory describes that the companies or firms are generally financed by both equities and debts.

Trade-off theory of capital structure primarily deals with the two concepts – cost of financial distress and agency costs. An important purpose of the trade-off theory of capital structure is to explain the fact that corporations usually are financed partly with debt and partly with equity.

It states that there is an advantage to financing with debt, the tax benefits of debt and there is a cost of financing with debt, the costs of financial distress including bankruptcy costs of debt and non-bankruptcy costs (e.g. staff leaving, suppliers demanding disadvantageous payment terms, bondholder/stockholder infighting, etc.).

The marginal benefit of further increases in debt declines as debt increases, while the marginal cost increases, so that a firm that is optimizing its overall value will focus on this trade-off when choosing how much debt and equity to use for financing.

Modigliani and Miller in 1963 introduced the tax benefit of debt. Later work led to an optimal capital structure which is given by the trade-off theory. According to Modigliani and Miller, the attractiveness of debt decreases with the personal tax on the interest income. A firm experiences financial distress when the firm is unable to cope with the debt holders' obligations. If the firm continues to fail in making payments to the debt holders, the firm can even be insolvent. The first element of Trade-off theory of capital structure, considered as the cost of debt is usually the financial distress costs or bankruptcy costs of debt. It is important to note that this includes the direct and indirect bankruptcy costs.

Trade-off theory of capital structure can also include the agency costs from agency theory as a cost of debt to explain why companies don't have 100% debt as expected from Modigliani and Miller. 95% of empirical papers in this area of study look at the conflict between managers and shareholders. The others look at conflicts between debt holders and shareholders. Both are equally important to explain how the agency theory is related to the Trade-off theory of capital structure.

The direct cost of financial distress refers to the cost of insolvency of a company. Once the proceedings of insolvency starts, the assets of the firm may be needed to be sold at distress price, which is generally much lower than the current values of the assets. A huge amount of administrative and legal costs are also associated with the insolvency. Even if the company is not insolvent, the financial distress of the company may include a number of indirect costs like – cost of employees, cost of customers, cost of suppliers, cost of investors, cost of managers and cost of shareholders.

The firms may often experience a dispute of interests among the management of the firm, debt holders and shareholders. These disputes generally give birth to agency problems that in turn give rise to the agency costs. The agency costs may affect the capital structure of a firm. There may be two types of conflicts – shareholders-managers conflict and shareholders-debt-holders conflict. The introduction of a dynamic Trade-off theory of capital structure makes the predictions of this theory a lot more accurate and reflective of that in practice.

Traditional Theory of Capital Structure

The Traditional Theory of Capital Structure states that when the Weighted Average Cost of Capital (WACC) is minimized, and the market value of assets is maximized, an optimal structure of capital exists. This is achieved by utilizing a mix of both equity and debt capital. The Traditional Theory of Capital Structure says that a firm's value increases to a certain level of debt capital, after which it tends to remain constant and eventually begins to decrease if there is too much borrowing. This decrease in value after the debt tipping point happens because of over leveraging. A blend of equity and debt financing can lead to a firm's optimal capital structure.

'Traditional Theory of Capital Structure'

The Traditional Theory of Capital structure tells us that wealth is not just created through investments in assets that yield a positive return on investment; purchasing those assets with an optimal blend of equity and debt is just as important. Several assumptions are at work when this theory is employed, such as, there are only debt and equity financing available for the firm; the firm pays all of its earnings as a dividend; the firm's total assets and revenues are fixed and do not change; the firm's financing is fixed and does not change; investors behave rationally; and there are no taxes. Based on this list of assumptions it is probably easy to see why there are several critics.

The traditional theory can be contrasted with the Modigliani and Miller (MM) theory which argues that other forces will indicate the optimal capital structure of a firm, such as corporate tax rates.

References

- An-introduction-to-capital-structure-357496: thebalance.com, Retrieved 20 June 2018
- Why-capital-structure-matters: axial.net, Retrieved 19 June 2018
- Capital-structure-meaning-concept-importance-and-factors-accounting-65150: yourarticlelibrary.com, Retrieved 10 July 2018
- How-to-determine-your-capital-structure: structuringfinance.com, Retrieved 19 May 2018
- Multiple-capital-structure: investopedia.com, Retrieved 10 April 2018
- Optimal-capital-structure, accounting-dictionary: myaccountingcourse.com, Retrieved 11 March 2018
- Complex-capital-structure, accounting-dictionary: myaccountingcourse.com, Retrieved 21 April 2018

3

Corporate Bond, Debt and Stock

A corporate bond is the bond that is issued by a corporation for raising finance/capital. A company may use different kinds of debts for financing its operations as part of its corporate finance strategy. The simplest corporate debt can be in the form of a term loan. The stock of a corporation is the capital that is raised by a corporation through the subscription and issuance of shares. The stock of a corporation refers to the equity stock of the owners of the corporation. The diverse aspects of corporate bond, debt and stock have been thoroughly discussed in this chapter, such as convertible bond, bearer bond, shares outstanding, common stock, preferred stock, etc.

Corporate Bond

A corporate bond is a debt security issued by a corporation and sold to investors. The backing for the bond is usually the payment ability of the company, which is typically money to be earned from future operations. In some cases, the company's physical assets may be used as collateral for bonds.

Corporate bonds are considered to have a higher risk than government bonds. As a result, interest rates are almost always higher on corporate bonds, even for companies with top-flight credit quality.

Corporate Bond Debt Funds

Corporate bonds are a good choice for investors who are looking for a fixed but higher income from a safe avenue. It is a low-risk investment vehicle, compared to debt funds as it ensures capital protection. If you opt for corporate bond funds that put majorly put money in high quality debt instruments, it can serve your financial goal.

Long-term debt funds often tend to become riskier when the interest rate fluctuates beyond expectations. Therefore, corporate bond funds invests in scrips to reduce this volatility. They usually go for an investment horizon of 1-4 years. This can be an extra benefit, if you remain invested up to 3 years. It can also prove to be more tax-efficient if you belong to the highest income tax slab.

Types of Corporate Bond Funds

Broadly, there are two types of corporate bond funds.

Type One: Type One Corporate Bond sticks to high-rated companies – public sector unit (PSU) companies and banks.

Type Two: Second type invests in slightly lower rated companies such as 'AA-' and below.

Let's take a simple example to understand this. Suppose, a CRISIL "A" rated bond with 1-year residual maturity has a 0.56% chance of defaulting, whereas a CRISIL "A" rated bond with a 3-year residual maturity has a 4.79% chance of defaulting. Considering that Corporate Bond Funds typically allocate at least half their portfolios to bonds that are ranked AA or lower, there's always the risk of some of its portfolio bonds defaulting, resulting in a drag on portfolio returns.

Features and Benefits of Corporate Bond Funds

a. Components of corporate bonds

Corporate bond funds invest significantly in debt paper. Companies issue the debt papers, which include bonds, debentures, commercial papers and structured obligations. Each of the components carries a unique risk profile and maturity date.

b. Price of the bond

Every bond has a price and it is never static. You can buy the same bond at different prices, based on the time you choose to buy. Check how it varies from par value – it will tell you about the market movement.

c. Par Value of the bond

This is the amount the company (bond issuer) gives you when the bond matures. Basically, it is the loan principal. In our country, a corporate bond's par value is normally Rs. 1000.

d. Coupon (interest)

When you buy a bond, the company will pay you interest regularly until you exit the corporate bond. This interest is called coupon, which is a specific percentage of the par value.

e. Current Yield

The annual returns you make from the bond is called current yield. For example, if coupon rate of a bond with Rs. 1000 par value is 20%, then the firm must pay you Rs. 200 as interest per year.

f. Yield to Maturity (YTM)

This is the in-house rate of returns of all the cash-flows in the bond, the present bond price, the coupon payments till maturity and the principal. Greater the YTM, higher will be your returns and vice versa.

g. Tax-efficiency

If you are holding your corporate bond fund for less than 3 years, you must pay short-term capital gains tax based on your tax slab. On the other hand, Section 112 of the Indian Income Tax mandates 20% long-term capital gains tax for larger investment horizon. This is applicable to those who hold the bond for more than 3 years.

h. Exposure & allocation

Corporate Bond Funds sometimes do take very small exposures to government securities as well. But usually they do so only when no suitable opportunities in the credit space are available. On an average, Corporate Bond Funds will have approximately 5.22% allocation to sovereign fixed income.

Risk Factors and Returns

There's always the possibility of bond issuer defaulting on its obligations. This default risk is higher for lower rated securities, and goes up exponentially with increasing maturities. If your fund manager invests only in highly-rated companies, expect an average returns of 8-10%. Here, the risk is also minimal.

On the other hand, if you invest in a slightly low-rated but a well-managed, fund, it can be rewarding. For instance, the companies tend to give slightly higher coupon rates to attract more investors. However, there is also a chance that the fund manager's call on the company goes wrong. Example, if it defaults on interest payments or principal repayment or the company gets downgraded further), it can cause a setback for investors.

Ways by which Corporate Bonds Make Returns

Like the Fixed Deposits (FDs) that individuals invest in, mutual funds invest in bonds that are tradable. Just like shares are traded in stock market! Similarly, there is also a debt market where you can trade various bonds. In this market, the prices of different bonds can rise or fall, just like they do on the stock markets. For instance, a mutual fund buys a bond and its price subsequently rises. Then it can make additional money over and above what it would have made out of the interest income alone. However, it could also go the other way round.

Things to Remember before Investing in Corporate Bond Funds

a. You must always review Corporate Bond Funds as a long term investment vehicle. This is because these funds invest in corporate debenture and bonds of medium to long term tenure.

b. If you are not a seasoned debt fund investor, it will be difficult for you to understand potential risks and market.

c. Remember that a large number of defaults within a fund's portfolio can lead to a serious drag in returns. If you decide to invest into them, don't be swayed by past returns.

d. In case of corporate bond funds, it is better to stick to the offerings of large AMCs, preferably, the top 5 funds. New investors are advised to stick to highly rated, short term debt funds with lower credit risk instead.

Convertible Bond

Convertible bonds are fixed-income debt securities that companies issue to raise capital, and they pay interest at regular intervals. What sets convertible bonds apart from most debt securities is that the owner can convert their bond holdings into a certain number of shares of common stock of the issuing company. That feature gives convertible bonds much greater upside than regular bonds, and for that reason, most investors treat convertible bonds as a hybrid between a fixed-income investment and a stock investment.

Types of Convertible Bonds

Convertible bonds can be turned into stock, subject to various restrictions. Like all bonds, they pay a coupon, or interest, rate and return their face value when they mature. Zero-coupon convertible bonds pay all interest at maturity. The distinctive feature of convertible bonds is their linkage to an underlying stock. If the stock price rises, it can propel the bond price higher. Convertible bonds are often used by sophisticated hedgers to offset positions in the underlying stock. For example, if you are positioned to profit from a lower stock price, the convertible bond will offset some of your losses if the stock price rises.

Vanilla Convertible

The basic - or vanilla - convertible bond is issued with a conversion price - the price that the underlying stock must attain to make the conversion profitable. Convertibles are normally issued with conversion prices that are substantially higher than the underlying stock price. If the bond is converted, the investor's unpaid accrued interest is forfeited. For this reason, investors often wait until qualifying for the next interest payment before converting the bond to stock.

Embedded Options

Convertibles can be embedded with a put option, a call option, or both. A call option gives the issuer the right to forcibly redeem the bonds before maturity for a preset price. The call date is usually staggered several years after the issue date. Call options are not attractive to investors, who require extra yield above the yields on vanilla or basic convertibles. Put options give the investor the right to sell the bond back to the issuer for an agreedon price. This creates a floor price under the bond, is attractive to investors and thus lowers the required yield on the bond. Many convertible bonds offer both options.

Mandatory Convertible

Companies issue mandatory convertible bonds with specified conversion dates. Investors must convert their bonds to the underlying stock no later than this date. These bonds usually have relatively short durations.

Exchangeable Bonds

The special feature of an exchangeable bond is that the underlying stock and the bond are from different issuers. Exchangeable bonds can have all the other features of convertible bonds.

Contingent Convertibles

Known as "co-cos," these bonds must attain a price above the conversion price before they can be converted. The required price is usually some fixed percentage above the conversion price, and the stock must trade at the required price for a specified period before conversions are allowed.

Foreign Currency Convertible Bond

These convertibles are denominated in a currency other than the one used in the issuer's country. For example, a convertible bond for a U.K. company might be denominated in U.S dollars rather than British pounds. This feature would make the bond more attractive to Americans, because interest payments would not be subject to fluctuations in the exchange rate that result in fewer dollars per pound.

Example of Working of a Convertible Bond Works

Let's say Acme Company issues a 5-year convertible bond with a $1,000 par value and a coupon of 5%. The "conversion ratio"—or the number of shares that the investor receives if he or she exercises the conversion – option is 25. The effective conversion price is, therefore, $40 per share, or $1000 divided by 25. The investor holds on to the convertible bond for three years and receives $50 in income each year. At that point, the stock has risen well above the conversion price and is trading at $60.

The investor converts the bond and receives 25 shares of stock at $60 per share, a total value of $1,500. In this way, the convertible bond offered both income and a chance to participate in the upside of the underlying stock.

Keep in mind, most convertible bonds are callable—meaning that the issuer can call the bonds away and thereby cap the investors' gain. As a result, convertibles don't have the same unlimited upside potential as common stock.

On the other hand, let's say that Acme's stock weakens during the life of the security—rather than rising to $60, it falls to $25. In this case, the investor wouldn't convert – since the stock price is less than the conversion price—and would hold on to the security until maturity as though it were a corporate bond. In this example, the investor receives $250 in income over the five-year period, and then receives his or her $1000 back upon the bond's maturity.

Investment in Convertible Bonds

Investors who are prepared to do the appropriate research can invest in individual convertible securities through their broker. A number of major fund companies offer mutual funds that invest in convertibles. Among the largest are Calamos Convertible A (ticker: CCVIX), Fidelity Convertible Securities (FCVSX), Vanguard Convertible Securities (VCVSX), and Franklin Convertible Securities (FISCX). Investors can also opt for the exchange-traded funds (ETFs) SPDR Barclays Capital Convertible Bond ETF (ticker: CWB) or PowerShares Convertible Securities Portfolio (CVRT).

Keep in mind, large portfolios of convertible securities—which funds and ETFs represent—tend to track the stock market fairly closely over time. As such, they perform more like a high-dividend equity fund. These products can provide an element of diversification and upside potential relative to traditional bond portfolios but are not necessarily the best way to diversify for someone whose portfolio is primarily invested in stocks.

Contingent Convertible Bond

Contingent capital or contingent convertible bonds ('CoCos") are debt instruments with the special feature that they will be written-off to zero, or mandatorily converted into ordinary shares of the issuer, usually banks or insurance companies, when one or more triggers are met. Such a trigger could include reaching a certain threshold in the required capital ratio or "non-viability" triggers such as failure to repay a liability when it falls due. In this regard CoCos are, in effect, capital insurance bonds, similar to catastrophe insurance bonds.

The main purpose of CoCo's is to increase the issuer's capital in times of distress in order to try to protect depositors in the bank or policy holders in an insurance company. If the trigger is never met, CoCos are normal debt instruments which can count towards a bank's (or insurer's) subordinated debt or Additional Tier 1 (AT1) capital, provided the relevant regulator approves it. The requirement for banks to issue CoCo's was contained in the Basel III rules, which came into effect in January 2013, with different bank regulators in different countries having different rules about how CoCos are structured to qualify as capital, what constitutes a trigger event and what proportion of capital can be in the form of CoCos compared with more traditional regulatory capital.

Typically investors in a debt instrument rank ahead of ordinary shareholders in a winding up and they could expect to receive a higher payout than ordinary shareholders. Holders of CoCos, on the other hand, will either rank equally with shareholders (as their CoCos will be compulsorily converted into ordinary shares) or in some CoCo offers, CoCo holders can actually rank behind ordinary shareholders and incur the first loss if they are completely written off under a trigger event which only impacts the CoCo and not the shares.

For example, British bank Barclays issued CoCo securities several years ago where investors could lose all their CoCo debt investment if Barclays' Common Equity Tier 1 (CET1) capital ratio falls below 7% of risk-weighted assets. This could result from large write downs in the loan book that could reduce the capital ratio to say 6.5% resulting in a total loss by CoCo debt holders but in such a scenario Barclays could remain viable, undertake a fresh capital raising and the ordinary shares could still have value.

Structure and Design of CoCos

The structure of CoCos is shaped by their primary purpose as a readily available source of bank capital in times of crisis. In order to achieve that objective, they need to possess several characteristics. First, CoCos need to automatically absorb losses prior to or at the point of insolvency. Second, the activation of the loss absorption mechanism must be a function of the capitalisation levels of the issuing bank. Finally, their design has to be robust to price manipulation and speculative attacks.

CoCos have two main defining characteristics – the loss absorption mechanism and the trigger that activates that mechanism. CoCos can absorb losses either by converting into common equity or by suffering a principal writedown. The trigger can be either mechanical (ie defined numerically in terms of a specific capital ratio) or discretionary (ie subject to supervisory judgment).

Triggers

One of the most important features in the design of a CoCo is the definition of the trigger (ie the point at which the loss absorption mechanism is activated). A CoCo can have one or more triggers. In case of multiple triggers, the loss absorption mechanism is activated when any trigger is breached.

Triggers can be based on a mechanical rule or supervisors' discretion. In the former case, the loss absorption mechanism is activated when the capital of the CoCo-issuing bank falls below a pre-specified fraction of its risk-weighted assets. The capital measure, in turn, can be based on book values or market values.

Book-value triggers, also known as accounting-value triggers, are typically set contractually in terms of the book value of Common Equity Tier 1 (CET1) capital as a ratio of risk-weighted assets (RWA). The effectiveness of book-value triggers depends crucially on the frequency at which the above ratios are calculated and publicly disclosed, as well as the rigour and consistency of internal risk models, which can vary significantly across banks and time. As a result, book-value triggers may not be activated in a timely fashion.

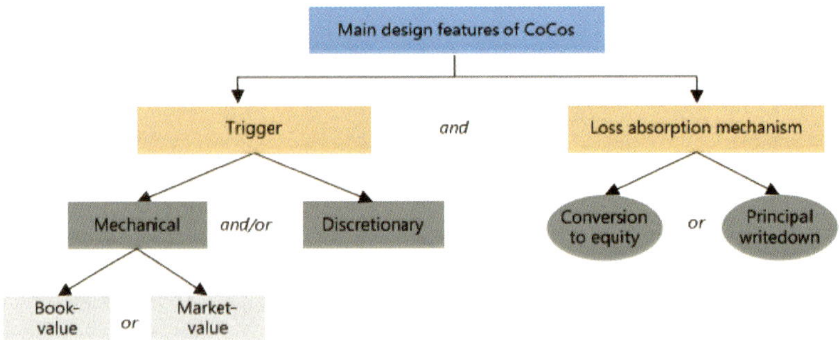

Market-value triggers could address the shortcoming of inconsistent accounting valuations. These triggers are set at a minimum ratio of the bank's stock market capitalisation to its assets. As a result, they can reduce the scope for balance sheet manipulation and regulatory for bearance.

However, market-value triggers may be difficult to price and could create incentives for stock price manipulation. The pricing of conversion-to-equity CoCos with a market-value trigger could suffer from a multiple equilibria problem.[7] More specifically, since CoCos must be priced jointly with common equity, a dilutive CoCo conversion rate could make it possible for more than one pair of CoCo prices and equity prices to exist for any given combination of bank asset values and non-CoCo debt levels. Furthermore, under certain circumstances, holders of CE CoCos may have an incentive to short-sell the underlying common stock in order to generate a self-fulfilling death spiral and depress the share price to the point at which the market-value trigger is breached.

Finally, discretionary triggers, or point of non-viability (PONV) triggers, are activated based on supervisors' judgment about the issuing bank's solvency prospects. In particular, supervisors can activate the loss absorption mechanism if they believe that such action is necessary to prevent the issuing bank's insolvency. PONV triggers allow regulators to trump any lack of timeliness or unreliability of book-value triggers. However, unless the conditions under which regulators will exercise their power to activate the loss absorption mechanism are made clear, such power could create uncertainty about the timing of the activation.

Loss Absorption Mechanism

The loss absorption mechanism is the second key characteristic of each CoCo. A CoCo can boost the issuing bank's equity in one of two ways. A conversion-toequity (CE) CoCo increases CET1 by converting into equity at a pre-defined conversion rate. By contrast, a principal writedown (PWD) CoCo raises equity by incurring a writedown.

For CoCos with a CE loss absorption mechanism, the conversion rate can be based on

(i) The market price of the stock at the time the trigger is breached;

(ii) A Pre-specified price (often the stock price at the time of issuance); or

(iii)A combination of (i) and (ii).

The first option could lead to substantial dilution of existing equity holders as the stock price is likely to be very low at the time the loss absorption mechanism is activated. But this potential for dilution would also increase the incentives for existing equity holders to avoid a breach of the trigger. By contrast, basing the conversion rate on a pre-specified price would limit the dilution of existing shareholders, but also probably decrease their incentives to avoid the trigger being breached. Finally, setting the conversion rate equal to the stock price at the time of conversion, subject to a pre-specified price floor, preserves the incentives for existing equity holders to avoid a breach of the trigger, while preventing unlimited dilution.

The principal writedown of a PWD CoCo could be either full or partial. Most PWD CoCos have a full writedown feature. However, there are exceptions. For example, in the case of the CoCo bond issued by Rabobank in March 2010, holders of CoCos would lose 75% of the face value and receive the remaining 25% in cash. One criticism of this type of loss absorption mechanism is that the issuer would have to fund a cash payout while in distress.

Factors Influencing the Size of the CoCo Investor Base

Increasing participation of traditional institutional investors like asset management companies, insurance companies and pension funds is necessary for the CoCo market to become a deep and liquid source of capital for banks. However, several factors are holding back demand from these investors.

The absence of a complete set of credit ratings for CoCos has been a significant hurdle on the growth path of this young market. The mandates of many institutional investors prevent them from holding financial instruments that do not have a credit rating or are rated below a certain level. In addition, an investment grade credit rating is a necessary condition for the inclusion of any security in many of the major bond indices.

Three main factors can explain credit rating agencies' initial reluctance to rate CoCos. First, the heterogeneity in the regulatory treatment of CoCos across jurisdictions hinders the creation of consistent rating methodologies. In addition, credit rating agencies are concerned that certain high-trigger CoCos have the potential to invert the traditional hierarchy of investors. Finally, the existence of discretionary triggers creates valuation uncertainty, which further complicates the ratings process.

More than half of all CoCos are currently unrated. Until recently, only Standard & Poor's and Fitch rated (some, but not all) CoCos. Moody's did not rate them until May 2013, when it started rating some low-trigger CoCos. According to the S&P rating methodology, a CoCo rating should be at least two to three notches below the issuer's credit rating and cannot exceed BBB+.12 Further downward notching is applied to instruments with triggers near or at the point of non-viability and to those that have a discretionary trigger. On average, CoCo ratings are approximately one notch lower than those of other subordinated debt and more than five notches below those of senior unsecured debt of the same issuer.

An additional factor limiting demand for CoCos is the inherent tension between the objectives of issuing banks' regulators and the regulators of potential CoCo bondholders. On the one hand, issuing banks' regulators aim to provide an automatic source of high-quality capital for banks in times of stress. This translates into a preference for instruments with greater loss absorption capacity. On the other hand, the regulators of prospective CoCo buyers are primarily concerned about the potential losses that those institutions might suffer on their CoCo holdings. As a result, they are likely to steer them towards instruments with a smaller loss absorption capacity.

Increasing the congruency and clarity of the regulatory treatment of CoCos across jurisdictions and fine-tuning their design could help to enhance the investor base by attracting more traditional fixed income investors. However, the risksharing capacity of these instruments also depends on the scope for diversification they offer and on the systemic importance of their buyers.

CoCos can provide strong diversification benefits only if the issuing banks' tail risk has low correlation with the portfolios of CoCo bondholders. Insurance of natural catastrophes is a useful analogy to assess the capacity limits of CoCos. Though the monetary costs of such events are high, their occurrence is independent from the business cycle. This implies that exposure to natural disaster risk through securities like catastrophe bonds provides diversification benefits for traditional investors. Unlike natural catastrophes, however, bank failures are correlated with the business cycle, limiting CoCos' diversification capacity in that regard.

The ability of CoCos to reduce systemic risks depends heavily on whether their buyers are themselves systemically important. As a consequence, regulators may want to discourage CoCo holdings by banks. At the same time, the systemic risk associated with other large institutional investors should also be taken into consideration. More specifically, CoCo holdings should be distributed not in a way that simply shifts the concentration of risk across different sectors of the financial system, but rather in a manner that reduces the amount of systemic risk.

Primary Market Pricing of CoCos

The main determinants of the pricing of CoCos are their position in the bank's capital structure, the loss absorption mechanism and the trigger.

The yields on CoCos are consistent with their place in the bank's capital structure. CoCos are subordinated to other debt instruments as they incur losses first. Accordingly, the average CoCo yield to maturity (YTM) at issuance tends to be greater than that of other debt instruments (eg other subordinated debt and senior unsecured debt). The YTM of newly issued CoCos is on average 2.8% higher than that of non-CoCo subordinated debt and 4.7% higher than that of senior unsecured debt of the same issuer.

The preferences of CoCo bondholders and equity holders diverge when it comes to the trigger level. All else the same, CoCos with relatively low triggers offer more favourable terms to holders of CoCos than to equity holders since the trigger is less likely to be breached and the former group is less likely to absorb losses. By contrast, for a given YTM level, equity holders prefer high-trigger CoCos since they are more likely to lead to early loss absorption by holders of CoCos. As a consequence, one can expect that the yields of high-trigger CoCos would on average be higher than those of low-trigger CoCos.

The interests of CoCo bondholders and equity holders also differ when it comes to PONV triggers. Issuing banks prefer these triggers since they are a necessary condition for regulatory capital eligibility under Basel III. Conversely, holders of CoCo favour instruments without PONV triggers because, all else the same, they increase the probability of the loss absorption mechanism being activated.

CoCo and equity holders also have conflicting interests when it comes to the loss absorption mechanism. All else the same, equity holders find PWD CoCos more attractive, since they avoid dilution and shift the cost of financial distress to CoCo bondholders. Conversely, for a given YTM level, holders of CoCos tend to prefer the CE clause over the PWD clause since the former gives them partial compensation, in the form of shares, when the trigger is breached, whereas the latter does not. That said, some CoCo holders seem to find the PWD feature attractive because it provides more clarity about the loss absorption amount than the CE feature. In addition, the PWD clause is favoured by those institutional fixed income investors that have mandates which prevent them from holding equity instruments.

Table below presents data on the pricing of several groups of CoCo bonds, divided according to their two principal characteristics, ie the trigger level and the loss absorption mechanism.

CoCos with a PWD clause tend to have higher YTMs at issuance than those with a CE clause. On average, the YTM of PWD CoCos is approximately 3.9% higher than that of non-CoCo subordinated debt of the same bank. By contrast, the comparable spread for CE CoCos is only 2.5%.

Low-trigger CoCos tend to command a lower yield premium than high-trigger ones. The average YTM spread at issuance for high-trigger CoCos over other

Table Primary market pricing of CoCo bonds			
YTM[1] spread at issuance over non-CoCo subordinated bonds, in per cent[2]			
	All	Conversion to equity (CE)	Principal writedown (PWD)
All	2.8	2.5	3.9
Low-trigger[3]	2.5	2.3	4.8
High-trigger[4]	3.6	3.5	3.6

[1] YTM = yield to maturity. [2] Weighted averages based on issued amounts. [3] Mechanical trigger level ≤6% (CET1/RWA). [4] Mechanical trigger level >6% (CET1/RWA).

Subordinated debt is 3.6%. By contrast, that spread is only 2.5% for low-trigger CoCos.

Consistent with the preferences of issuers and investors, the CoCos that are least costly to issue are those that feature a combination of a low trigger and a CE loss absorption mechanism. The average spread on that CoCo type over other subordinated debt of the same bank is 2.3%. By contrast, the corresponding average spread for CE CoCos with a high trigger is 3.5%. High-trigger CoCos with a PWD feature are even costlier – their average YTM spread at issuance over nonCoCo subordinated debt is 3.6%. Finally, the most expensive group of CoCos in our sample are those that have a PWD feature and a low trigger. Their average YTM spread at issuance is 4.8%.

Table above contains a pair of relative pricing metrics that is puzzling at first glance. Namely, PWD CoCos with a low trigger command a higher yield than their hightrigger counterparts (column 1), even though economic intuition suggests that the opposite should be true. One possible explanation for that apparent pricing anomaly is that most of the low-trigger PWD CoCos in our sample have a PONV clause, whereas the majority of the high-trigger PWD CoCos do not. As discussed above, the PONV clause raises the probability that the loss absorption mechanism will be activated, which causes investors to demand a higher premium for holding CoCos with a PONV clause.

Secondary Market Trading of CoCos

The trading of CoCos on secondary markets can provide further insights into the properties of these instruments. In order to gauge the degree of co-movement between CoCos and other debt and equity instruments of the same bank, we have calculated the correlation between the daily changes in the CoCo bond spread, on the one hand, and the daily changes in the non-CoCo subordinated debt spread, the CDS spread (on senior unsecured debt) and the equity price of the same issuer, on the other hand. Several patterns stand out.

First, CoCo spreads are most strongly correlated with the spreads of other subordinated debt. The average correlation coefficient for that pair of instruments in our sample is 0.44. The correlations of CoCos with CDS spreads and equity prices, although significant, are not as strong (0.38 and –0.25, respectively). These general observations are in line with the conclusions of a case study on the reactions of the share price of Credit Suisse and the spreads on its bonds to adverse news about the bank's level of capitalisation.

Correlations between CoCo bond spreads1 and prices/spreads of other instruments of the same issuer[2]

Table 2

	Subordinated bond spread[3]	CDS spread[4]	Equity prices[5]
All	0.44	0.38	-0.25
Low-trigger[6]	0.50	0.42	-0.25
High-trigger[7]			-0.26

[1] Daily changes in the spread between the yield to maturity (YTM) of a CoCo bond and a corresponding government bond (matched by currency and maturity). [2] Weighted averages based on issued amounts. [3] Daily changes in the spread between the YTM of a nonCoCo subordinated bond and a corresponding government bond (matched by currency and maturity). [4] Daily changes. [5] Daily percentage changes. [6] Mechanical trigger level ≤6% (CET1/RWA). [7] Mechanical trigger level >6% (CET1/RWA).

Debt, CoCo and Equity Price Reactions to News about Capital

On 14 June 2012, the Swiss National Bank (SNB) criticised in its Financial Stability Report the low level of capitalisation of Credit Suisse, urging the bank to increase its capital by suspending dividends and/or by raising fresh capital through a rights issue. We examine how the SNB announcement, which came as a surprise to financial markets, affected the prices of various debt and equity instruments issued by Credit Suisse.

The reaction of CoCo bond spreads was consistent with the place of that type of instrument in the capital structure. Their market value was more sensitive to the news than the market values of other, more senior, debt instruments, but less sensitive than the market value of equity, which is a more junior claim. On the day the SNB report was published, the equity price of Credit Suisse dropped by more than 10% while the yield on the bank's CoCos maturing in February 2041 rose by 39 basis points or 5.8%. By comparison, the yield to maturity on non-CoCo subordinated debt with a similar remaining maturity as the CoCo increased by 23 basis points while the yields on more senior debt issues and CSD spreads hardly moved.

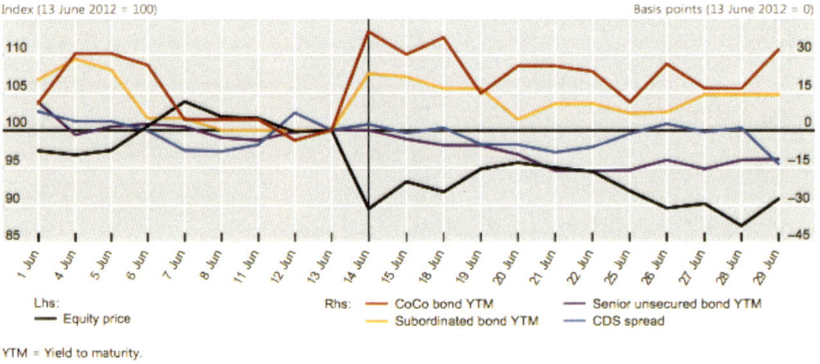

Second, non-CoCo subordinated debt spreads and CDS spreads tend to be more correlated with the spreads of low-trigger CoCos than with those of high-trigger CoCos. The average correlation coefficient between low-trigger CoCos and non-CoCo subordinated debt in our sample (0.50) is considerably higher than the one between high-trigger CoCos and non-CoCo subordinated debt (0.32). Similarly, the average correlation coefficient between lowtrigger CoCos and CDS spreads (0.42) is substantially higher than the one between high-trigger CoCos and CDS spreads (0.30). Intuitively, low-trigger CoCos are likely to suffer losses at the same point as other subordinated debt – the point of insolvency. By contrast, high-trigger CoCos are likely to suffer losses much earlier than non-CoCo subordinated debt.

Finally, the trigger level does not appear to affect the correlations between CoCo spreads and equity prices. This result is somewhat surprising since, all else the same, high-trigger CoCos should be more informationally sensitive than low-trigger ones due to the fact that the former are more likely to absorb losses. Therefore, one could expect that high-trigger CoCos would behave more like equity than low-trigger CoCos. Yet the average correlation coefficient between low-trigger CoCos and equity prices (−0.25) is almost the same as the one between high-trigger CoCos and equity prices (−0.26).

Embedded Risks

CoCos carry a wide spectrum of risk, including market, credit, and regulatory risk. As a result, the valuation and risk modeling of these complex securities is difficult. First, modeling the trigger event itself is challenging. The accounting trigger contains in its denominator the value of RWA, which is a function of a bank's internal models, reported at most on a quarterly basis. Thus, different banks compute RWA differently for identical portfolios of assets. As a result, the trigger may not accurately indicate impeding insolvency. Moreover, because the accounting triggers are lagged, they will not provide an early warning during a bank crisis.

Extension and missed-coupon risk for AT1 capital is important to acknowledge. As described earlier, callable AT1 CoCos must have the first call date at least five years after issuance. After the first call, the coupon payments typically switch from fixed to float. Thus, modeling assumptions about redemption are required to compute yields and spreads for CoCos. One can compute yields by using a simple approach such as yield-to-worst or -first or from a standard interest rate model that handles arbitrary coupon structures. Missed-coupon or coupon cancellation risk is the risk of the bank not paying interest to CoCo investors. Recall that Deutsche Bank's perceived inability to make future coupon payments after the February sell-off caused turmoil for its contingent capital investors.

Finally, there is regulatory risk. Recall that a discretionary trigger may accompany an accounting trigger. Anticipating when regulators will use a discretionary trigger or when they will permit redemption, even if it makes sense economically from the bank's perspective, is virtually impossible. In addition, when regulatory capital definitions change, the issuer can call at the prevailing market price (regulatory call provision). At times, the price of CoCos has soared when investors anticipated an issuer call due to the reclassification of regulatory capital. An interesting case involves Swiss regulators in October 2015, when they proposed that only high-trigger CoCos be classified as AT1 capital. Consequently, investors anticipated a regulatory call of a low-trigger AT1 Coco issued by Credit Suisse. This drove its price above par until the regulators decided to grandfather this particular CoCo as an AT1.

Table: Embedded risks for CoCo bonds

Key Risk	
Interest rates	Currently minimal in low-rate environment
Credit spread	Systematic and issuer specific
Coupon cancellation	AT1 capital is subject to missed coupon payments
Extension risk	Most AT1 CoCos are callable
Regulatory risk	- timing of discretionary trigger - discretionary coupon cancellation - extension risk - regulatory call provision: issuer can call if regulatory capital definitions change

Bearer Bond

Bearer bonds or unregistered bonds are bonds that are not registered to a holder and do not identify a holder on the face of the bond. In other words, when a company issues bearer bonds, it does not register the buyer of the bonds when they are issued. Bearer bonds are unregistered. This means that the interest and principle for the bearer bond are due to whoever is in possession of the bond.

Think bearer bonds like cash. Whoever is in possession of cash is its owner. So if you found 10 dollars on the street, you could pick it up and be the owner of those 10 dollars. The same is true for bearer bonds. Since the issuing company does not register each bondholder with each bond, the ownership of the bond transfers with possession on the bond.

That is why is important to secure bearer bonds in particular. If they were stolen, the thief could collect the interest payments. It is important to keep all bonds, especially bearer bonds, in a safe.

Example

Registered bonds, on the other hand, are registered with the issuing company. Each registered bond is listed with the name and address of the bondholder in the company's bond record. Many registered bonds are not issued with certificates because the bond registration can be used for bond payment information. A certificate is often unnecessary.

Bearer bonds can be issued as term bonds or serial bonds and secured bonds or unsecured bonds.

A bearer bond is often called a coupon bond. The coupons grant interest payments to the holder from the borrower.

Working

Actual bearer bonds are uncommon today because nearly all bonds are registered electronically rather than in certificate form. (although some bondholders still choose to receive paper certificates). Therefore, the term coupon refers to the interest rate of a bond rather than the physical nature of the certificate.

In the 1980s, some financial institutions started buying bearer bonds and selling the coupons as separate securities, called strips.

Let's assume you purchase a $1,000 XYZ Company bearer bond. The coupon rate on the bond is 5%, which means the issuer will pay you 5% interest per year, or $50, on the face value of the bond ($1,000 x 0.05). Even if your bond trades for less than $1,000 (or more than $1,000), the issuer is still responsible for paying you $50 per year. To claim your interest payment, you would simply clip off the appropriate coupon from the bond's certificate and show it to an agent of the issuer.

Importance

Coupon bonds are called bearer bonds for a reason. That is, anyone who presents the coupon to the issuer is entitled to the interest payment even if that person is not the owner of the bond. Therefore, since bearer bonds offer many fraud and tax evasion opportunities, they are nearly unheard of today.

Instead, modern bonds are usually registered bonds or book entry bonds. Registered bonds are bonds with physical certificates that describe the terms of the debt, and the registered holder receives interest payments automatically from the issuer. Book entry bonds are bonds that are electronically registered to the financial institution acting on behalf of the investor. The investor receives a receipt for his or her bond in lieu of a certificate, and the investor's account at the financial institution receives the interest payment.

The appeal of anonymity: Bearer bonds' anonymity historically made them appealing in several ways:

- Hiding assets and income was relatively easy with bearer bonds. With no record of purchases and sales, it's easy to move money and store wealth. The physical bond certificates had high-dollar denominations ($5,000 to more than $1 billion), making it easy to take substantial sums overseas and earn significant income. Tax evasion was also relatively easy, as individuals could store money in bonds instead of mainstream financial accounts and earn interest.
- Money laundering has been a problem with bearer bonds. To reduce crime, regulators rely on paper trails (or electronic records). But bearer bonds make it possible to hand over billions of dollars in a relatively small package. The money can later be re-inserted into the financial system from a legitimate-looking source.
- Theft and forgery are tempting because bearer bonds are essentially one step away from cash. Thieves who stole bearer bonds could redeem the bonds and spend the proceeds with little risk of getting caught. Indeed, several movie plots center on bearer bond theft. For example, the 1988 action move "Die Hard" features thieves stealing $640 million of bearer bonds in just a few duffel bags. What's more fake bearer bonds provide an opportunity for skilled printers to convert worthless paper into real money.

For investors who don't need to hide assets and income, bearer bonds now have few advantages. If they get stolen, there is no way to recover your money. Natural disasters and fires can also cause significant losses. As a result, it's wise to store bearer bonds in safe deposit boxes and other protected locations (with security, fire mitigation, protection from hurricanes, etc.). But it's probably safer to have a financial institution with redundant data backups track your ownership electronically.

Mechanics of Bearer Bonds

Bearer bonds, like other bonds, are debt instruments. Governments, businesses, and other organizations issue bonds to raise money, which they use to fund operations and growth.

When somebody buys a bond, they "lend" money to the issuer. Just like your bank or mortgage lender, they get repaid in two ways (assuming the bond's issuer does not default on the obligations):

Return of principal: Bonds have a maturity date when the buyer receives their original investment. With bearer bonds, the bondholder redeems the bond by submitting the paper that the bond is printed on. In some cases, bonds are "called" before their maturity date, at which point interest payments stop, and the bondholder redeems early. However, because bearer bonds are unregistered, buyers might not know when bearer bonds get called.

Interest payments: Issuers pay interest periodically (annually, for example). Bearer bonds have coupons attached for each interest payment. To collect payments, bondholders remove a coupon and submit it to the bond issuer (or "clip coupons").

Shares Outstanding

Outstanding shares are the shares owned by stockholders, company officials, and investors in the public domain, including retail investors, institutional investors, and insiders. However, stocks outstanding does not include treasury stock.

A company also often keeps a portion of its outstanding shares of stock in its own treasury, from both the initial stock issue as well as stock repurchases. These are called "treasury shares," and are not included in outstanding stocks balance. Increasing treasury shares will always result in decreases of outstanding shares (and vice-versa).

Outstanding Shares Formula

Outstanding Shares = Issued Stock - Treasury Stock

- The number of stocks outstanding is equal to the number of issued shares minus the number of shares held in the company's treasury.
- It's also equal to the float (shares available to the public and excludes any restricted shares, or shares held by company officers or insiders) plus any restricted shares.

For example, if a company issues a total of 1000 shares. 600 shares are issued as floating shares to the general public, 200 shares are issued as restricted shares to company insiders, and 200 are kept in the company's treasury. In this case, the company has a total of 800 outstanding shares and 200 treasury shares.

Working

Shares outstanding is also referred to as outstanding shares, or issued shares.

Shares that are outstanding include stock owned by the firm's shareholders and owners. Shares outstanding does not include treasury stock, which are stock shares that are repurchased by the company. It also does not include unissued shares.

The number of shares outstanding is listed on a company's balance sheet as "Capital Stock" and is reported on the company's quarterly filings with the US Securities and Exchange Commission. The number of shares outstanding can also be found in the capital section of a company's annual report.

Types of Shares Outstanding

There are primarily two types of shares outstanding:

1. Basic Share Outstanding
2. Fully Diluted Share Outstanding

Basic shares mean the number of outstanding stocks currently outstanding, while the fully diluted number takes into account things such as warrants, capital notes, and convertible stock. In other words, the fully diluted number of shares outstanding tells you how many outstanding stocks there could potentially be.

Warrants are instruments that give the holder a right to purchase more outstanding shares of stock from the company's treasury. Whenever warrants are activated, stocks outstanding increase while the number of treasury stocks decreases. For example, suppose XYZ issues 100 warrants. If all these warrants are activated, then XYZ will have to sell 100 shares from its treasury to the warrant holders.

Reason by which Share Outstanding Keep on Changing

Outstanding stocks will increase when the company increases its share capital by selling new stock to the public or when it declares a stock split (company divides its existing shares into multiple shares to improve liquidity).

Conversely, stocks outstanding will decrease if a firm completes a share buyback (repurchase of its own shares by the company which decreases the number of outstanding stocks in the public and increases the treasury shares amount) or a reverse split (consolidation of a corporation's shares according to a predetermined ratio).

Ways by which Shares Outstanding Affect Investors

A greater number of shares outstanding means a more stable company given greater price stability as that it takes many more shares traded to create a significant movement in the stock price. Contrary to this, the outstanding shares of stock with a much lower number of outstanding stocks could be more vulnerable to price manipulation, requiring much fewer shares to be traded up or down to move the stock price.

A number of outstanding stocks are an important value for any investors as it is included in the latest market capitalization and earning per share calculation as shown below:

- Outstanding shares Formula: Shares issued – treasury shares – restricted shares = 25,800 – 5,500 – (2 x 2,000) = 16,300.
- Suppose, stock is currently at $35.65. Therefore, the market capitalization of the firm is 16,300 x $35.65 = $581,095.
- Company A has a net income of $12,500 as per the latest financials. Therefore, the firm's earnings per share is $12,500 / 16,300 = $0.77.
- After three months, the company's management decides a share buyback of 1,000 shares. The outstanding shares of stock price after 3 months is $36.88.
- Therefore outstanding shares of stock after three months = 16,300 – 1, 000 = 15,300.
- Market cap after three months = 15,300 x $36.88 = $564,264
- EPS after three months = $12,500 / 15,300 = 0.82

B17 fx =B4/B14

	A	B
1	Total Issue size (X)	25800
2	Shares to partners (Y)	4000
3	Treasury stock (Z)	5500
4	Net Income of the last full year	$12,500.0
5		
6	At time=0	
7	Outstanding Shares (X-Y-Z)	16300
8	Stock Price per share	$35.65
9	Market Capitalization	$581,095
10	Earning per share	$0.77
11		
12	After 3 months	
13	No of shares buyback	1000
14	Shares Outstanding	15300
15	Stock price after 3 months	$36.88
16	Market Capitalization	$564,264
17	Earning per share	$0.82

- As the number of outstanding shares of the stock decreases by 1,000, the company's EPS increases by 6.54%.
- Also, stocks outstanding is an important parameter used in the calculation of Price to book value (P/B ratio) which is an indicator of how much shareholders are paying for the net assets of a company.

Corporate Debt

Debt represents borrowed funds in which the borrower promises to make interest payments and to repay the principal in accordance with an agreed upon schedule. Along with equity (common stock plus retained earnings), debt represents one of the two major sources of capital for business enterprises.

The primary raisers of funds in the debt market are the U.S. Department of the Treasury, federally sponsored credit agencies, state and local governments, and corporations. Historically, the amount of new, long-term debt financing issued in the United States greatly exceeds the volume of equity financing. Corporate bonds constitute a smaller amount of long-term borrowing than either federal government and agency issues or the issues of state and local governments. Corporations also engage in extensive short-term borrowing, such as through commercial loans.

The money market is the market for debt instruments with a maturity of one year or less at the time of issuance. The primary example of a corporate money market instrument is commercial paper. Commercial paper represents short-term pure discount obligations issued by the largest and most creditworthy industrial and financial firms. Commercial paper can be issued directly by the corporation or through a broker/dealer. Ford Credit recently became the first direct issuer to sell commercial paper via the Internet.

Senior Debt

Senior debt is borrowed money that a company must repay first if it goes out of business. Each type of financing has a different priority level in being repaid if the company goes out of business. If a company goes bankrupt, the issuers of senior debt, which are often bondholders or banks that have issued revolving credit lines, are most likely to be repaid, followed by junior debt holders, preferred stock holders and common stock holders, possibly by selling collateral held for debt repayment.

Senior Debt

Senior debt is a company's first tier of liabilities, typically secured by a lien against some type of collateral. Senior debt is secured by a business for a set interest rate and time period. The company provides regular principal and interest payments to lenders based on a preset schedule. This makes the debt less risky, but also commands a lower return for lenders.

Senior debt holders may be able to voice their opinions on how much subordinated debt a company assumes. If the company becomes insolvent, carrying too much debt may mean the business cannot pay all of its creditors. For this reason, senior debt holders typically want to keep other debt at a minimum.

Secured and Unsecured Senior Debt

Secured senior debt is backed by an asset that was pledged as collateral. For example, lenders may place liens against equipment, vehicles or homes when issuing loans. If the loan goes into default, the asset may be sold to cover the debt. Conversely, unsecured debt is not backed by an asset pledged as collateral. If a business becomes insolvent, unsecured debt holders file claims against the company's general assets.

Senior and Subordinated Debt

If a company files for bankruptcy, senior debt claims are paid first. All other debt is subordinated. Collateral from asset-backed debts may be sold to pay off senior secured debt. Senior unsecured debt is then paid using other company assets. If any assets remain, subordinated debt is paid. For this reason, subordinated creditors may lose some or all of the principal and interest payments that they are owed.

Example of Senior Debt

In July 2016, Alejandro Garcia Padilla, governor of Puerto Rico, announced that Puerto Rico would default on $779 million in constitutionally-backed general obligation debt, its most senior debt. The Commonwealth had been focusing on covering services required for its citizens rather than paying its debt obligations. The previous month, President Barack Obama signed into law a bill providing a debt restructuring process, which stopped any litigation that would have resulted from the default. A federal oversight board was also implemented to manage Puerto Rico's finances. The general obligation (GO) debt is a category of debt that the United States had not defaulted on in decades.

Limitations to Seniority

Secured Parties may Receive Preference to Unsecured Senior Lenders

Notwithstanding the senior status of a loan or other debt instrument, another debt instrument (whether senior or otherwise) may benefit from security that effectively renders that other instrument more likely to be repaid in an insolvency than unsecured senior Lenders of a secured debt instrument (regardless of ranking) receive the benefit of the security for that instrument until they are repaid in full, without having to share the benefit of that security with any other lenders. If the value of the security is insufficient to repay the secured debt, the residual unpaid claim will rank according to its documentation (whether senior or otherwise), and will receive pro rata treatment with other unsecured debts of such rank.

Super-senior Status

Senior lenders are theoretically (and usually) in the best position because they have first claim to unsecured assets.

However, in various jurisdictions and circumstances, nominally "senior" debt may not rank pari passu with all other senior obligations. For example, in the 2008 Washington Mutual Bank seizure, all assets and most (including deposits, covered bonds, and other secured debt) of Washington Mutual Bank's liabilities were assumed by JPMorgan Chase. However other debt claims, including unsecured senior debt, were not. By doing this, the Federal Deposit Insurance Corporation (FDIC) effectively subordinated the unsecured senior debt to depositors, thereby fully protecting depositors while also eliminating any potential deposit insurance liability to the FDIC itself. In this and similar cases, specific regulatory and oversight powers can lead to senior lenders being subordinated in potentially unexpected ways.

Additionally, in US, new lenders can come in to fund the continuing operation of companies and be granted status super-senior to other (even senior secured) lenders, so-called "debtor in possession" status. Similar regimes exist in other jurisdictions.

"Senior" debt at holding company is structurally subordinated to all debt at the subsidiary

A senior lender to a holding company is in fact subordinated to any lenders (senior or otherwise) at a subsidiary with respect to access to the subsidiary's assets in a bankruptcy. The collapse of Washington Mutual bank in 2008 highlighted this priority of claim, as lenders to Washington Mutual, Inc. received no benefit from the assets of that entity's bank subsidiaries.

Subordinated Debt

Subordinated Debt is a type of debt that is risky and is secondary in position with respect to repayment of loan, in case of default by the borrower. In other words a subordinated debt that ranks below other securities or loans when the phase of loan repayment occurs.

If the company is under heavy loan and it faces bankruptcy, the borrowers will pay the other loans first and keep the subordinate debt at the last number in the queue. It is very risky as compared to unsubordinated debts. The priority of the subordinated debt is low and it gets repaid after the senior debts get repaid.

Getting a subordinated debt for a company with low credit rating is very difficult. For the acceptance of a subordinated debt it is essential that the borrower company must have goof future cash flows and ratings. Usually companies take a subordinate debt when the chance of getting a normal debt narrows because of the risk factor. These debts have a higher rate of return due to the risk that the lender has to face. Even the subordinated bonds have lower credit rating than senior bonds as they are risk sensitive.

An example of subordinated debt can be seen in the banking sector these days where the lenders easily give away the credit. This is only because of the reason that the lenders have a claim on the bank's assets after the settlement with the senior debts. Due to the banks financial position regularly monitored in the market the lenders have access to early warning process that makes them realize if their debt is going to repaid or not. Another example is the asset-backed securities often issued in tranches however, in that case to the senior tranches get repaid first.

Subordinated debts are very risky because of the priority aspects and corporate lenders tend to avoid subordinated bonds. However when there is no option left they issue it with a strict monitoring policy. Subordinated bonds have some negative aspects but the lender has the chance of greater returns if the borrower is stable enough to repay it.

Types of Subordination Debt

The importance of subordination increases when the debtor owes more than one creditor and the total value of assets remains insufficient to pay all the liabilities at the time of default. Broadly, there are three types of subordinations:

- Collateral subordination
- Structural subordination
- Contractual subordination

Let us understand the first two types with the help of an example. A conglomerate "ABC Ltd" has 4 operating subsidiaries, OS1, OS2, OS3, and OS4. The amount of debt and assets at the parent and its subsidiaries is shown below:

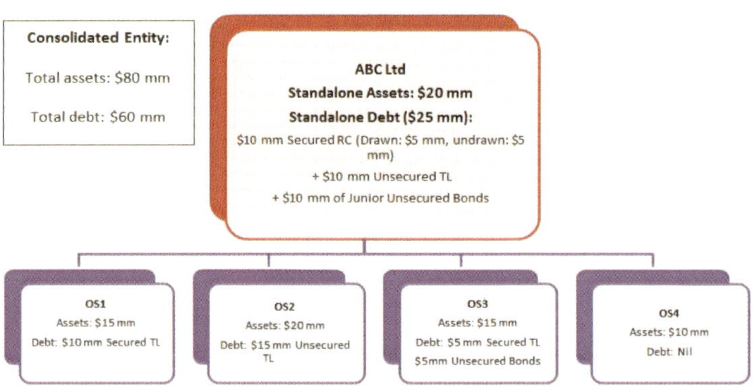

Collateral Subordination Debt

In this example, the priority order of claims of various debt facilities on the assets of the standalone parent ABC in descending order would be: 1) $5 mm Secured Revolving credit, 2) $10 mm Unsecured Term loan, and 3) $10 mm Junior Unsecured Bonds. Hence, the $10 mm of Bonds is collaterally subordinated compared to the RC and TL, whereas the TL is collaterally subordinated to the RC. This is based on the priority of these debt structures over the assets of the standalone parent assuming a liquidation scenario. Likewise, at OS3 the $5 mm Unsecured Bonds are collaterally subordinated to the $5 mm Secured TL. Thus, in a credit tranche, ranging from senior secured to junior subordinated, the subordinated tranche could act as protective layers for the senior tranche which usually remains unaffected.

Elimination of Collateral Subordination Risk

The most common way to avoid collateral subordination risk is over collateralisation, which means the amount of debt issued is limited to a smaller portion of the fair value of the underlying assets. In this case, a decline in value of the assets could still leave enough cushion for the secured debt to get repaid.

Structural Subordination Debt

We note that the operating subsidiaries OS1-OS4 are typically expected to service their own debt from their operating cash flows, and then upstream only the remaining portion (likely in the form of dividends) to its parent entity. This is intuitive as the equity shareholders (i.e the parent) are most subordinated of all the liabilities. Hence, considering the consolidated entity, in a typical scenario, the liability at the parent is structurally subordinated to the debt at OS1-OS4. We note that out of the total consolidated debt of $60 mm, $35 mm (or 58% of the total consolidated debt) is structurally senior to the debt at standalone entity. This can impact the LGD (or the loss given default) of the debt at the parent level, considering that the assets at the parent were insufficient to service its own debt.

Ring Fencing

The extreme scenarios where the operating subsidiaries are financially independent of the parent are termed as ring fencing. This can be ensured through covenants at ring fenced assets, and limit on dividend and inter-company cash transfers from the operating subsidiaries to the parent. This arrangement is typically done for regulatory reasons and taxation purpose. One example of a ring fenced entity is a public utility business which is required to be separated from a parent company in a non-regulated business. This is done mainly to protect the customers of the basic services from financial instability in the parent business. As a matter of fact, the 2008 financial crisis highlighted the fact that the banks should ring-fence their retail operations so as to protect the retail deposits from the meltdown of the corporations.

Non-recourse

Conversely, the debt at the operating subsidiaries could be non-recourse in nature, which means that the lender to the operating subsidiary OS2 cannot claim the parent's assets in a default scenario, in case OS2's assets are insufficient to fund its liabilities. However, in majority of cases, if a business (represented by the operating subsidiary) goes through a difficult time (leading to suppressed cash flows for a long time) due to its cyclical nature, the parent may come to rescue its operating subsidiary. This is more the case when the subsidiary is of a strategic importance for the parent, shares the name of the parent, and when the parent's reputation is at stake which could impact the stakeholders' confidence. For instance, a L'Oreal India entity shares the name with the L'Oreal brand – the French parent, and is also a strategically important subsidiary for L'Oreal considering its presence in a high growth emerging country India. These scenarios are usually documented in the credit agreement in the form of parent support – verbal or written. In a parent support clause, a verbal support shows the parent's intention to support the capital needs of its subsidiary in an implicit way, without having a legal obligation. In this case, a parent may also help its subsidiary in the form of equity injection. A written support is a stronger form of support, which could set a legal obligation on the parent to rescue its subsidiaries, leading to improved confidence of the lenders to lend to the operating subsidiary.

Elimination of Structural Subordination Risk

We note that the debt at an operating subsidiary can become pari-passu (i.e at equal priority) with the debt at the parent, when the operating subsidiary provides an upstream guarantee to the parent. An upstream guarantee is one of the ways to tackle structural subordination and fetch better financing terms for the Company. For instance, if the $15 mm Unsecured TL at OS2 is bundled in the same financing package with the $10 mm Unsecured TL to the parent along with upstream guarantees from the subsidiaries OS2 and OS4, the total debt at parent, OS2, and OS4 would be $40 mm against the total assets of $50 mm, which would place parent at a more favourable position by the creditors. Of course the creditors would restrict future borrowings at the operating subsidiaries, so as to avoid weakening of the guarantees. Various international firms with international operations are inclined to undertake debt locally at its operating subsidiaries, and then have the foreign subsidiaries guarantee the debt of the parent. The upstream guarantee could also be given in different financing packages at various levels such as below:

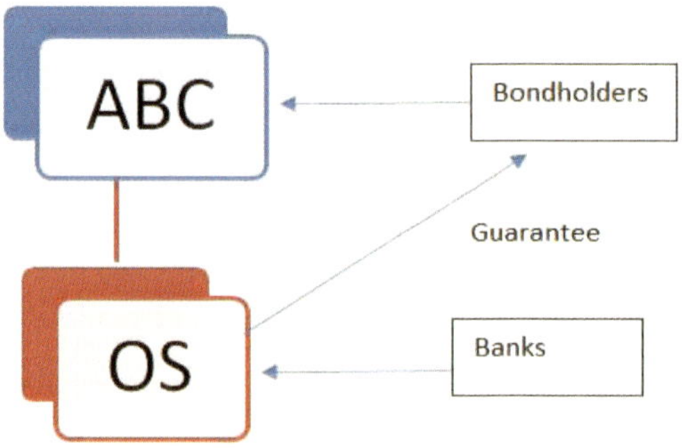

An alternate way to remove structural subordination risk involves the use of inter-company loans, under which the debt and assets at consolidated level would still add upto the same. In this case ABC (i.e. the parent) would act both as a creditor as well as shareholder to its subsidiaries. This arrangement could look like below:

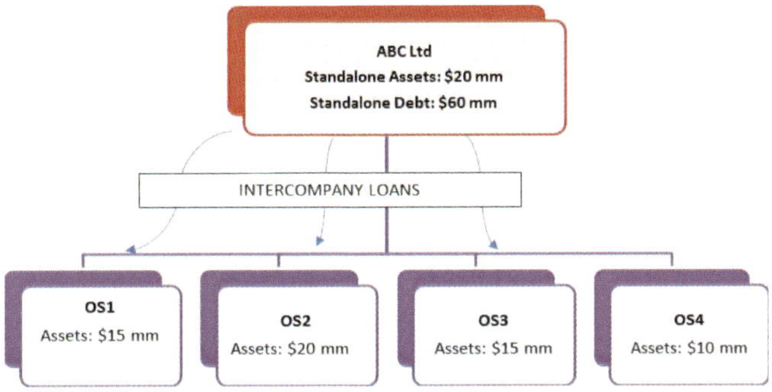

Contractual Subordination Debt

This type of subordination arises when there is an explicit contractual agreement between a group of creditors, where a certain group of creditors (who are subordinated) wilfully provide protection to another group (senior) in the event of bankruptcy. In this case, the senior creditors are entitled to receive the bankruptcy distributions before the subordinated group. The subordinated group, which could be the existing creditors or corporate insiders (such as management) may be motivated to do so to gain higher risk-return (in case of IPO/FPO), as well as attract financing during corporate restructuring. In a more regular scenario, the liabilities (related to working capital) as well as payments to employees could have priority in the payment waterfall.

Examples

A particularly important example of subordinated bonds can be found in bonds issued by banks. Subordinated debt is issued periodically by most large banking corporations in the U.S. Subordinated debt can be expected to be especially risk-sensitive because subordinated debt holders have claims on bank assets only after senior debtholders and they lack the upside gain enjoyed by shareholders.

This status of subordinated debt makes it perfect for experimenting with the significance of market discipline, via the signalling effect of secondary market prices of subordinated debt (and, where relevant, the issue price of these bonds initially in the primary markets).

From the perspective of policy-makers and regulators, the potential benefit from having banks issue subordinated debt is that the markets and their information-generating capabilities are enrolled in the "supervision" of the financial condition of the banks. This, hopefully, creates both an early-warning system, like the so-called "canary in the mine", and, also hopefully, an incentive for bank management to act prudently, thus helping to offset the moral hazard that can otherwise exist, especially in a circumstance where banks have limited equity and deposits are insured. This role of subordinated debt has attracted increasing attention from policy analysts in recent years.

For a second example of subordinated debt, consider asset-backed securities. These are often issued in tranches. The senior tranches get paid back first; the subordinated tranches later.

A third example is mezzanine debt.

Sustainable Subordinated Debt

A business can only take on so much debt. So how much subordinated debt can a company handle?

There are several measures to typically estimate a company's maximum subordinated debt:

- Total debt to EBITDA ratio of 5-6 times. As mentioned above, senior debt typically accounts for 2-3 times debt to EBITDA, hence the remaining for subordinated debt
- EBITDA to cash interest of about 2 times
- Minimum equity funding of 30%-35%

Mezzanine Capital

Mezzanine capital is a form of financing that is part debt and part equity. It incorporates equity-based options, such as warrants, with a lower-priority debt to provide flexible long term capital for use in buy-outs or growth financings. Frequently unsecured, it usually bears interest at a higher rate than secured loans and often gives the lender a stake in the equity of the company. Mezzanine debt is often used to finance acquisitions, buyouts and accelerated growth. Its repayment profile is often back ended over a 5 to 7 year period.

Structure

Mezzanine financings can be completed through a variety of different structures based on the specific objectives of the transaction and the existing capital structure in place at the company. The basic forms used in most mezzanine financings are subordinated notes and preferred stock. Mezzanine lenders, typically specialist mezzanine investment funds, look for a certain rate of return which can come from (each individual security can be made up of any of the following or a combination thereof):

- Cash interest: A periodic payment of cash based on a percentage of the outstanding balance of the mezzanine financing. The interest rate can be either fixed throughout the term of the loan or can fluctuate (i.e., float) along with LIBOR or other base rates.
- PIK interest: Payable in kind interest is a periodic form of payment in which the interest payment is not paid in cash but rather by increasing the principal

amount by the amount of the interest (e.g., a $100 million bond with an 8% PIK interest rate will have a balance of $108 million at the end of the period, but will not pay any cash interest).

- Ownership: Along with the typical interest payment associated with debt, mezzanine capital will often include an equity stake in the form of attached warrants or a conversion feature similar to that of a convertible bond. The ownership component in mezzanine securities is almost always accompanied by either cash interest or PIK interest, and, in many cases, by both.

Mezzanine lenders will also often charge an arrangement fee, payable upfront at the closing of the transaction. Arrangement fees contribute the least return, and their purposes are primarily to cover administrative costs or as an incentive to complete the transaction.

The following are illustrative examples of mezzanine financings:

- $100 million of senior subordinated notes with warrants (10% cash interest, 3% PIK interest and warrants representing 4% of the fully diluted ownership of the company)
- $50 million of redeemable preferred stock with warrants (0% cash interest, 14% PIK interest and warrants representing 6% of the fully diluted ownership of the company)

In structuring a mezzanine security, the company and lender work together to avoid burdening the borrower with the full interest cost of such a loan. Because mezzanine lenders will seek a return of 14% to 20%, this return must be achieved through means other than simple cash interest payments. As a result, by using equity ownership and PIK interest, the mezzanine lender effectively defers its compensation until the due date of the security or a change of control of the company.

Mezzanine financings can be made at either the operating company level or at the level of a holding company (also known as structural subordination). In a holding company structure, as there are no operations and hence no cash flows, the structural subordination of the security and the reliance on cash dividends from the operating company introduces additional risk and typically higher cost. This approach is taken most often as a result of the company's existing capital structure.

Uses

Leveraged Buyouts

In leveraged buyouts, mezzanine capital is used in conjunction with other securities to fund the purchase price of the company being acquired. Typically, mezzanine capital will be used to fill a financing gap between less expensive forms of financing (e.g., senior loans, second lien loan, high yield financings) and equity. Often, a financial sponsor will exhaust other sources of capital before turning to mezzanine capital.

Financial sponsors will seek to use mezzanine capital in a leveraged buyout in order to reduce the amount of the capital invested by the private equity firm; because mezzanine lenders typically have a lower target cost of capital than the private equity investor, using mezzanine capital can potentially enhance the private equity firm's investment returns. Additionally, middle market companies may be unable to access the high yield market due to high minimum size requirements, creating a need for flexible, private mezzanine capital.

Real Estate Finance

In real estate finance, mezzanine loans are often used by developers to secure supplementary financing for development projects (typically in cases where the primary mortgage or construction loan equity requirements are larger than 10%). These sorts of mezzanine loans are often secured by a second ranking real property mortgage (that is, ranking subordinate to the first mortgage lenders). Standard mortgage foreclosure proceedings can take more than a year, depending upon the relationship between the first mortgage lenders and the mezzanine debt lender, governed by an Intercreditor Deed.

Mezzanine capital is the layer that sits below the company's senior secured debt and above owner's equity. It has attributes resembling both of its capital "cousins." Like debt, mezzanine capital is a fixed obligation to repay over a term and accrues interest. Like equity, mezzanine financing has little or no collateral, is subordinate in right of payment to the senior debt, has more flexible repayment terms and a longer maturity than senior bank loans but earns enhanced equity-like returns through higher interest rates and limited participation in the capital appreciation of the company through warrants and other short-term payouts.

Business owners often ask when it is appropriate to consider mezzanine financing. Why would a company use it rather than using traditional bank financing or simply putting in more equity? There are three situations where mezzanine financing is most useful:

(i) As a funding source to enable asset diversification for owners of closely-held companies who are seeking liquidity,

(ii) For management-led buyouts/buy-ins and other similar ownership transition transactions and

(iii) To fund the acquisition of another company.

In these transactions, mezzanine capital is useful as a complement to senior bank financing, not in lieu of it. However, inclusion of a mezzanine financing layer has several beneficial effects on the senior debt and the equity layers in the capital structure. These include the ability to obtain senior debt financing without personal guarantees, enhanced returns on equity capital and the ability to put more liquidity into the hands of owners and sellers at closing.

Unsecured Debt

An unsecured debt is an obligation or debt that does not have specific property—like your house or car—serving as collateral for payment of the debt. If you fail to make payment on an unsecured debt, the creditor can't take any of your property without first suing you and getting a court judgment (subject to a few exceptions).

A secured debt, on the other hand, has a piece of property serving as collateral for the debt. If you fail to make payments, the creditor can take the property.

Common Types of Unsecured Debts

Common types of unsecured debts include:

- Most department store and other credit card charges
- Student loans
- Telephone, electric, and other utility bills (except to the extent that you're required to post a deposit)
- Medical bills
- Personal loans that you weren't required to execute a security agreement or mortgage to obtain
- Court judgments that have not yet been enforced through remedies such as garnishment or attachment
- Income taxes (unless they're so seriously delinquent that they've gone into collection and become subject to a governmental lien), and
- Back rent (except in states that allow landlord liens).

Most debts are unsecured. The primary exceptions are home and auto loans, which are almost always secured.

Advances on lines of credit can be unsecured claims. Some lines of credit are unsecured, backed only by your promise to repay advances taken against them. Obligations on home equity lines of credit, on the other hand, are typically secured claims (secured by your home).

Consequences of not Paying an Unsecured Debt

If you fail make payment on an unsecured debt, the creditor can contact you to try to obtain payment, report the delinquent debt to a credit reporting agency, or file a lawsuit against you. Generally, a nongovernmental, unsecured creditor can't seize any of your assets without a court judgment.

Ways through which Unsecured Creditors can get a Court Judgment

To obtain a judgment, a creditor must file a complaint in state or federal court and serve you with a copy, which is the start of the lawsuit. You have the right to file an answer to the complaint and contest the lawsuit before a judgment can be entered.

Remedies Once the Creditor has a Judgment

Once a creditor obtains a court judgment against you, it can proceed with collection remedies. Collection remedies and procedures are governed primarily by state law. A judgment creditor may, among other things:

- Take your examination under oath to obtain information about your income, other obligations, and assets
- Garnish your wages and bank accounts, and
- Attach and sell real and personal property.

The percentage of your wages that can be garnished varies from state to state. State and federal law also exempt some real and personal property from collection. Creditors can't garnish or collect from assets to the extent that they are covered by exemptions. Exemptions available to you may protect your home equity, household furniture, pension plans, and other items of property from your creditors' collection efforts.

Exceptions to the Court Judgment Rule

If you default on a federally-insured student loan, the Department of Education can garnish up to 15% of your disposable income without a court judgment. State and federal tax authorities also may undertake collection remedies without first going to court.

Characteristics of Unsecured Loans

To distinguish unsecured from secured loans, you can use the following characteristics as reference.

Absence of Collateral

Unsecured loans is a type of debt that is characterized by the lack of collateral requirement. Collateral acts as something that you will put on the line for your lender's security. If you are suddenly unable to pay for your debt, they have the authority to take the collateral from you. Usually, this is something of value to you – like a your home for instance.

High Interest Rates

In an unsecured loan, lenders basically have nothing to hold against you if you are unable to pay for your debt. If you refuse to pay them, the only way they can force you is to go to court. This means a higher risk loan that the lenders counteract by imposing high interest rates or strict requirements prior to approval.

No Tax Benefits

Another characteristic of this loan type is the lack of tax benefits. In a secure type of loan, you can deduct the interest rate from your income tax. With an unsecured loan, the interest accrued is not tax deductible.

Lower Loan Amount

This type of loan usually involves a smaller amount of money as compared to secured loans. Unexpected expenses like medical bills or funeral costs are typical reasons to get this type of loan – both of which require a small amount only. If you need a bigger amount, like hundreds of thousands, you need to apply for a different type of loan.

Short Payment Term

Because of the small loan amount, the payment term is relatively short as well. And speaking of the method of payment, unsecured debts may or may not be given fixed terms. This depends on the specific loan purpose and the agreed terms with the lender. For instance, if a loan is given a specific payment term like a signature loan, it is considered a fixed term or non-revolving debt. On the other hand, credit card debt, which is another form of unsecured loan is a revolving debt because the monthly payments and interest rate is variable and can change month on month.

Unsecured loans are perfect for a person who does not have equity to put on the line. It is a great option for people who have a good credit standing. By having a high credit score, you can negotiate the interest rate of your loan. You also have the opportunity of being approved for a bank loan.

This does not mean that people with bad credit will not be approved of this loan. There are lenders who will agree to provide you with financial assistance but there are repercussions. For one, the interest rate is usually higher than those who have a good credit standing. Also, you may find that your choices of lenders will be limited. Not all financial institutions (esp. banks) will lend money to a person with a bad credit score.

Borrowers who are in need of fast cash are also ideal candidates for this type of loan – especially if you are getting a payday loan or using your credit card to pay off purchases.

Tips when Getting Unsecured Loans

Before you finalize your intention to get unsecured loans, or any loan for that matter, you need to check your budget first. Analyze your income and deduct any current expense that you have. These expenses include your basic necessities, utility bills and other payments for current debts. Anything that is left is the amount that you can afford to pay the new loan that you want to take. If this comes out to be a negative amount, think twice before you proceed with the loan. You run the risk of defaulting on the new loan.

If you are getting a loan because of an immediate need, see how you can save on your current expenses first. Check the expenses that you can live without and consider if you have anything of value to put up as collateral.

Bottom line is, if your income is not enough to cover your current expenses, getting another loan to pay for that emergency need may not be approved.

Stock

A stock (also known as "shares" and "equity) is a type of security that signifies ownership in a corporation and represents a claim on part of the corporation's assets and earnings.

There are two main types of stock: common and preferred. Common stock usually entitles the owner to vote at shareholders' meetings and to receive dividends. Preferred stockholders generally do not have voting rights, though they have a higher claim on assets and earnings than the common stockholders. For example, owners of preferred stock receive dividends before common shareholders and have priority in the event that a company goes bankrupt and is liquidated.

A holder of stock (a shareholder) has a claim to a part of the corporation's assets and earnings. In other words, a shareholder is an owner of a company. Ownership is determined by the number of shares a person owns relative to the number of outstanding shares. For example, if a company has 1,000 shares of stock outstanding and one person owns 100 shares, that person would own and have claim to 10% of the company's assets.

Stocks are the foundation of nearly every portfolio. Historically, they have outperformed most other investments over the long run.

Common Stock

Common stock is a type of security that represents ownership of equity in a company. There are other terms – such as common share, ordinary share, or voting share – that are equivalent to common stock.

Holders of common stock own the rights to claim a share in the company's profits and exercise control over it by participating in the elections of the board of directors, as well as in the voting regarding important corporate policies.

Common stock owners can profit from the capital appreciation of the securities. On average, the shares offer a higher return relative to preferred stock or bonds. However, the higher returns come with the higher risks associated with such securities.

Shareholder Rights

The main sources of shareholder rights are legislation in the company's incorporation, corporate charter and governance documents. Therefore, the rights of shareholders can vary from one jurisdiction to another and from one corporation to another.

Nevertheless, there are few shareholder rights that are almost uniform for every corporation. First, it is the right of shareholders to claim a portion of company's profits. The shareholders usually receive a portion of profits through dividends. In addition, in case of a company's liquidation, holders of common stock own rights to the company's assets. However, since common shareholders are at the bottom of the priority ladder, it is very unlikely that they would receive something.

Moreover, common shareholders can participate in important corporate decisions through voting. They can participate in the election of the board of directors and vote on different corporate matters such as corporate objectives, policies, and stock splits.

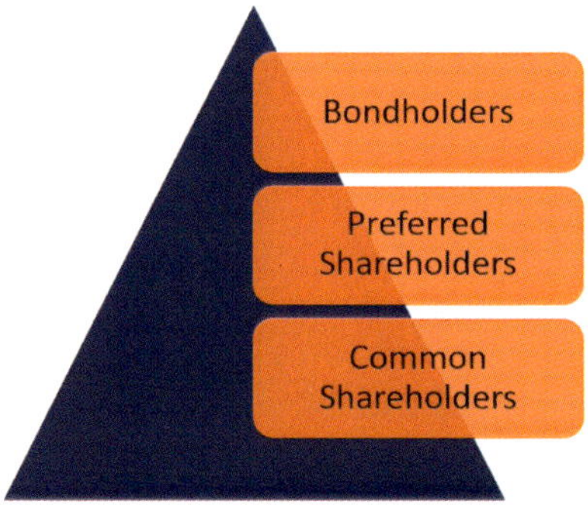

Classifications of Common Stock

There is no unified classification of common stock. However, some companies can issue two classes of common stock. In most cases, a company will issue one class of voting shares and another class of non-voting (or with lesser voting power) shares. Dual classification is generally used when the company becomes public. The main rationale for using the classification is to preserve control over the company.

Despite the difference in voting rights, different classes of common stock usually enjoy the same rights to the company's profits.

Preferred Stock

Preferred stock is an investment security which, depending on the issuing company, can represent ownership in a corporation along with being a debt instrument of the company. The fact that preferred stock can be represented on both sides of the company's balance sheet - representing ownership as well as a liability - indicates that preferred stock can be construed as a hybrid investment security.

When purchasing preferred stock, think as though you are loaning the company money. When loaning money to a friend, you expect to be paid back with interest. Preferred stock works in a very similar fashion. A preferred stock may be issued at $25 per share and may trade on the stock market. Preferred stock dividends typically must be paid prior to a corporation issuing dividends to common stockholders.

Working

The primary difference between preferred stock and common stock relates to the order in which shareholders are paid in the event of bankruptcy or other corporate restructuring. If the issuing company seeks bankruptcy protection, then the owners of preferred shares take priority over common shareholders when it comes time to pay dividends and liquidate the company's assets.

The other main difference between preferred and common shares relates to dividends. Although dividends paid on common stock are not guaranteed and can fluctuate from quarter to quarter, preferred shareholders are usually guaranteed a fixed dividend paid on a regular basis. As a result, preferred stocks often act similar to bonds. The average dividend yield paid out on preferred stock has recently ranged from 5% to 7%. That compares to historical yields of around 6% for investment quality corporate bonds, and roughly 2% to 3% dividends for common stocks.

Importance

Preferred stock is a good alternative for risk-averse investors wanting to buy equities. In general, they are less volatile then common stock and provide a better stream of dividends. Most preferred shares are also callable, meaning the issuer can redeem the shares at any time, so they provide investors with more options than common shares. But for all of these advantages, preferred stock has one downside -- its shareholders generally do not enjoy the same voting privileges as the holders of common stock. Not all investors actively participate in voting, but it may be a deterent for some investors.

Types

In addition to straight preferred stock, there is diversity in the preferred stock market. Additional types of preferred stock include:

- Prior preferred stock: Many companies have different issues of preferred stock outstanding at one time; one issue is usually designated highest-priority. If the company has only enough money to meet the dividend schedule on one of the preferred issues, it makes the payments on the prior preferred. Therefore, prior preferred have less credit risk than other preferred stocks (but usually offers a lower yield).
- Preference preferred stock: Ranked behind a company's prior preferred stock (on a seniority basis) are its preference preferred issues. These issues receive preference over all other classes of the company's preferred (except for prior preferred). If the company issues more than one issue of preference preferred, the issues are ranked by seniority. One issue is designated first preference; the next-senior issue is the second and so on.
- Convertible preferred stock: These are preferred issues which holders can exchange for a predetermined number of the company's common-stock shares. This exchange may occur at any time the investor chooses, regardless of the market price of the common stock. It is a one-way deal; one cannot convert the common stock back to preferred stock. A variant of this is the anti-dilutive convertible preferred recently made popular by investment banker Stan Medley who structured several variants of these preferred for some forty plus public companies. In the variants used by Stan Medley the preferred share converts to

either a percentage of the company's common shares or a fixed dollar amount of common shares rather than a set number of shares of common. The intention is to ameliorate the bad effects investors suffer from rampant shorting and dilutive efforts on the OTC markets.

- Cumulative preferred stock—If the dividend is not paid, it will accumulate for future payment.
- Exchangeable preferred stock: This type of preferred stock carries an embedded option to be exchanged for some other security.
- Participating preferred stock: These preferred issues offer holders the opportunity to receive extra dividends if the company achieves predetermined financial goals. Investors who purchased these stocks receive their regular dividend regardless of company performance (assuming the company does well enough to make its annual dividend payments). If the company achieves predetermined sales, earnings or profitability goals, the investors receive an additional dividend.
- Perpetual preferred stock: This type of preferred stock has no fixed date on which invested capital will be returned to the shareholder (although there are redemption privileges held by the corporation); most preferred stock is issued without a redemption date.
- Putable preferred stock: These issues have a "put" privilege, whereby the holder may (under certain conditions) force the issuer to redeem shares.
- Monthly income preferred stock: A combination of preferred stock and subordinated debt.
- Non-cumulative preferred stock: Dividends for this type of preferred stock will not accumulate if they are unpaid; very common in TRuPS and bank preferred stock, since under BIS rules preferred stock must be non-cumulative if it is to be included in Tier 1 capital.
- Supervoting stock: a "class of stock that provides its holders with larger than proportionate voting rights compared with another class of stock issued by the same company." It enables a limited number of stockholders to control a company. Usually, the purpose of the super voting shares is to give key company insiders greater control over the company's voting rights, and thus its board and corporate actions. The existence of super voting shares can also be an effective defense against hostile takeovers, since key insiders can maintain majority voting control of their company without actually owning more than half of the outstanding shares.

Usage

Preferred stocks offer a company an alternative form of financing—for example through pension-led funding; in some cases, a company can defer dividends by going into arrears with little penalty or risk to its credit rating, however, such action could have a negative impact on the company meeting the terms of its financing contract. With traditional debt, payments are required; a missed payment would put the company in default.

Occasionally companies use preferred shares as means of preventing hostile takeovers, creating preferred shares with a poison pill (or forced-exchange or conversion features) which are exercised upon a change in control. Some corporations contain provisions in their charters authorizing the issuance of preferred stock whose terms and conditions may be determined by the board of directors when issued. These "blank checks" are often used as a takeover defense; they may be assigned very high liquidation value (which must be redeemed in the event of a change of control), or may have great super-voting powers.

When a corporation goes bankrupt, there may be enough money to repay holders of preferred issues known as "senior" but not enough money for "junior" issues. Therefore, when preferred shares are first issued their governing document may contain protective provisions preventing the issuance of new preferred shares with a senior claim. Individual series of preferred shares may have a senior, pari-passu (equal), or junior relationship with other series issued by the same corporation.

Users

Preferred shares are more common in private or pre-public companies, where it is useful to distinguish between the control of and the economic interest in the company. Government regulations and the rules of stock exchanges may either encourage or discourage the issuance of publicly traded preferred shares. In many countries, banks are encouraged to issue preferred stock as a source of Tier 1 capital. On the other hand, the Tel Aviv Stock Exchange prohibits listed companies from having more than one class of capital stock. A company may issue several classes of preferred stock. It may undergo several rounds of financing, with each round receiving separate rights and having a separate class of preferred stock. Such a company might have "Series A Preferred," "Series B Preferred," "Series C Preferred" and common stock.

In the United States there are two types of preferred stocks: straight preferreds and convertible preferred. Straight preferred are issued in perpetuity (although some are subject to call by the issuer, under certain conditions) and pay a stipulated rate of interest to the holder. Convertible preferred in addition to the foregoing features of a straight preferred contain a provision by which the holder may convert the preferred into the common stock of the company (or, sometimes, into the common stock of an affiliated company) under certain conditions (among which may be the specification of a future date when conversion may begin, a certain number of common shares per preferred share or a certain price per share for the common stock).

There are income-tax advantages generally available to corporations investing in preferred stocks in the United States.

But for individuals, a straight preferred stock, a hybrid between a bond and a stock, bears some disadvantages of each type of securities without enjoying the advantages of either. Like a bond, a straight preferred does not participate in future earnings and dividend growth of the company, or growth in the price of the common stock. However, a bond has greater security than the preferred and has a maturity date at which the principal is to be repaid. Like the common, the preferred has less security protection than the bond. However, the potential increase in the market price of the common (and its dividends, paid from future growth of the company) is lacking for the preferred. One advantage of the preferred to its issuer is that the preferred receives better equity credit at rating agencies than straight debt (since it is usually perpetual). Also, certain types of preferred stock qualify as Tier 1 capital; this allows financial institutions to satisfy regulatory requirements without diluting common shareholders. Through preferred stock, financial institutions are able to gain leverage while receiving Tier 1 equity credit.

If an investor paid par ($100) today for a typical straight preferred, such an investment would give a current yield of just over six percent. If, in a few years, 10-year Treasuries were to yield more than 13 percent to maturity (as they did in 1981) these preferreds would yield at least 13 percent; since the rate of dividend is fixed, this would reduce their market price to $46, a 54-percent loss. The difference between straight preferreds and Treasuries (or any investment-grade Federal-agency or corporate bond) is that the bonds would move up to par as their maturity date approaches; however, the straight preferred (having no maturity date) might remain at these $40 levels (or lower) for a long time.

Advantages of straight preferreds may include higher yields and—in the U.S. at least—tax advantages; they yield about 2 percent more than 10-year Treasuries, rank ahead of common stock in case of bankruptcy and dividends are taxable at a maximum rate of 15% rather than at ordinary-income rates (as with bond interest).

Advantages of Preference Shares

1. No obligation for dividends: A company is not bound to pay a dividend on preference shares if its profits in a particular year are insufficient. It can postpone the dividend in case of cumulative preference shares also. No fixed burden is created on its finances.

2. No interference: Generally, preference shares do not carry voting rights. Therefore, a company can raise capital without dilution of control. Equity shareholders retain exclusive control over the company.

3. Trading on equity: The rate of dividend on preference shares is fixed. Therefore, with the rise in its earnings, the company can provide the benefits of trading on equity to the equity shareholders.

4. No charge on assets: Preference shares do not create any mortgage or charge on the assets of the company. The company can keep its fixed assets free for raising loans in future

5. Variety: Different types of preference shares can be issued depending on the needs of investors. Participating preference shares or convertible preference shares may be issued to attract bold and enterprising investors.

Participating Preferred Stock

Participating preferred stock is a share that gives its holder participation in the additional earnings of a business. The participation feature increases the value of such a share, which allows the issuer to sell it at a higher price. This participation is in addition to the usual fixed dividend associated with most types of preferred stock. Participation can take several forms, such as the following:

- Earnings rights. If the business generates a certain amount of income, the holder of participating preferred shares will be paid a certain proportion of that income, in addition to the normal dividend.
- Liquidation rights. If the business is sold, the holder of participating preferred shares will be paid a certain proportion of the net sale price received.

These additional payments are usually made in the form of dividends. Also, participation rights are sometimes activated only when the amounts that a company earns, either through its operations or sale of the business, exceeds a certain threshold level. Depending on the level of the threshold, participation payments may be relatively rare.

Participating preferred stock agreements may or may not include other features, such as:

- Holders of the shares may have the authority to approve certain actions, such as the sale of the business or larger assets.
- Holders of the shares may have voting rights similar to those held by the holders of common stock.
- The shares may be cumulative, so that unpaid dividends must be paid before any dividends can be issued to the holders of common stock.

If participation rights are likely to generate a return, the price of participating preferred stock can be quite high, which makes it an attractive feature for investors holding these shares. However, it reduces the amount of funds that might be distributed to the holders of common stock, so it tends to depress the price of common stock.

An investor should buy participating preferred stock when he believes that a business is likely to have unusually strong earnings or be sold for a high price, so that he can participate in those gains.

As an example of the terms of this type of stock, ABC Company issues 100,000 shares of participating preferred stock, which entitles the holder of each share to an annual dividend of $5.00. In addition, the holder is entitled to his pro rata share of 20% of all company earnings that exceed a baseline earnings level of $10 million per year.

Restricted Stock

Restricted stock refers to unregistered shares of ownership in a corporation that are issued to corporate affiliates, such as executives and directors. Restricted stock is non-transferable and must be traded in compliance with special Securities and Exchange Commission (SEC) regulations. It typically becomes available for sale under a graded vesting schedule that lasts several years.

Restricted stock is also referred to as "letter stock" and "section 1244 stock."

Restricted stock became more popular in the mid-2000s as companies were required to expense stock option grants. It is often used as a form of employee compensation, in which case, it typically becomes transferrable, that is, vests, upon the satisfaction of certain conditions, such as continued employment for a period of time or the achievement of particular product-development milestones, earnings per share (EPS) goals, or other financial targets.

Insiders are given restricted stock after merger and acquisition activity, underwriting activity, and affiliate ownership in order to prevent premature selling that might adversely affect the company. An executive may have to forfeit restricted stock if he leaves the company, fails to meet corporate or personal performance goals, or runs afoul of SEC trading restrictions. The SEC regulations that govern the trading of restricted stock are outlined under SEC Rule 144, which describes the registration and public trading of restricted stock and the limits on holding periods and volume.

Restricted Stock Units vs. Restricted Stock Awards

Two variations of restricted stock are restricted stock units (RSUs) and restricted stock awards. A restricted stock unit is a promise made to an employee by an employer to grant a given number of shares of the company's stock to the employee at a predetermined time in the future. Since RSUs are not actually stocks, but only a right to the promised stock, they carry no voting rights. An RSU must be exercised in order to receive the stock. An RSU that is converted to stock carries the standard voting rights for the class of stock issued.

A restricted stock award is similar to an RSU in a number of ways, except for the fact that the award also comes with voting rights. This is because the employee owns the stock immediately once it is awarded. Generally, an RSU represents stock, but in some cases an employee can elect to receive the cash value of the RSU in lieu of a stock award. This is not the case for restricted stock awards, which cannot be redeemed for cash.

Taxation of Restricted Stock

The taxation of restricted stock is complex and is governed by Section 1244 of the Internal Revenue Code (IRC). Restricted stock holders pay tax on the capital gain or loss represented by the difference between the stock's price on the date it vests and the date it is sold. In addition, restricted stock is taxable as ordinary income in the year it vests. This is converse to stock options which are taxed when the employee exercises his or her option, not when they are vested.

The amount on restricted stock that must be declared as income is the stock's fair market value on the vesting date minus its original exercise price. However, the restricted stock holder may do a Section 83(b) election, which lets him or her use the price on the grant date, not the vesting date, for the purposes of calculating ordinary income tax. The tax bill must be paid sooner in this case, but it may be substantially lower if the stock appreciates between the grant date and the vesting date. The risk of taking this election is that if the restricted stock holder leaves the company before the shares vest, the shares are forfeited, and taxes already paid are non-refundable.

Tracking Stock

A tracking stock is a special type of stock issued by a company to represent a particular division or segment of the business. Tracking stocks allow management to retain control of the operation without having to sell ownership or create a separate legal entity that is spun off to shareholders, with its own board of directors and management team, while allowing investors the opportunity to value various aspects of an enterprise on different terms and price-to-earnings multiples.

At the time they were used, they were effectively the result of ambitious management teams trying to cash in on the obscene (and stupid) once-in-several-generations valuation levels that seemed to be hitting new highs on an almost daily basis back during the dot-com bubble. Even stable, old-fashioned blue-chip stocks got in on the madness.

An Example of One Particularly Popular Tracking Stock

In what now seems like a lifetime ago and long before its meltdown, Sprint was one of the most attractive telecommunication companies in the United States. Its traditional landline businesses were highly profitable and paid a rich dividend and it had a new, exciting division that specialized in cell phones, which management was convinced would replace landlines someday; a notion that seemed strange to the typical citizen at the time but one that was often discussed with increasing frequency in the Form 10-K filings.

As the Internet boom got out of control, pushing the stock price ever-higher to the point even the dividend yield became non-enticing, Sprint saw that cellular companies were being valued at crazy multiples. The already-richly valued telecommunication utility decided to divide its common stock into two classes of tracking stock trading under two ticker symbols, FON and PCS, somewhat resembling a dual class stock setup but very different from what the classical version of such a capital structure actually represents.

Its classic landline business, the cash cow gushing money from local and long distance plans, was assigned to FON. Meanwhile, the cellular business was assigned to PCS. Shareholders were given 1 share of PCS for every 2 shares of FON they held.

After hitting the market, the demand for PCS was incredible and a lot of employees in the formerly sleepy world of switchboards and telephone poles became millionaires as speculators drove the price of the cellular division's tracking stock higher. Things like fundamentals - paying attention to balance sheets and income statements - no longer mattered to people.

When the bottom fell out and the growth couldn't match a reasonable dividend-adjusted PEG, Sprint's stock began to collapse along with the rest of the overvalued equities on the New York Stock Exchange and Nasdaq (in fact, it took fifteen years for the latter to reach its former high). The company's board decided to exercise its authority and reassemble the tracking stocks into a single ticker, FON, by exchanging shares of PCS for it, hunkering down to try and make it through the storm. In 2005, Sprint merged with Nextel.

It didn't do much good for Sprint's long-term equity holders who have suffered a catastrophic loss of purchasing power over the past twenty years.

Understanding the Pros and Cons of Tracking Stocks

There are several benefits to tracking stocks:

- A tracking stock can allow management to unlock value by increasing the total stock market capitalization and enterprise value of the business through expansion in the overall p/e ratio. This makes existing shareholders wealthier as they can sell their appreciated shares to buy other investments, pay down debt, send their children or grandchildren to college, donate to charity, build a new home, take a vacation, or any number of other things. It also gives the board of directors an appreciated currency in the form of two different shares it can use when making acquisitions, letting it to expand while giving up less intrinsic value.

- Management retains control over the tracked operating segment or business.

On the flip side, there are several drawbacks to tracking stocks:

- Tracking stocks often have greatly reduced or non-existent voting rights.
- An owner of a tracking stock might not actually own the specific aspect of the operating segment that is being tracked. In the event of a corporate bankruptcy, the assets of the particular division their tracking stock was supposed to represent would be fair game for the creditors even if the division associated with the tracking stock was extremely profitable and growing rapidly. This is not the case with traditional spin-offs. For example, look at the bankruptcy of Eastman Kodak and how it had no effect on its former subsidiary Eastman Chemical.
- If the market goes south, the tracking stock can be absorbed back into the main stock at a price that may appear unattractive to either or both the owners of the tracking stock and the original corporate stock.

Treasury Stock

Treasury shares are the shares which are bought back by the issuing company, reducing the number of shares outstanding on the open market.

All companies have an authorized amount of equity capital that it can issue legally. Of this amount, the total number of shares owned by investors, including the officers and insiders of the company, are called outstanding shares. The amount of equity which is available to the public for sale and purchase on the stock market is known as float. Treasury shares are the shares which were ones part of the float and outstanding shares, but were subsequently bought back by the company.

The shares which have been bought back by a company can either be canceled or held for reissue. Technically speaking, the repurchased shares are a company's own shares that have been bought back after having been issued and fully paid. Treasury share do not pay any dividends and they do not have any voting rights. The possession of these shares does not give the company the right to either receive any assets on company liquidation, or to exercise pre-emptive rights as a shareholder.

They should not be included in the calculations of outstanding shares. The amount of treasury shares can not exceed the maximum proportion of total capitalization specified by laws and regulations.

In essence, the treasury shares are the same as unissued equity capital. They are not classified as an asset on the balance sheet, because assets should have probable future economic benefits. These shares simply reduce ordinary share capital. They are usually presented under the equity capital in balance sheet as a negative number.

When the shares are bought back, they have a positive effect on the earning per share ratio and price earnings ratio because the number of outstanding shares is reduced. Although these ratios improve but the value of shares do not change because there is an equal increase in the market risk.

Shares buy back is a good way of distributing cash to the shareholders instead of dividends because it is tax efficient. They are also bought back to protect the company from hostile takeovers. If the shares are undervalued, some companies buy back their shares to benefit the shareholders.

Limitations of Treasury Stock

- No voting rights
- Not entitled to receive dividends
- Not included in the calculation of outstanding shares
- Does not exercise preemptive rights as a shareholder
- Not entitled to receive net assets in case the company liquidates
- In some countries, the number of treasury stocks held by companies is regulated – total treasury stock cannot exceed the maximum proportion of capitalization specified by law.

References

- Types-convertible-bonds-7344: finance.zacks.com, Retrieved 15 June 2018
- What-are-convertible-bonds-416834: thebalance.com, Retrieved 16 March 2018
- Overview-of-bearer-bonds-4160421: thebalance.com, Retrieved 25 June 2018
- Outstanding-shares-stocks: wallstreetmojo.com, Retrieved 25 June 2018
- Mezzanine-capital-the-middle-in-middle-market-finance: metzlewis.com, Retrieved 14 July 2018
- What-is-preferred-stock-definition-types-advantages: study.com, Retrieved 25 March 2018
- What-is-participating-preferred-stock: accountingtools.com, Retrieved 10 April 2018
- What-is-a-tracking-stock-357649: thebalance.com, Retrieved 15 May 2018

4

Interest Rate, Time and Income Analysis

An interest rate refers to the interest due per a specific period, for an amount of money lent, borrowed or deposited. The elements of time value of money and income analysis are also integral to the field of corporate finance. The topics elaborated in this chapter on nominal interest rate, real interest rate, time value of money, bond valuation, bond convexity and bond duration will help in developing a better perspective of interest rate, time and income analysis.

Interest Rate

An interest rate is the percent of principal charged by the lender for the use of its money. The principal is the amount of money lent. As a result, banks pay you an interest rate on deposits. They are borrowing that money from you.

Anyone can lend money and charge interest, but it's usually banks. They use the deposits from savings or checking accounts to fund loans. They pay interest rates to encourage people to make deposits.

Banks charge borrowers a little higher interest rate than they pay depositors so they can profit. At the same time, banks compete with each other for both depositors and borrowers. The resulting competition keeps interest rates from all banks in a narrow range of each other.

Working of Interest Rates

The bank applies the interest rate to the total unpaid portion of your loan or credit card balance. It's critical to know what your interest rate is. It's the only way to know how much it adds to your outstanding debt. You must pay at least the interest each month. If not, your outstanding debt will increase even though you are making payments.

Although interest rates are very competitive, they aren't the same. A bank will charge higher interest rates if it thinks there's a lower chance the debt will get repaid. For that reason, banks will always assign a higher interest rate to revolving loans, like credit cards. These types of loans are more expensive to manage. Banks also charge higher rates to people they consider risky. It's important to know what your credit score is and how to improve it. The higher your score, the lower the interest rate you will have to pay.

Banks charge fixed rates or variable rates. It depends on whether the loan is a mortgage, credit card, or unpaid bill. The actual interest rates are determined by either the 10-year Treasury note or by the fed funds rate.

Fixed rates remain the same throughout the life of the loan. Your initial payments consist mostly of interest payments. As time goes on, you pay a higher and higher percentage of the debt principal. If you make an extra payment, it all goes toward principal. You can pay the debt off sooner that way. Most conventional mortgages are fixed-rate loans.

Variable rates change with the prime rate. When the rate rises, so will the payment on your loan. With these loans, you must pay attention to the prime rate, which is based on the fed funds rate. If you make extra payments, it will also go towards paying off the principal.

Annual Percentage Rate

Annual percentage rate allows you to compare the cost of different borrowing options. The APR includes any fees a bank may charge. These one-time fees are called "points" because they the bank calculates them as a percentage point of the total. The APR can help you compare a loan that only charges an interest rate to one that charges a lower interest rate plus points.

Interest Rates Drive Economic Growth

A country's central bank sets interest rates. In the United States, the fed funds rate is that guiding rate. It's what banks charge each other for overnight loans. The Federal Reserve requires banks to maintain 10 percent of total deposits in reserve each night. Otherwise, they would lend out every single penny they have. That would not allow enough of a buffer for the next day's withdrawals. The fed funds rate affects the nation's money supply and thus the health of the economy.

Interest rates make loans more expensive. When interest rates are high, fewer people and businesses can afford to borrow. That lowers the amount of credit available to fund purchases, slowing consumer demand. At the same time, it encourages more people to save because they receive more on their savings rate. High-interest rates also reduce the capital available to expand businesses, strangling supply. This reduction in liquidity slows the economy.

Low-interest rates have the opposite effect on the economy. Low mortgage rates have the same effect as lower housing prices, stimulating demand for real estate. Savings rates fall. When savers find they get less interest on their deposits, they might decide to spend more. They might also put their money into slightly riskier, but more profitable, investments. That drives up stock prices. Low-interest rates make business loans more affordable. That encourages business expansion and new jobs.

Interest

Interest is the charge for the privilege of borrowing money, typically expressed as annual percentage rate (APR). Interest can also refer to the amount of ownership a stockholder has in a company, usually expressed as a percentage.

Two main types of interest can be applied to loans: simple and compound. Simple interest is a set rate on the principle originally lent to the borrower that the borrower has to pay for the ability to use the money. Compound interest is interest on both the principle and the compounding interest paid on that loan. The latter of the two types of interest is the most common.

Some of the considerations that go into calculating the type of interest and the amount a lender will charge a borrower include:

- Opportunity cost or the cost of the inability of the lender to use the money they're lending out
- Amount of expected inflation
- Risk that the lender is unable to pay the loan back because of default
- Length of time that the money is being lent
- Possibility of government intervention on interest rates
- Liquidity of the loan being made

A quick way to get a rough understanding of how long it will take in order for an investment to double is to use the rule of 72. Divide the number 72 by the interest rate, 72/4 for instance, and you'll double your investment in 18 years.

Simple Interest

Simple interest means interest that is earned or paid on a fixed amount. Simple interest is calculated once. It is calculated for the full term on the principle amount. To calculate how much interest a person will earn on an amount of R5000 at a simple interest rate of 10% for 3 months, the following formula will be used:

Amount × 10% = interest a person will earn.

Compound Interest

The money a person earns in interest becomes part of the principle amount and also starts to earn interest. Compound interest is calculated during the term. To calculate the interest a person will earn on an amount of Rs 5000 at a compound interest of 10% for a year the same formula is used as normal interest.

Nominal Interest Rate

The nominal interest rate is the percentage yield of a security or a loan without considering the effect of inflation. In other words, it's the actual rate that borrowers pay to lenders to use their money.

The coupons that bond investors receive are calculated with a nominal interest rate because they measure the percentage yield of the bond based on its face value.

Therefore, a 25-year municipal bond with a face value of $5,000 and an 8% coupon ratethat pays interest every year, will return the bondholder $5,000 x 8% = $400 annually for 25 years. If we subtract inflation from the nominal interest rate, we derive the real interest rate, which is the rate that the deposits are calculated on.

Let's look at an example.

Example

At the beginning of 2015, Markus deposits $1,500 in a checking account with a 6% annual interest rate. At the end of the year, the value of his deposit is $1,500 x (1 + 6%) = $1,590.

If inflation were 0%, the general price level would not change during the year; therefore, Markus would be able to buy 6% more goods and services that he was able to buy a year earlier with $1,500. Therefore, the nominal interest rate would be 6%.

However, with an inflation rate of 6%, Markus has $1,590, but the real value of his deposit this year is not higher than the value of his deposit a year earlier. Markus can buy the same goods and services that he could buy a year earlier although he has more money.

In fact, an inflation rate of 6 percent essentially means that the products and services are more expensive by 6% on average. Therefore, Markus receives a nominal interest rate of 6% and a real interest rate of 6% – 6% = 0%.

Real Interest Rate

The real interest rate is the nominal interest rate – inflation rate. The formula allows the calculation of a real interest rate for a given period, using an estimated rate of inflation. It is known under the name of Fisher equation.

Formula

$$i_r = \frac{1 + i_{nom}}{1 + r_{inf}^{est}} - 1$$

Legend

nom	Nominal interest rate
est inf	Estimated rate of inflation

For example, if the Bank of England set base rates of 5.5% and the CPI inflation rate is 3.4%. Then the real interest rates is said to be 2.1%.

A higher real interest rate is good for savers and bad for borrowers.

Note, even if nominal interest rates were high e.g. 11%, savers would see a decline in their real value of money if inflation was 12%. This is why the real interest rate is important

Real interest rates can be negative if inflation is higher than nominal interest rates.

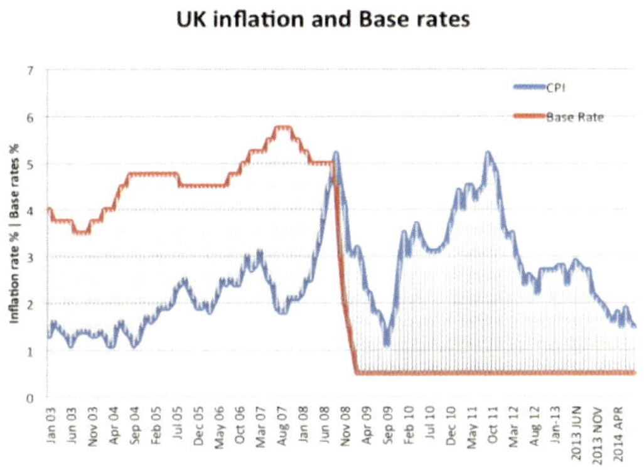

- E.g. in 2007, nominal interest rates were 5.5%, inflation 3%. In this case, we have a real interest rate of + 2.5%.
- In May 2011, inflation was close to 5%, base rates were 0.5%. Therefore in theory, we have negative real interest rates of – 4.5%.

Importance of Real Interest Rates

If inflation is 7%, this may sound very bad for savers. It means the value of money is declining by 7% a year. However, if interest rates are 9%, then savers can still protect their saving. This is because the interest on their savings outweighs the decline in the value of money.

If inflation was 7%, but savers only got 4% interest, then savers would lose out.

Inflation and Saving Rates

Note, the actual saving rates that banks pay. Don't always mirror Bank of England base rates. In the credit crunch, banks were slow to cut interest rates. They needed to attract deposits. Therefore, real interest rates were better for savers than indicated by looking at base rates.

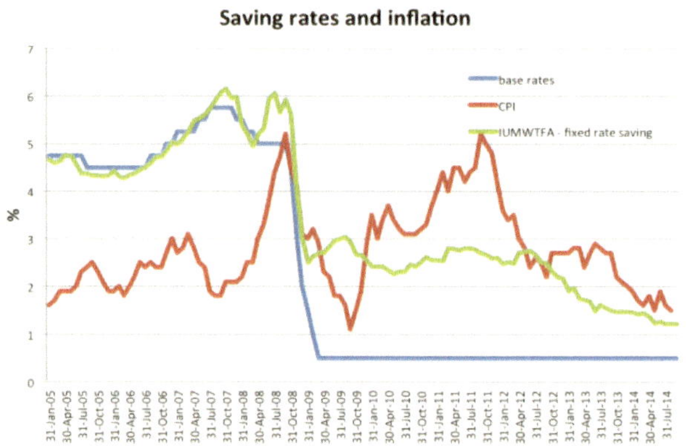

In a liquidity trap, lower interest rates may be ineffective in boosting demand because there are many other factors at work.

- Fall in exports due to global downturn.
- Commercial banks not wanting to lend because of the credit crunch.
- Fall in house prices due to lack of mortgage availability.

This reflects the scale of the recession and how loose monetary policy has been insufficient to prevent the rapid decline in output and fall in inflation.

Also, there is always an issue of time lag. It can take 18 months for interest rate cuts to have an effect.

Bank Rates and base Rates

Another issue is that commercial banks may not pass base rate cuts onto consumers. Therefore, the effective real interest rate may be different to the actual real interest rate, using Bank of England base rate.

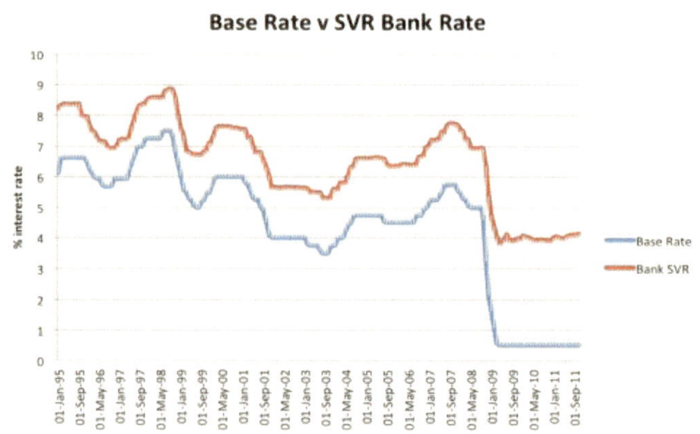

For example, although base rates in 2010 were 0.5%, banks may offer savers a rate of 4%. This is because banks needed to attract saving and deposits.

Effective Interest Rate

The Effective Annual Rate (EAR) is the rate of interest actually earned on an investment or paid on a loan as a result of compounding the interest over a given period of time. It is usually higher than the nominal rate and is used to compare different financial products that calculate annual interest with different compounding periods – weekly, monthly, yearly, etc. Increasing the number of compounding periods makes the effective annual interest rate increase as time goes by.

Effective Annual Rate

$$\left[1 + \frac{\text{Nominal interest rate}}{\text{\# of compounding periods}}\right]^{\wedge\text{(number of compounding periods)}} -1$$

The effective annual rate is normally higher than the nominal rate because the nominal rate quotes a yearly percentage rate regardless of compounding. Increasing the number of compounding periods increases the effective annual rate as compared to the nominal rate. To spin it in another light, an investment that is compounded annually will have an effective annual rate that is equal to its nominal rate. However, if the same investment was instead compounded quarterly, the effective annual rate would then be higher.

Formula for the Effective Annual Rate

The formula for the EAR is:

Effective Annual Rate = (1 + (nominal interest rate / number of compounding periods)) ^ (number of compounding periods) – 1

For example:

Union Bank offers a nominal interest rate of 12% on its certificate of deposit to Mr. Obama, a bank client. The client initially invested $1,000 and agreed to have the interest compounded monthly for one full year. As a result of compounding, the effective interest rate is 12.683%, in which the money grew by $126.83 for one year, even though the interest is offered at only 12%.

Effective Annual Rate Calculator

Below is a figure of CFI's free effective annual rate (EAR) calculator.

As you can see in the example above, a nominal interest rate of 8.0% with 12 compounding periods per year equates to an effective annual percentage rate (EAPR) of 8.3%.

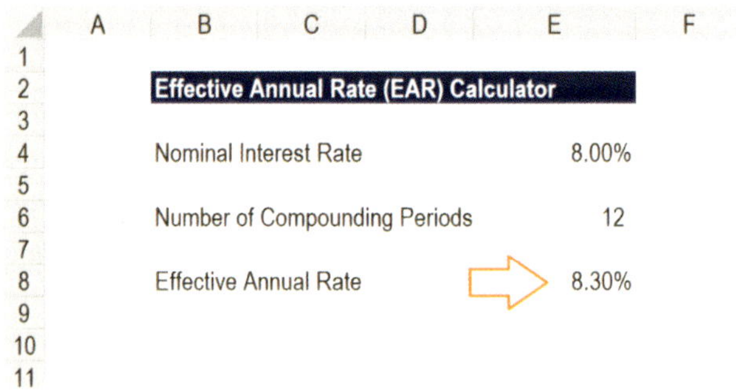

Time Value of Money

Time value of money is the concept that the value of a dollar to be received in future is less than the value of a dollar on hand today. One reason is that money received today can be invested thus generating more money. Another reason is that when a person opts to receive a sum of money in future rather than today, he is effectively lending the money and there are risks involved in lending such as default risk and inflation. Default risk arises when the borrower does not pay the money back to the lender. Inflation is the rise in general level of prices.

Time value of money principle also applies when comparing the worth of money to be received in future and the worth of money to be received in further future. In other words, TVM principle says that the value of given sum of money to be received on a particular date is more than same sum of money to be received on a later date.

Few of the basic terms used in time value of money calculations are:

Present Value

When a future payment or series of payments are discounted at the given rate of interest up to the present date to reflect the time value of money, the resulting value is called present value.

Future Value

Future value is amount that is obtained by enhancing the value of a present payment or a series of payments at the given rate of interest to reflect the time value of money.

Interest

Interest is charge against use of money paid by the borrower to the lender in addition to the actual money lent.

The basic formula for the time value of money is as follows:

PV = FV ÷ (1+I)^N).

Application of Time Value of Money Principle

There are many applications of time value of money principle. For example, we can use it to compare the worth of cash flows occurring at different times in future, to find the present worth of a series of payments to be received periodically in future, to find the required amount of current investment that must be made at a given interest rate to generate a required future cash flow, etc.

Bond Valuation

Bond valuation is a technique for determining the fair price of a bond. The theoretical fair value is the present value of the stream of cash flows expected. Bond valuation includes calculating the present value of the bond's cash flow (future interest payments), and the bond's par value (value upon maturity).

A bond's par value and cash flow are fixed, so investors need simply to look to bond valuation to determine whether an investment in a particular bond would be worthwhile. It's only one of the factors investors consider in determining whether to invest in a particular bond, though. Other important considerations are: the issuing company's creditworthiness, the bond's price appreciation potential, prevailing market interest rates, etc.

Bond Valuation Formula

Firstly, the present value of the bond's future cash flows should be determined. The present value is the amount that would have to be invested today in order to generate said future cash flow. It's dependent on both the timing of the cash flow and the interest rate. To figure out the value, the present value of each individual cash flow must be found. Then, you'll simply add the cash flows together.

$$P = \left(\frac{C}{1+i} + \frac{C}{(1+i)^2} + \ldots + \frac{C}{(1+i)^N} \right) + \frac{M}{(1+i)^N}$$

$$= \left(\sum_{n=1}^{N} \frac{C}{(1+i)^{-n}} \right) + \frac{M}{(1+i)^N}$$

$$= C\left(\frac{1-(1+i)^{-N}}{i}\right) + M(1+i)^{-N}$$

F = face values

iF = contractual interest rate

C = F * iF = coupon payment (periodic interest payment)

N = number of payments

i = market interest rate, or required yield, or observed / appropriate yield to maturity

M = value at maturity, usually equals face value

P = market price of bond

Present Value Approach

Below is the formula for calculating a bond's price, which uses the basic present value (PV) formula for a given discount rate:

$$P = \left(\frac{C}{1+i} + \frac{C}{(1+i)^2} + \ldots + \frac{C}{(1+i)^N}\right) + \frac{M}{(1+i)^N}$$

$$= \left(\sum_{n=1}^{N} \frac{C}{(1+i)^{-n}}\right) + \frac{M}{(1+i)^N}$$

$$= C\left(\frac{1-(1+i)^{-N}}{i}\right) + M(1+i)^{-N}$$

where:

F = face values

iF = contractual interest rate

C = F * iF = coupon payment (periodic interest payment)

N = number of payments

i = market interest rate, or required yield, or observed / appropriate yield to maturity

M = value at maturity, usually equals face value

P = market price of bond.

Relative Price Approach

Under this approach—an extension of the above—the bond will be priced relative to a benchmark, usually a government security; see Relative valuation. Here, the yield to maturity on the bond is determined based on the bond's Credit rating relative to a government security with similar maturity or duration. The better the quality of the bond, the smaller the spread between its required return and the YTM of the benchmark. This required return is then used to discount the bond cash flows, replacing i in the formula above, to obtain the price.

Arbitrage-free Pricing Approach

As distinct from the two related approaches above, a bond may be thought of as a "package of cash flows"—coupon or face—with each cash flow viewed as a zero-coupon instrument maturing on the date it will be received. Thus, rather than using a single discount rate, one should use multiple discount rates, discounting each cash flow at its own rate. Here, each cash flow is separately discounted at the same rate as a zero-coupon bond corresponding to the coupon date, and of equivalent credit worthiness (if possible, from the same issuer as the bond being valued, or if not, with the appropriate credit spread).

Under this approach, the bond price should reflect its "arbitrage-free" price, as any deviation from this price will be exploited and the bond will then quickly reprice to its correct level. Here, we apply the rational pricing logic relating to "Assets with identical cash flows". In detail:

(1) The bond's coupon dates and coupon amounts are known with certainty. Therefore,

(2) Some multiple (or fraction) of zero-coupon bonds, each corresponding to the bond's coupon dates, can be specified so as to produce identical cash flows to the bond. Thus

(3) The bond price today must be equal to the sum of each of its cash flows discounted at the discount rate implied by the value of the corresponding ZCB. Were this not the case,

(4) The arbitrageur could finance his purchase of whichever of the bond or the sum of the various ZCBs was cheaper, by short selling the other, and meeting his cash flow commitments using the coupons or maturing zeroes as appropriate.

(5) His "risk free", arbitrage profit would be the difference between the two values.

Stochastic Calculus Approach

When modelling a bond option, or other interest rate derivative (IRD), it is important to recognize that future interest rates are uncertain, and therefore, the discount rate(s) referred to above, under all three cases—i.e. whether for all coupons or for each individual coupon—is not adequately represented by a fixed (deterministic) number. In such cases, stochastic calculus is employed.

The following is a partial differential equation (PDE) in stochastic calculus which is satisfied by any zero-coupon bond.

$$\frac{1}{2}\sigma(r)^2\frac{\partial^2 P}{\partial r^2}+[a(r)+\sigma(r)+\varphi(r,t)]\frac{\partial P}{\partial r}+\frac{\partial P}{\partial t}-rP=0$$

The solution to the PDE—given in Cox —is:

$$P[t,T,r(t)]=E_t^*[e^{-R(t,T)}]$$

where E_t^* is the expectation with respect to risk-neutral probabilities, and $R(t,T)$ is a random variable representing the discount rate.

To actually determine the bond price, the analyst must choose the specific short rate model to be employed. The approaches commonly used are:

- The CIR model
- The Black-Derman-Toy model
- The Hull-White model
- The HJM framework
- The Chen model.

Note that depending on the model selected, a closed-form solution may not be available, and a lattice- or simulation-based implementation of the model in question is then employed.

Clean and Dirty Price

When the bond is not valued precisely on a coupon date, the calculated price, using the methods above, will incorporate accrued interest: i.e. any interest due to the owner of the bond since the previous coupon date. The price of a bond which includes this accrued interest is known as the "dirty price" (or "full price" or "all in price" or "Cash price"). The "clean price" is the price excluding any interest that has accrued. Clean prices are generally more stable over time than dirty prices. This is because the dirty price will drop suddenly when the bond goes "ex interest" and the purchaser is no longer entitled to receive the next coupon payment. In many markets, it is market practice to quote bonds on a clean-price basis. When a purchase is settled, the accrued interest is added to the quoted clean price to arrive at the actual amount to be paid.

Yield and Price Relationships

Once the price or value has been calculated, various yields relating the price of the bond to its coupons can then be determined.

Yield to Maturity

The yield to maturity (YTM) is the discount rate which returns the market price of a bond without embedded optionality; it is identical to i (required return) in the above equation. YTM is thus the internal rate of return of an investment in the bond made at the observed price. Since YTM can be used to price a bond, bond prices are often quoted in terms of YTM.

To achieve a return equal to YTM, i.e. where it is the required return on the bond, the bond owner must:

- Buy the bond at price P_0,
- hold the bond until maturity, and
- redeem the bond at par.

Coupon Rate

The coupon rate is simply the coupon payment *C* as a percentage of the face value *F*.

$$\text{Coupon rate} = \frac{C}{F}$$

Coupon yield is also called nominal yield.

Current Yield

The current yield is simply the coupon payment *C* as a percentage of the (current) bond price *P*.

$$\text{Current yield} = \frac{C}{P_0}.$$

Relationship

The concept of current yield is closely related to other bond concepts, including yield to maturity, and coupon yield. The relationship between yield to maturity and the coupon rate is as follows:

- When a bond sells at a discount, YTM > current yield > coupon yield.
- When a bond sells at a premium, coupon yield > current yield > YTM.
- When a bond sells at par, YTM = current yield = coupon yield.

Price Sensitivity

The sensitivity of a bond's market price to interest rate (i.e. yield) movements is measured by its duration, and, additionally, by its convexity.

Duration is a linear measure of how the price of a bond changes in response to interest rate changes. It is approximately equal to the percentage change in price for a given change in yield, and may be thought of as the elasticity of the bond's price with respect to discount rates. For example, for small interest rate changes, the duration is the approximate percentage by which the value of the bond will fall for a 1% per annum increase in market interest rate. So the market price of a 17-year bond with a duration of 7 would fall about 7% if the market interest rate (or more precisely the corresponding force of interest) increased by 1% per annum.

Convexity is a measure of the "curvature" of price changes. It is needed because the price is not a linear function of the discount rate, but rather a convex function of the discount rate. Specifically, duration can be formulated as the first derivative of the price with respect to the interest rate, and convexity as the second derivative. Continuing the above example, for a more accurate estimate of sensitivity, the convexity score would be multiplied by the square of the change in interest rate, and the result added to the value derived by the above linear formula.

Accounting Treatment

In accounting for liabilities, any bond discount or premium must be amortized over the life of the bond. A number of methods may be used for this depending on applicable accounting rules. One possibility is that amortization amount in each period is calculated from the following formula:

$$n \in \{0,1,\ldots,N-1\}$$

a_{n+1} = amortization amount in period number "n+1"

$$a_{n+1} = |iP - C|(1+i)^n$$

Bond Discount or Bond Premium $= |F - P| = a_1 + a_2 + \ldots + a_N$

Bond Discount or Bond Premium $= F\,|i - i_F|\,(\frac{1-(1+i)^{-N}}{i})$

Bond Convexity

Convexity in Bonds measures the degree of the non-linear relationship between the price and yield of the bond. As we know the bond price and the yield are inversely related i.e. as yield increases the price decreases. However, this relation is not a straight line but is a convex curve. Convexity measures the curvature in this relationship i.e. how the duration changes with a change in yield of the bond.

Duration of a bond is the linear relationship between the bond price and interest rates where, as interest rates increase bond price decreases. Simply put, a higher duration implies that the bond price is more sensitive to rate changes. For a small and sudden change in bond yield duration is a good measure of the sensitivity of the bond price. However, for larger changes in yield, the duration measure is not effective as the relationship is non-linear and is a curve. There are four different types of Duration measures namely Macaulay's Duration, Modified Duration, Effective duration and Key rate duration which all measure how long it takes for the price of the bond to be paid off by the internal cash flows. What they differ is in how they treat the interest rate changes, embedded bond options and bond redemption options. They however, do not take into account the non-linear relationship between price and yield.

Convexity measures the sensitivity of the bond's duration to change is yield. Convexity is a good measure for bond price changes with greater fluctuations in the interest rates. Mathematically speaking, convexity is the second derivative of the formula for change in bond prices with a change in interest rates and a first derivative of the duration equation.

Bond Convexity Formula

Formula for bond convexity:

$$Convexity = \frac{1}{P \times (1+y)^2} \sum_{t=1}^{T} \left[\frac{CF_t}{(1+y)^t} (t^2 + t) \right]$$

P = Bond price.

Y = Yield to maturity in decimal form.

T = Maturity in years.

CF_t = Cash flow at time t.

Convexity Adjustment = Convexity × 100 × (Δy)2

Calculation of Convexity Example

For a Bond of Face Value USD 1,000 with a semi-annual coupon of 8.0% and a Yield of 10% and 6 years to maturity and a present price of 911.37, the duration is 4.82 years, the modified duration is 4.59 and the calculation for Convexity would be:

Time (t)	Cash Flow	Present value (PV) of cash Flow	Weight = PV of Cash flow / Price	Convexity = Sum of [t x (t+1) x weight x $\frac{1}{(1+y)^2}$]
1	40.00	38.10	4.61%	0.0835
2	40.00	36.28	3.98%	0.2167
3	40.00	34.55	3.79%	0.4127
4	40.00	32.91	3.61%	0.6550
5	40.00	31.34	3.44%	0.9358
6	40.00	29.85	3.28%	1.2477
7	40.00	28.43	3.12%	1.5843
8	40.00	27.07	2.97%	1.9400
9	40.00	25.78	2.83%	2.3095
10	40.00	24.56	2.69%	2.6884
11	40.00	23.39	2.57%	3.0724
12	1,040.00	579.11	63.54%	89.9113
				Sum: 105.0573

Annual Convexity: Semi Annual Convexity/ 4= 26.2643Semi Annual Convexity: 105.0573

In the above example a convexity of 26.2643 can be used to predict the price change for a 1% change in yield would be:

If only modified duration is used:

*Change in price = – Modified Duration *Change in yield*

*Change in price for 1% increase in yield = (– 4.59*1%) = -4.59%*

So the price would decrease by 41.83

To accommodate the convex shape of the graph the change in price formula changes to:

*Change in price = [–Modified Duration *Change in yield] +[1/2 * Convexity*(change in yield)^2]*

*Change in price for 1% increase in yield = [-4.59*1 %] + [1/2 *26.2643* 1%] = -4.46%*

So the price would decrease by only 40.64 instead of 41.83

This shows how for the same 1% increase in yield the predicted price decrease, changes if only duration is used as against when the convexity of the price yield curve is also adjusted.

So the price at a 1% increase in yield as predicted by Modified duration is 869.54 and as predicted using modified duration and convexity of the bond is 870.74. This difference of 1.12 in the price change is due to the fact that the price yield curve is not linear as assumed by the duration formula.

Convexity Approximation Formula

As seen in the convexity calculation can be quite tedious and long especially f the bond is long term and has numerous cash flows. The formula for convexity approximation is as follows:

$$\text{Convexity Approximation} = \frac{P_{+} + P_{-} - 2P_{0}}{2 \times P_{0}(\Delta y)^{2}}$$

P_0= Bond price.

p_-= Bond price when interest rate in incremented.

P_+= Bond price when interest rate in decremented.

Δy = Change in interest rate in decimal form.

Convexity Adjustment = Convexity/2 × 100 × (Δy)2 .

Convexity and Risk Management

As can be seen from the formula Convexity is a function of the bond price, YTM (Yield to maturity), Time to maturity and the sum of the cash flows. The number of coupon flows (cash flows) change the duration and hence the convexity of the bond. The duration of a zero bond is equal to its time to maturity but as there still exists a convex relationship between its price and yield, zero coupon bonds have the highest convexity and its prices most sensitive to changes in yield.

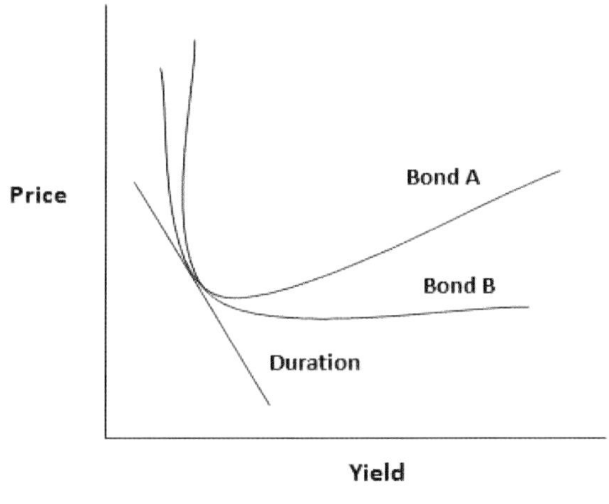

In the above graph Bond A is more convex than Bond B even though they both have the same duration and hence Bond A is less affected by interest rate changes.

Convexity is a risk management tool used to define how risky a bond is as more the convexity of the bond, more is its price sensitivity to interest rate movements. A bond with a higher convexity has larger price change when the interest rate drops than a bond with lower convexity. Hence when two similar bonds are evaluated for investment with similar yield and duration the one with higher convexity is preferred in a stable or falling interest rate scenarios as price change is larger. In a falling interest rate scenario again a higher convexity would be better as the price loss for an increase in interest rates would be smaller.

Positive and Negative Convexity

Convexity can be positive or negative. A bond has positive convexity if the yield and the duration of the bond increase or decrease together, i.e. they have a positive correlation. The yield curve for this typically moves upward. This typical is for a bond which does not have a call option or a prepayment option. Bonds have negative convexity when the yield increases the duration decreases i.e. there is a negative correlation between yield and duration and the yield curve moves downward. These are typically bonds with call options, mortgage-backed securities and those bonds which have a repayment option. If the bond with prepayment or call option has a premium to be paid for the early exit then the convexity may turn positive.

The coupon payments and the periodicity of the payments of the bond contribute to the convexity of the bond. If there are more periodic coupon payments over the life of the bond then the convexity is higher making it more immune to interest rate risks as the periodic payments help in negating the effect of the change in the market interest rates. If there is a lump sum payment then the convexity is the least making it a more risky investment.

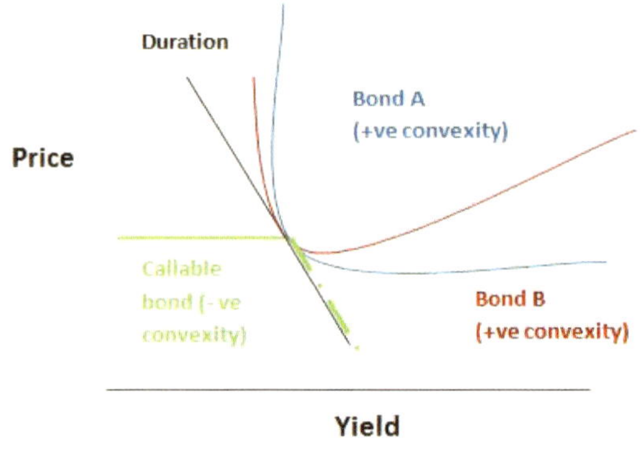

Convexity of a Bond Portfolio

For a bond portfolio the convexity would measure the risk of the all the bonds put together and is the weighted average of the individual bonds with no of bonds or the market value of the bonds being used as weights.

Even though Convexity takes into account the non-linear shape of price-yield curve and adjusts for the prediction for price change there is still some error left as it is only the second derivative of the price-yield equation. To get a more accurate price for a change in yield, adding the next derivative would give a price much closer to the actual price of the bond. Today with sophisticated computer models predicting prices, convexity is more a measure of the risk of the bond or the bond portfolio. More convex the bond or the bond portfolio less risky it is as the price change for a reduction in interest rates is less. So bond which is more convex would have a lower yield as the market prices in the lower risk.

Interest Rate Risk and Convexity

Risk measurement for a bond involves a number of risks. These include but are not limited to:

1. The market risk that is changes in the market interest rate in an unprofitable manner.
2. The prepayment risk that is the bond is prepaid earlier than the maturity date hence disrupting the cash flows.
3. Default risk that is the bond issuer would not pay the interest or the principal amount.

The interest rate risk is a universal risk for all bond holders as all increase in interest rate would reduce the prices and all decrease in interest rate would increase the price of the bond. This interest rate risk is measured by modified duration and is further refined by convexity. Convexity is a measure of systemic risk as it measures the effect of change in the bond portfolio value with larger change in the market interest rate while modified duration is enough to predict smaller changes in interest rates.

As mentioned earlier convexity is positive for regular bonds but for bonds with options like callable bonds, mortgage backed securities (which have prepayment option) the bonds have negative convexity at lower interest rates as the prepayment risk increases. For such bonds with negative convexity prices do not increase significantly wit decrease in interest rates as cash flows change due to prepayment and early calls.

As the cash flow is more spread out the convexity increases as the interest rate risk increases with more gap in between the cash flows. So convexity as a measure is more useful if the coupons are more spread out and are of lesser value. If we have a zero-coupon bond and a portfolio of zero coupon bonds, the convexity are as follows:

- The duration of the zero coupon bond which is equal to its maturity (as there is only one cash flow) and hence its convexity is very high.
- While the duration of the zero coupon bond portfolio can be adjusted as to the

that of a single zero coupon bond by varying the nominal and maturity value of the zero coupon bonds within the portfolio. However, the convexity of this portfolio is higher than the single zero coupon bond. This is because the cash flows of the bonds in the portfolio are more dispersed than that of a single zero coupon bond.

Convexity of bonds with a put option is positive while that of a bond with call option is negative. This is because when a put option is in the money then if the market goes down you can put the bond or if the market goes up you preserve all the cash flows. This makes the convexity positive, however, or a bond with call option the issuer would call the bond if market interest rate decreases s and if the market rate the increases the cash flow would be preserved. Due to the possible change in cash flows, the convexity of the bond is negative as interest rates decrease.

The measured convexity of the bond when there is no expected change in future cash flows is called modified convexity. When there are changes expected in the future cash flows the convexity that is measured is the effective convexity.

Bond Duration

Duration is a measure of a bond's sensitivity to interest rate changes. The higher the bond's duration, the greater its sensitivity to the change (also known as volatility) and vice versa.

Macaulay Duration

There is more than one way to calculate duration, depending on one's compounding assumptions, but the Macaulay duration (named after Frederick Macaulay, an economist who developed the concept in 1938) is the most common. The formula is:

$$\text{Macaulay duration} = \frac{\sum_{t=1}^{n} \frac{tC}{(1+y)^t} + \frac{nM}{(1+y)^n}}{P}$$

where,

t = period in which the coupon is received

C = periodic (usually semiannual) coupon payment

y = the periodic yield to maturity or required yield

n = number periods

M = maturity value (in $)

P = market price of bond

The formula is complicated, but what it boils down to is: Duration = Present value of a bond's cash flows, weighted by length of time to receipt and divided by the bond's current market value. For example, let's calculate the duration of a three-year, $1,000 Company XYZ bond with a semi-annual 10% coupon.

Period	Cash Flow	Period x Cash Flow	PV of $1 at 5%	Present Value of the Cash Flow
1	$50	$50	0.952	$47.62
2	$50	$100	0.907	$90.70
3	$50	$150	0.863	$129.58
4	$50	$200	0.822	$164.54
5	$50	$250	0.783	$195.88
6	$1,050	$6,300	0.746	$4,701.16
Total				**$5,329.48**

Notice in the table above that we first weighted the cash flows by the periods in which the occurred and then calculated the present value of each of these weighted cash flows (also, a measure of 5% is used instead of 10% because payments are semi-annual).

To calculate the Macaulay duration, we then divide the sum of the present values of these cash flows by the current bond price (which we are assuming is $1,000):

Company XYZ Macaulay duration = $5,329.48 / $1,000 = 5.33

As mentioned earlier, duration can help investors understand how sensitive a bond is to changes in prevailing interest rates. By multiplying a bond's duration by the change, the investor can estimate the percentage price change for the bond. For example, consider the Company XYZ bonds with duration of 5.53 years. If for whatever reason market yields increased by 20 basis points (0.20%), the approximate percentage change in the XYZ bond's price would be:

-5.53 x .002 = -0.01106 or -1.106%

Note that this is an approximation. The formula assumes a linear relationship between bond prices and yields even though the relationship is actually convex. Thus, the formula is less reliable when there is a large change in yield.

In general, six things affect a bond's duration:

- Bond's Price: Note that if the bond in the above example were trading at $900 today, then the duration would be $5,329.48 / $900 = 5.92. If the bond were trading at $1,200 today, then the duration would be $5,329.48 / $1,200 = 4.44.
- Coupon: The higher a bond's coupon, the more income it produces early on and thus the shorter its duration. The lower the coupon, the longer the duration

(and volatility). Zero-coupon bonds, which have only one cash flow, have durations equal to their maturities.

- Maturity: The longer a bond's maturity, the greater its duration (and volatility). Duration changes every time a bond makes a coupon payment. Over time, it shortens as the bond nears maturity.
- Yield to Maturity: The higher a bond's yield to maturity, the shorter its duration because the present value of the distant cash flows (which have the heaviest weighting) become overshadowed by the value of the nearer payments.
- Sinking Fund: The presence of a sinking fund lowers a bond's duration because the extra cash flows in the early years are greater than those of a bond without a sinking fund.
- Call Provision: Bonds with call provisions also have shorter durations because the principal is repaid earlier than a similar non-callable bond.

Modified Duration

In contrast to Macaulay duration, modified duration (sometimes abbreviated MD) is a price sensitivity measure, defined as the percentage derivative of price with respect to yield (the first order derivative of bond price with respect to yield). Modified duration applies when a bond or other asset is considered as a function of yield. In this case one can measure the logarithmic derivative with respect to yield:

$$ModD(y) \equiv -\frac{1}{V}\cdot\frac{\partial V}{\partial y} = -\frac{\partial ln(V)}{\partial y}$$

Thus for fixed payment bonds, when the yield is expressed continuously compounded, Macaulay duration and modified duration are equal.

First, consider the case of continuously compounded yields. If we take the derivative of price or present value, expression, $V = \sum_{i=1}^{n} PV_i = \sum_{i=1}^{n} CF_i \cdot e^{-y \cdot t_i}$
with respect to the continuously compounded yield y we see that:

$$\frac{\partial V}{\partial y} = -\sum_{i=1}^{n} t_i \cdot CF_i \cdot e^{-y \cdot t_i} = -MacD \cdot V,$$

In other words, for yields expressed continuously compounded,

$$ModD = MacD.$$

where,

i indexes the cash flows,

t_i is the time in years until the *ith* payment will be received,

V is the present value of all cash payments from the asset.

Periodically Compounded

In financial markets, yields are usually expressed periodically compounded (say annually or semi-annually) instead of continuously compounded. Then expression

$V = \sum_{i=1}^{n} PV_i = \sum_{i=1}^{n} CF_i \cdot e^{-y \cdot t_i}$ becomes:

$$V(y_k) = \sum_{i=1}^{n} PV_i = \sum_{i=1}^{n} \frac{CF_i}{(1+y_k/k)^{k \cdot t_i}}$$

$$MacD = \sum_{i=1}^{n} \frac{t_i}{V(y_k)} \cdot \frac{CF_i}{(1+y_k/k)^{k \cdot t_i}}$$

To find modified duration, when we take the derivative of the value V with respect to the periodically compounded yield we find

$$\frac{\partial V}{\partial y_k} = -\frac{1}{(1+y_k/k)} \cdot \sum_{i=1}^{n} t_i \cdot \frac{CF_i}{(1+y_k/k)^{k \cdot t_i}} = -\frac{MacD \cdot V(y_k)}{(1+y_k/k)}$$

Rearranging (dividing both sides by -V) gives:

$$\frac{MacD}{(1+y_k/k)} = -\frac{1}{V(y_k)} \cdot \frac{\partial V}{\partial y_k} \equiv ModD$$

which is the well-known relationship between modified duration and Macaulay duration:

$$ModD = \frac{MacD}{(1+y_k/k)}$$

where,

- i indexes the cash flows,
- k is the compounding frequency per year (1 for annual, 2 for semi-annual, 12 for monthly, 52 for weekly, etc.),
- CF_i is the cash flow of the *ith* payment from an asset,

- t_i is the time in years until the *ith* payment will be received (e.g. a two-year semi-annual would be represented by a t_i index of 0.5, 1.0, 1.5, and 2.0),
- yk is the yield to maturity for an asset, periodically compounded
- V is the present value of all cash payments from the asset.

This gives the well-known relation between Macaulay duration and modified duration quoted above. It should be remembered that, even though Macaulay duration and modified duration are closely related, they are conceptually distinct. Macaulay duration is a weighted average time until repayment (measured in units of time such as years) while modified duration is a price sensitivity measure when the price is treated as a function of yield, the percentage change in price with respect to yield.

Units

Mathematically, modified duration and Macaulay duration have the same units, as can be seen in the above equations.

Modified duration can be expressed as the percent change in price per one percentage point change in yield per year (for example yield going from 8% per year ($y = 0.08$) to 9% per year ($y = 0.09$)). This will give modified duration a value close to the Macaulay duration (and equal when rates are continuously compounded).

Formally, modified duration is semi-elasticity, the percent change in price for a unit change in yield, rather than elasticity, which is a percentage change in output for a percentage change in input. Modified duration is a rate of change, the percent change in price per change in yield.

In derivatives pricing ("The Greeks"), the closest analogous quantity is Rho, which is the derivative of the price with respect to interest rates.

Non-fixed Cash Flows

Modified duration can be extended to instruments with non-fixed cash flows, while Macaulay duration applies only to fixed cash flow instruments. Modified duration is defined as the logarithmic derivative of price with respect to yield, and such a definition will apply to instruments that depend on yields, whether or not the cash flows are fixed.

Finite Yield Changes

Modified duration is defined above as a derivative (as the term relates to calculus) and so is based on infinitesimal changes. Modified duration is also useful as a measure of the sensitivity of a bond's market price to finite interest rate (i.e., yield) movements. For a small change in yield Δy,

$$ModD \approx -\frac{1}{V}\frac{\Delta V}{\Delta y} \Rightarrow \Delta V \approx -V \cdot ModD \cdot \Delta y$$

Thus modified duration is approximately equal to the percentage change in price for a given finite change in yield. So a 15-year bond with a Macaulay duration of 7 years would have a Modified duration of roughly 7 years and would fall approximately 7% in value if the interest rate increased by one percentage point (say from 7% to 8%).

Fisher–Weil Duration

Fisher–Weil duration is a refinement of Macaulay's duration which takes into account the term structure of interest rates. Fisher–Weil duration calculates the present values of the relevant cashflows (more strictly) by using the zero coupon yield for each respective maturity.

Key Rate Duration

Key rate durations (also called partial DV01s or partial durations) are a natural extension of the total modified duration to measuring sensitivity to shifts of different parts of the yield curve. Key rate durations might be defined, for example, with respect to zero-coupon rates with maturity '1M', '3M', '6M', '1Y', '2Y', '3Y', '5Y', '7Y', '10Y', '15Y', '20Y', '25Y', '30Y'. Thomas Ho 1992 introduced the term key rate duration. Reitano covered multifactor yield curve models as early as 1991 and has revisited the topic in a recent review.

Key rate durations require that we value an instrument off a yield curve and requires building a yield curve. Ho's original methodology was based on valuing instruments off a zero or spot yield curve and used linear interpolation between "key rates", but the idea is applicable to yield curves based on forward rates, par rates, and so forth. Many technical issues arise for key rate durations (partial DV01s) that do not arise for the standard total modified duration because of the dependence of the key rate durations on the specific type of the yield curve used to value the instruments.

Formulas

For a standard bond with fixed, semi-annual payments the bond duration closed-form formula is:

$$\text{Dur} = \frac{1}{P}\left(C\frac{(1+ai)(1+i)^m - (1+i) - (m-1+a)i}{i^2(1+i)^{(m-1+a)}} + \frac{FV(m-1+a)}{(1+i)^{(m-1+a)}} \right)$$

- FV = par value
- C = coupon payment per period (half-year)

- i = discount rate per period (half-year)
- a = fraction of a period remaining until next coupon payment
- m = number of full coupon periods until maturity
- P = bond price (present value of cash flows discounted with rate i)

For a bond with coupon frequency *k* but an integer number of periods (so that there is no fractional payment period), the formula simplifies to:

$$MacD = \left[\frac{(1+y/k)}{y/k} - \frac{100(1+y/k)+m(c/k-100y/k)}{(c/k)[(1+y/k)^m-1]+100y/k}\right]/k$$

where,

- y = Yield (per year, in percent),
- c = Coupon (per year, in decimal form),
- m = Number of coupon periods.

Example

Consider a 2-year bond with face value of $100, a 20% semi-annual coupon, and a yield of 4% semi-annually compounded. The total PV will be:

$$V = \sum_{i=1}^{n} PV_i = \sum_{i=1}^{n} \frac{CF_i}{(1+y/k)^{k \cdot t_i}} = \sum_{i=1}^{4} \frac{10}{(1+.04/2)^i} + \frac{100}{(1+.04/2)^4}$$
$$= 9.804 + 9.612 + 9.423 + 9.238 + 92.385 = 130.462$$

The Macaulay duration is then

$$\text{MacD} = 0.5 \cdot \frac{9.804}{130.462} + 1.0 \cdot \frac{9.612}{130.462} + 1.5 \cdot \frac{9.423}{130.462} + 2.0 \cdot \frac{9.238}{130.462}$$

$$+ 2.0 \cdot \frac{92.385}{130.462} = 1.777 \text{years.}$$

The simple formula above gives (y/k =.04/2=.02, c/k = 20/2 = 10):

$$\text{MacD} = \left[\frac{(1.02)}{0.02} - \frac{100(1.02)+4(10-2)}{10[(1.02)^4-1]+2}\right]/2 = 1.777 \text{years}$$

The modified duration, measured as percentage change in price per one percentage point change in yield, is:

$$ModD = \frac{MacD}{(1+y/k)} = \frac{1.777}{(1+.04/2)} = 1.742$$

(% change in price per 1 percentage point change in yield)

The DV01, measured as dollar change in price for a $100 nominal bond for a one percentage point change in yield, is

$$DV01 = \frac{ModD \cdot 130.462}{100} = 2.27 \text{ (\$ per 1 percentage point change in yield)}$$

where the division by 100 is because modified duration is the percentage change.

Dollar duration, DV01, BPV, Bloomberg "Risk"

The dollar duration or DV01 or BPV or Bloomberg Risk is defined as negative of the derivative of the value with respect to yield:

$$D_{\$} = DV01 = -\frac{\partial V}{\partial y}.$$

so that it is the product of the modified duration and the price (value):

$$D_{\$} = DV01 = BPV = V \cdot ModD / 100 \text{ (\$ per 1 percentage point change in yield)}$$

Or

$$D_{\$} = DV01 = V \cdot ModD / 10000 \text{ (\$ per 1 basis point change in yield)}$$

The DV01 is analogous to the delta in derivative pricing (The Greeks) – it is the ratio of a price change in output (dollars) to unit change in input (a basis point of yield). Dollar duration or DV01 is the change in price in dollars, not in percentage. It gives the dollar variation in a bond's value per unit change in the yield. It is often measured per 1 basis point - DV01 is short for "dollar value of an 01" (or 1 basis point). The name BPV (basis point value) or Bloomberg "Risk" is also used, often applied to the dollar change for a $100 notional for 100bp change in yields - giving the same units as duration. PV01 (present value of an 01) is sometimes used, although PV01 more accurately refers to the value of a one dollar or one basis point annuity. (For a par bond and a flat yield curve the DV01, derivative of price with respect yield, and PV01, value of a one-dollar annuity, will actually have the same value.

DV01 or dollar duration can be used for instruments with zero up-front value such as interest rate swaps where percentage changes and modified duration are less useful.

Application to Value-at-risk (VaR)

Dollar duration $D_{\$}$ is commonly used for value-at-risk (VaR) calculation. To illustrate applications to portfolio risk management, consider a portfolio of securities dependent on the interest rates $r_1,\ldots,r_n$ as risk factors, and let

$$V = V(r_1,\ldots,r_n)$$

denote the value of such portfolio. Then the exposure vector $\omega = (\omega_1,\ldots,\omega_n)$ has components

$$\omega_i = -D_{\$,i} := \frac{\partial V}{\partial r_i}.$$

Accordingly, the change in value of the portfolio can be approximated as

$$\Delta V = \sum_{i=1}^{n} \omega_i \Delta r_i + \sum_{1 \le i,j \le n} O(\Delta r_i \Delta r_j),$$

that is, a component that is linear in the interest rate changes plus an error term which is at least quadratic. This formula can be used to calculate the VaR of the portfolio by ignoring higher order terms. Typically cubic or higher terms are truncated. Quadratic terms, when included, can be expressed in terms of (multi-variate) bond convexity. One can make assumptions about the joint distribution of the interest rates and then calculate VaR by Monte Carlo simulation or, in some special cases (e.g., Gaussian distribution assuming a linear approximation), even analytically. The formula can also be used to calculate the DV01 of the portfolio (cf. below) and it can be generalized to include risk factors beyond interest rates.

Risk – Duration as Interest Rate Sensitivity

The primary use of duration (modified duration) is to measure interest rate sensitivity or exposure. Thinking of risk in terms of interest rates or yields is very useful because it helps to normalize across otherwise disparate instruments. Consider, for example, the following four instruments, each with 10-year final maturity:

Description	Coupon ($ per year)	Initial Price (per $100 notional)	Final Principal Re-Payment	Yield	Macaulay Duration (years)	Modified Duration (% per 100bp yld ch)	BPV or DV01 ($ per 100bp yld ch)
5% semi-annual coupon bond	$5	$100	$100	5%	7.99yrs	7.79%	$7.79
5% semi-annual annuity	$5	$38.9729	$0	5%	4.84yrs	4.72%	$1.84
zero-coupon bond	$0	$61.0271	$100	5%	10yrs	9.76%	$5.95
5% fixed-floating swap, Receive fixed	$5	$0	$0	5%	NA	NA	$7.79

All four have a 10-year maturity but the sensitivity to interest rates, and thus the risk, will be different: the zero-coupon has the highest sensitivity and the annuity the lowest.

Consider first a $100 investment in each, which makes sense for the three bonds (the coupon bond, the annuity, the zero-coupon bond - it does not make sense for the interest rate swap for which there is no initial investment). Modified duration is a useful measure to compare interest rate sensitivity across the three. The zero-coupon bond will have the highest sensitivity, changing at a rate of 9.76% per 100bp change in yield. This means that if yields go up from 5% to 5.01% (a rise of 1bp) the price should fall by roughly 0.0976% or a change in price from $61.0271 per $100 notional to roughly $60.968. The original $100 invested will fall to roughly $99.90. The annuity has the lowest sensitivity, roughly half that of the zero-coupon bond, with a modified duration of 4.72%.

Alternatively, we could consider $100 notional of each of the instruments. In this case the BPV or DV01 (dollar value of an 01 or dollar duration) is the more natural measure. The BPV in the table is the dollar change in price for $100 notional for 100bp change in yields. The BPV will make sense for the interest rate swap (for which modified duration is not defined) as well as the three bonds.

Modified duration measures the size of the interest rate sensitivity. Sometimes we can be misled into thinking that it measures which part of the yield curve the instrument is sensitive to. After all, the modified duration (% change in price) is almost the same number as the Macaulay duration (a kind of weighted average years to maturity). For example, the annuity above has Macaulay duration of 4.8 years and we might think that it is sensitive to the 5-year yield. But it has a cash flows out to 10 years and thus will be sensitive to 10-year yields. If we want to measure sensitivity to parts of the yield curve we need to consider key rate durations.

For bonds with fixed cash flows a price change can come from two sources:

1. The passage of time (convergence towards par). This is of course totally predictable, and hence not a risk.

2. A change in the yield. This can be due to a change in the benchmark yield, and/or change in the yield spread.

The yield-price relationship is inverse, and the modified duration provides a very useful measure of the price sensitivity to yields. As a first derivative it provides a linear approximation. For large yield changes, convexity can be added to provide a quadratic or second-order approximation. Alternatively, and often more usefully, convexity can be used to measure how the modified duration changes as yields change. Similar risk measures (first and second order) used in the options markets are the delta and gamma.

Modified duration and DV01 as measures of interest rate sensitivity are also useful because they can be applied to instruments and securities with varying or contingent cash flows, such as options.

Embedded Options and Effective Duration

For bonds that have embedded options, such as putable and callable bonds, Modified duration will not correctly approximate the price move for a change in yield to maturity.

Consider a bond with an embedded put option. As an example, a $1,000 bond that can be redeemed by the holder at par at any time before the bond's maturity (i.e. an American put option). No matter how high interest rates become, the price of the bond will never go below $1,000 (ignoring counterparty risk). This bond's price sensitivity to interest rate changes is different from a non-putable bond with otherwise identical cashflows.

To price such bonds, one must use option pricing to determine the value of the bond, and then one can compute its delta (and hence its lambda), which is the duration. The effective duration is a discrete approximation to this later, and will require an option pricing model.

$$\text{Effective duration} = \frac{V_{-\Delta y} - V_{+\Delta y}}{2(V_0)\Delta y}$$

where Δ y is the amount that yield changes, and $V_{-\Delta y}$ and $V_{+\Delta y}$ are the values that the bond will take if the yield falls by y or rises by y, respectively. (Note that this value may vary depending on the value used for Δ y.)

These values are typically calculated using a tree-based model, built for the entire yield curve (as opposed to a single yield to maturity), and therefore capturing exercise behavior at each point in the option's life as a function of both time and interest rates.

Spread Duration

Sensitivity of a bond's market price to a change in Option Adjusted Spread (OAS). Thus the index, or underlying yield curve, remains unchanged. Floating rate assets that are benchmarked to an index (such as 1-month or 3-month LIBOR) and reset periodically will have an effective duration near zero but a spread duration comparable to an otherwise identical fixed rate bond.

Average Duration

The sensitivity of a portfolio of bonds such as a bond mutual fund to changes in interest rates can also be important. The average duration of the bonds in the portfolio is often reported. The duration of a portfolio equals the weighted average maturity of all of the cash flows in the portfolio. If each bond has the same yield to maturity, this equals the weighted average of the portfolio's bond's durations, with weights proportional to the bond prices. Otherwise the weighted average of the bond's durations is just a good approximation, but it can still be used to infer how the value of the portfolio would change in response to changes in interest rates.

Importance of Bond Duration

Understanding the duration formula is not nearly as important as understanding that duration is a measure of risk because it has a direct relationship with price volatility. The greater duration of the bond, the greater its percentage price volatility.

By providing a way to estimate the effect of certain market changes on a bond's price, duration can help you choose investments that might better meet your future cash needs. Duration also helps income investors who want to take on minimal interest rate risk (that is, they believe interest rates might rise) understand why they should consider bonds with high coupon payments and shorter maturities.

References

- "Coping with the Risk of Interest-Rate Fluctuations: Returns to Bondholders from Naive and Optimal Strategies." Lawrence Fisher and Roman L. Weil; Journal of Business, 1971, 44(4), pp. 408-31. JSTOR 2352056
- What-are-interest-rates-and-how-do-they-work-3305855: thebalance.com, Retrieved 10 June 2018
- Reitano, Robert R. (January 1991). "Multivariate Duration Analysis" (PDF). Transactions of the Society of Actuaries. XLIII: 335–391. Retrieved 2011.
- Formula-calculation-of-a-real-interest-rate-Fisher-equation: iotafinance.com, Retrieved 25 April 2018
- Ho, Thomas S.Y. (September 1992). "Key Rate Durations: Measures of Interest Rate Risks". Journal of Fixed Income. 2 (2): 29–44.
- Bond-valuation, starter-guides: wallstreetsurvivor.com, Retrieved 15 April 2018
- Convexity-of-a-bond-formula-duration: wallstreetmojo.com, Retrieved 13 May 2018

5

Dividend: Distribution of Profits

A dividend is the payment a corporation makes to its shareholders, usually in the form of a distribution of the profits earned or surplus achieved. This chapter discusses in detail the varied concepts and theories related to dividend and the distribution of profits, such as dividend policy, dividend yield and dividend payout ratio.

Dividend

Dividend is "a distribution to shareholders out of profits or reserves available for this purpose."

The term dividend refers to that portion of profit (after tax) which is distributed among the owners/shareholders of the firm. Dividend may be defined as the return that a shareholder gets from the company, out of its profits, on his shareholdings.

In other words, dividend is that part of the net earnings of a corporation that is distributed to its stockholders. It is a payment made to the equity shareholders for their investment in the company.

As per the section 2(22) of the Income Tax Act, 1961, dividend defined as:

Any distribution of accumulated profits whether capitalized or not, if such distribution entails a release of assets or part thereof.

Dividend is a reward to equity shareholders for their investment in the company. It is a basic right of equity shareholders to get dividend from the earnings of a company. Their share should be distributed among the members within the limit of an act and with rational behavior of directors.

Types of Dividends

Classifications of dividends are based on the form in which they are paid. Following given below are the different types of dividends:

Cash dividend

Companies mostly pay dividends in cash. A Company should have enough cash in its bank account when cash dividends are declared. If it does not have enough bank balance, arrangement should be made to borrow funds. When the Company follows a stable dividend policy, it should prepare a cash budget for the coming period to indicate the necessary funds, which would be needed to meet the regular dividend payments of the company. It is relatively difficult to make cash planning in anticipation of dividend needs when an unstable policy is followed. The cash account and the reserve account of a company will be reduced when the cash dividend is paid. Thus, both the total assets and net worth of the company are reduced when the cash dividend is distributed. The market price of the share drops in most cases by the amount of the cash dividend distributed.

Bonus Shares

(OR Stock -dividend in USA) An issue of bonus share is the distribution of shares free of cost to the existing shareholders, In India, bonus shares are issued in addition to the cash dividend and not in lieu of cash dividend. Hence, Companies in India may supplement cash dividend by bonus issues. Issuing bonus shares increases the number of outstanding shares of the company. The bonus shares are distributed proportionately to the existing shareholder. Hence there is no dilution of ownership.

The declaration of the bonus shares will increase the paid-up Share Capital and reduce the reserves and surplus retained earnings) of the company. The total net-worth (paid up capital plus reserves and surplus) is not affected by the bonus issue. Infect, a bonus issue represents a recapitalization of reserves and surplus. It is merely an accounting transfer from reserves and surplus to paid up capital.

The following are advantages of the bonus shares to shareholders:

1) Tax benefit: One of the advantages to shareholders in the receipt of bonus shares is the beneficial treatment of such dividends with regard to income taxes.

2) Indication of higher future profits: The issue of bonus shares is normally interpreted by shareholders as an indication of higher profitability.

3) Future dividends may increase: if a Company has been following a policy of paying a fixed amount of dividend per share and continues it after the declaration of the bonus issue, the total cash dividend of the shareholders will increase in the future.

4) Psychological Value: The declaration of the bonus issue may have a favorable psychological effect on shareholders. The receipt of bonus shares gives them a chance sell the shares to make capital gains without impairing their principal investment. They also associate it with the prosperity of the company.

Special dividend

In special circumstances Company declares Special dividends. Generally company declares special dividend in case of abnormal profits.

Extra- dividend: An extra dividend is an additional non-recurring dividend paid over and above the regular dividends by the company. Companies with fluctuating earnings payout additional dividends when their earnings warrant it, rather than fighting to keep a higher quantity of regular dividends.

Annual dividend: When annually company declares and pay dividend is defined as annual dividend.

Interim dividend: During the year any time company declares a dividend, it is defined as Interim dividend.

Regular cash dividends

Regular cash dividends are those the company exacts to maintain every year. They may be paid quarterly, monthly, semi-annually or annually.

Scrip dividends: These are promises to make the payment of dividend at a future date: Instead of paying the dividend now, the firm elects to pay it at some later date. The 'scrip' issued to stockholders is merely a special form of promissory note or notes payable.

Liquidating dividends

These dividends are those which reduce paid-in capital: It is a pro-rata distribution of cash or property to stockholders as part of the dissolution of a business.

Property dividends

These dividends are payable in assets of the corporation other than cash. For example, a firm may distribute samples of its own product or shares in another company it owns to its stockholders.

The Dividend Decision

The company's Board of Directors makes dividend decisions. They are faced with the decision to pay out dividends or to reinvest the cash into new projects.

The tradeoff between paying dividends and retaining profits within the company The dividend policy decision is a trade-off between retaining earnings v/s paying out cash dividends. Dividend policies must always consider two basic objectives:

- Maximizing owners' wealth
- Providing sufficient financing While determining a firm's dividend policy, management must find a balance between current income for stockholders (dividends) and future growth of the company (retained earnings).

In applying a rational framework for dividend policy, a firm must consider the following two issues:

- How much cash is available for paying dividends to equity investors, after meeting all needs-debt payments, capital expenditures and working capital (i.e. Free Cash Flow to Equity - FCFE)
- To what extent are good projects available to the firm (i.e. Return on equity - ROE > Required Return) The potential combinations of FCFE and Project Quality and the generalizations of the dividend policy to be adapted in each situation are presented below:

Factors	**FCFE> Dividends**	**FCFE<Dividends**
ROE> Cost of Equity	Good Projects Cash flow surplus No Change	Good Projects Decrease Dividends Invest in Projects
ROE< Cost of Equity	Poor Projects Cash flow surplus Increase Dividends Reduce Investment	Poor Projects Cash flow Deficit Decrease Dividends Reduce Investment

Figure: Dividend Decision Matrix

Dividend Payment Procedures

The firm's board of directors normally meets quarterly to evaluate financial performance and decide whether, and in what amount, dividends should be paid.

If dividend is to be paid the declaration date, record date etc. have to be established.

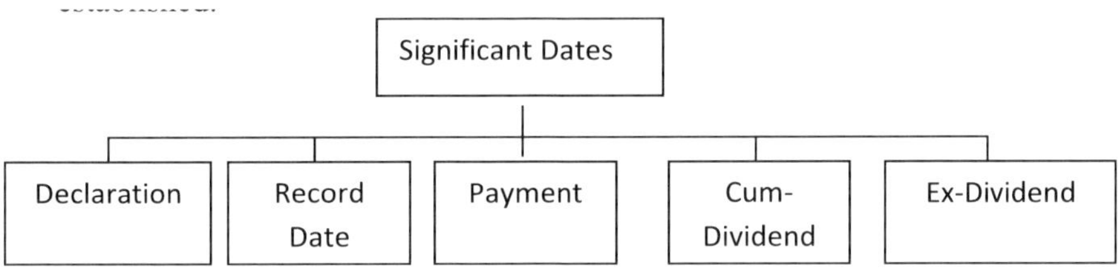

Figure: Dividend Payment Dates

Declaration date: This is the day on which the board of directors declares a payment of dividend.

Date of Record: This is the day on which all persons whose names are recoded as stockholders will receive the dividend.

Payment date: The dividend checks are mailed to shareholders of record.

Cum Dividend date: This is the last say on which the buyer who buys the stock is entitled to get the dividend.

Ex-Dividend date: Shares become ex dividend on the date seller is entitled to keep the dividend. This is the first date on which the buyer who buys the stock is not entitled to dividend.

Dividend Models

The various models that support the above-mentioned theories of dividend relevance and irrelevance are as follows:

Modigliani Miller Approach

According to them the price of a share of a firm is determined by its earning potentiality and investment policy and not by the pattern of income distribution. The model given by them is as follows:

$$Po = D1 + P1/\ (1/Ke)$$

Where, Po = Prevailing market price of a share

Ke = Cost of equity capital

D1 = Dividend to be received at the end of period one

P1 = Market price of a share at the end of period one.

According to the MM hypothesis, market value of a share before dividend is declared is equal to the present value of dividends paid plus the market value of the share after dividend is declared.

Walter's Approach

According to Prof. James E. Walter, in the long run, share prices reflect the present value of future+ dividends. According to him investment policy and dividend policy are inter related and the choice of a appropriate dividend policy affects the value of an enterprise. His formula for determination of expected market price of a share is as follows:

$$P = D + r/k(E\text{-}D)\ K$$

Where,

P = Market price of equity share

D = Dividend per share E = Earnings per share

(E-D) = Retained earnings per share

r = Internal rate of return on investment

k = cost of capital

Gordon's Approach

Dividend Yield Basis

The value of a share, like any other financial asset, is the present value of the future cash flows associated with ownership. On this view, the value of the share is calculated as the present value of an infinite stream of dividends.

Myron Gordon's Dividend Growth Model explains how dividend policy of a firm is a basis of establishing share value. Gordon's model uses the dividend capitalization approach for stock valuation. The formula used is as follows:

$$P_0 = E_1 (1-b) / K - br$$

Where,

P_0 = price per share at the end of year 0

E_1 = earnings per share at the end of year 1

$(1-b)$ = fraction of earnings the firm distributes by way of dividends

b = fraction of earnings the firm ploughs back

k = rate of return required by shareholders

r = rate of return earned on investments made by the firm

br = growth rate of dividend and earnings

The models, provided by Walter and Gordon lead to the following implications:

If $r > k$ Price per share increases as dividend payout ratio decreases

If $r = k$ Price per share remains unchanged with changes in dividend payout ratio

If $r < k$ Price per share increases as dividend payout ratio increases.

This further implies that:

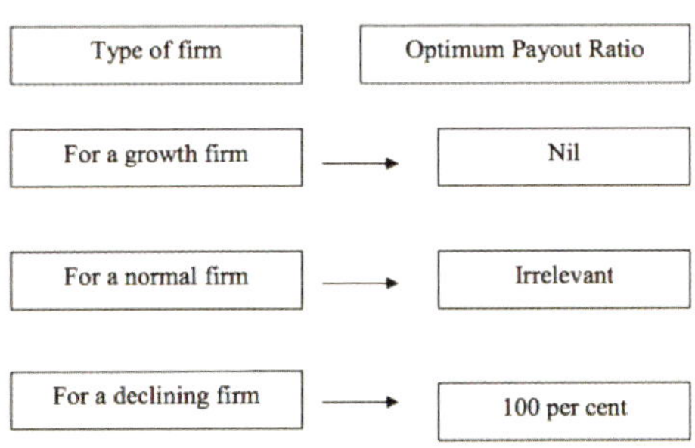

Figure: Optimum Payout Ratio

Steps to be Followed in Setting Dividends

The points considered by the BOD while making the dividend decision has already been discussed earlier in The Dividend Decision. The dividend payment procedure involves determination of a firm's profitable investment opportunities over a reasonable time horizon; projection of the firm's operating cash flows necessary for financing the projects; estimation of the residual funds which can be made available for distribution; finalizing the target payout rates keeping in view industry trends, financial soundness of business, future prospects, borrowing capacity etc. among other factors; and finally setting a feasible payout rate for the current year.

The steps to be followed by a firm in setting dividends are briefly listed as follows:

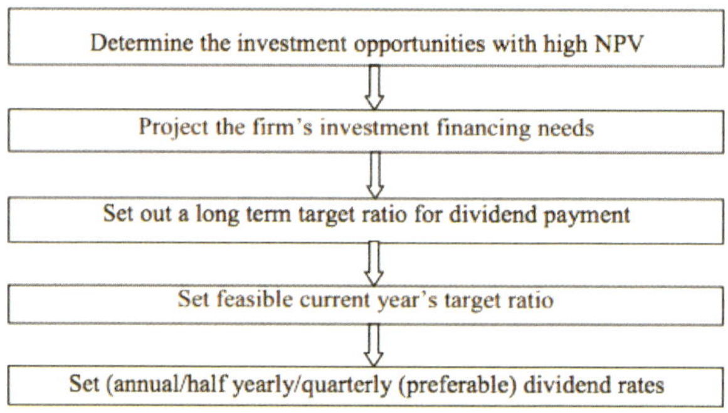

Figure: Steps for setting dividends

Dividend and a Firm's Life Cycle

The payout policy of firms undergoes systematic changes over their life cycle. New firms or firms that are in the growth stage pay very low or no dividends as during this initial growth period firms retain funds to finance investment. Mature firms that are no longer in a growth phase often pay high and increasing dividends. Thus, dividend payout keeps increasing as firms grow more mature and finally d stage arises where a firm's cash flow exceeds its capital needs, and during this liquidation stage, excess cash is distributed generously in the form of cash dividends to the shareholders.

Stage of Growth			
Stage I	Stage II	Stage III	Stage IV
Introduction	Rapid Growth	Maturity	Decline
Dividend Policy			
No Dividend	Low Dividend Payout Policy	Growing or Increasing Payout Policy	Generous Dividend Payout Policy

Figure: Dividend and a firm's life cycle

Special Dividend

When a company finds that it has a large amount of excess cash, it might decide to distribute that cash to its shareholders through a special dividend. Unlike a regular dividend, a special dividend is a one-time payment. One well-known example of a special dividend is when Microsoft paid shareholders a total of $32 billion in special dividends in November of 2004.

While special dividends can be a nice bonus for investors, they also have certain drawbacks.

Special Dividends versus Normal Dividends

Special dividends should not be confused with normal dividends, which are typically paid quarterly and in uniform installments. While a company can raise its regular dividends, special dividends usually represent a payout that is significantly larger than a company's normal dividend payment.

When a company raises its normal dividend, investors expect to continue receiving higher regular payments on an ongoing basis. This is why companies are careful to announce special dividends -- to keep investors' expectations in check. Special dividends generally don't impact a company's stock valuation or dividend yield because they're one-time events.

Reason for Declaring Special Dividends by Companies

A company might choose to make a special dividend payment after a period of particularly strong earnings. Generally speaking, dividend payments are a way for companies to share their profits with stockholders. Special dividends are often regarded as a form of sharing a bit of extra wealth. In other situations, a company might announce a special dividend payment at a time when it wants to change its financial structure.

Special Dividend Taxes

Unlike most regular dividends, which are taxed as qualified dividends (and thus as long-term capital gains), special dividends can be made up of a mixture of capital gains, ordinary income, and returns of capital.

The exact breakdown of the special dividend is spelled out in the 1099-DIV form sent to you by the company at tax time, but in general most special dividends are treated as returns of capital.

Rather than paying taxes on dividends classified as a return of capital, you lower the cost basis of your shares and only get taxed when you sell them.

However, this aspect of special dividend taxes also means that special dividends held in tax-deferred accounts, such as IRAs or 401(k)s, will miss out on the tax benefit.

That's because any money withdrawn from these accounts after the age of 59.5 will be taxed as ordinary income.

Special Dividend Rules

The usual rules about holding periods don't necessarily apply to special dividends.

For example, with normal dividends the company will issue three dates: the ex-dividend date, the record date, and the pay date.

This means that anyone who is a shareholder of record (i.e. your broker's clearing house has a record of you owning shares) will get the dividend on the pay date.

The ex-dividend date is the first day that you won't get the dividend if you purchase shares that day.

In other words, in order to get the most recently announced regular dividend, you must purchase shares the day before the ex-div date.

Special Dividend Impact on Stock Price

In theory, a company's stock price will automatically fall by the special dividend amount on the ex-dividend date because the company's distribution of this cash represents a decrease in the value of the company.

Take a look at FutureFuel, for example. FutureFuel (FF) declared a special dividend of $2.29 per share at the end of 2016.

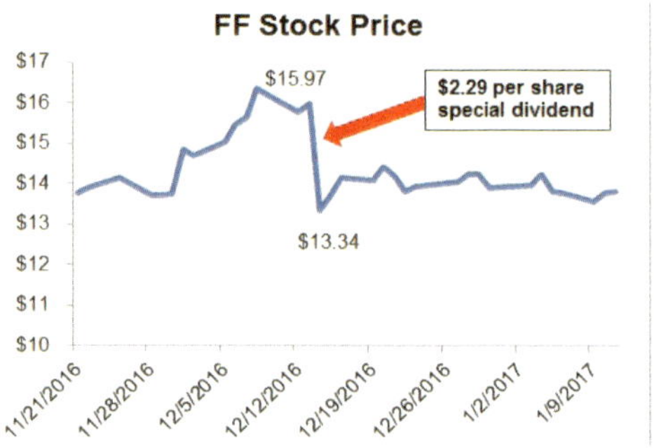

Immediately before FutureFuel's ex-dividend date, its stock price was $15.97 per share. Then, the company's stock price immediately dropped to $13.34 per share, a decrease of $2.63 (somewhat more than the special dividend amount).

If you had purchased shares of FutureFuel prior to the ex-dividend date just to get the special dividend, the market value of your investment would have actually dropped by slightly more than the special dividend you received.

You never know how a stock's price will respond to a special dividend, making this dividend capture strategy a risky one to pursue.

Now here's where special dividends differ from regular dividends. Since special dividends can be very large (sometimes as much as 25% to 30% of a company's share price), stock markets need to avoid having a share price collapse by that much, which could trigger stop loss orders or margin calls.

Thus markets will adjust a company's dividend dates with a "due bill" document. This represents a promissory note whose new ex-dividend date is set by the exchange, via its own complicated rules (not the dividend-paying company's), which are designed to minimize the potential disruption caused by special dividends.

Basically what this means is that the exact dates at which you need to buy and sell a dividend stock in order to "capture" the special dividend can be complicated and different than the ex-dividend date stated in a company's press release.

That's just one of the main reasons why this strategy, of specifically buying a stock just to get the special dividend, is a poor one.

Don't Chase Special Dividends

When a company announces a large special dividend, many investors are initially drawn to the idea of buying shares to get the special payment.

However, this strategy, a derivative of the regular dividend capture idea, is usually not a good idea.

That's because after the bill due ex-dividend date, the share price will almost always decrease by the special dividend amount. In other words, from a total return perspective you gain nothing from a special dividend, as the total value of your investment is unchanged (you collect the dividend, but the price of your investment decreases by an equal amount).

In addition, you need to remember that a special dividend represents a return of capital to investors, meaning the cash paid out will no longer be available to grow the business.

This also applies to regular dividend stocks. However, the difference is that a regular dividend, especially one that grows along with a company's earnings and free cash flow, is a sustainable, long-term way of boosting shareholder value.

That's because historically around 40% of the stock market's gains have come from dividends, including dividend reinvestment.

In fact, studies have shown that the long-term total returns of steady dividend growers, such as dividend achievers, aristocrats, and kings, generally follows the formula dividend yield + earnings growth.

This makes intuitive sense because over time a high quality dividend stock will have a stable payout ratio and yield.

For example, say a company grows its earnings by 7.2% per year for a decade. That will lead to earnings doubling over that time period, and the share price will naturally rise as investors are attracted to the company's growing profits.

However, a special dividend has no long-term benefit, specifically because it is a one-time event. This makes intuitive sense because the intrinsic value of a stock is the future discounted cash flow the company can be expected to generate.

So a major special dividend, even one that represents a one-time 30% yield, won't raise the long-term value of a stock.

This is why special dividends, except for rare exceptions such as in the case of Main Street Capital or Ford, are often a bad idea.

The only reason that those companies' special dividend policies are ideal for long-term shareholders is because these special dividends are regular; they can be extrapolated out into the future to a degree and thus discounted to a present fair value.

On the other hand, take the example of National Grid, which sold off a major and steady cash flow asset to pay its special dividend. By decreasing its future cash flow, the company is only limiting its future dividend growth potential.

But what if a company is simply piling up so much cash on its balance sheet that it can't possibly spend it all? Apple (AAPL) has over $200 billion in cash and cash equivalents and generates annual free cash flow of over $50 billion, for example. The company could pay a substantial special dividend if it wanted to.

However, Apple instead announced a $100 billion buyback authorization and has continued to raise its regular dividend at a fast pace.

Consistent buybacks of undervalued shares provide a great, permanent way to boost long-term earnings per share and help keep the payout ratio low.

Not only does that help to maintain a highly secure dividend, but it also allows the company to maintain a faster payout growth rate for longer.

This approach creates far more incentive for income investors to buy its shares and drive solid long-term total returns.

Liquidating Dividend

The term liquidating dividend refers to the process of providing shareholders with a partial or full distribution of their capital investment in the company. Liquidating dividends are typically paid when a company is going out of business or has sold a portion of the enterprise.

Also known as liquidating distributions, a liquidating dividend is a return of the company's shareholders' capital investment. This concept is different than regular dividends, which are paid from the company's profits or retained earnings.

This difference has income tax implications to shareholders. While regular dividends are taxable, liquidating dividends are not taxable since they are merely the return of the shareholder's investments. Companies will issue IRS Form 1099-DIV, which clarifies the tax implications of the distribution.

Companies will pay liquidating dividends under the following circumstances:

- The company has filed for bankruptcy and decided the best course of action would be to liquidate the net assets of the company.
- The company has decided to exit a business and has sold the operation's assets to another entity.
- Distributions can only be made to shareholders after the money owed to creditors has been paid. Cash can only be paid to shareholders if the company's net assets are positive.

Example

The management team at Company A has decided to declare a dividend of $2.00 per share and has 800,000 shares of common stock outstanding. The company balance sheet shows $400,000 in retained earnings and $5,000,000 in paid in capital in excess of par. The following entry is required:

Cash Paid = Shares of Common Stock x Dividend

= 800,000 x $2.00, or $1,600,000

The entry to record the transaction would be:

	Debit	Credit
Retained Earnings	$400,000	
Paid-In Capital in Excess of Par	$1,200,000	
Cash		$1,600,000

In the above example, shareholders would need to be informed that $400,000 / 800,000, or $0.50 per share were regular dividends, while $1.50 per share represents a liquidating dividend.

Calculating Liquidating Dividends

Let's assume that the Tablet Universe Company has a retained earnings balance of $200,000 and a paid-up capital balance of $1,500,000. On May 1, the company declares a dividend of $3.00 per share on the company's 200,000 shares outstanding.

The total dividend is:

= $3.00 x 200,000 shares

= $600,000

The total dividend will be $600,000. The company must use its retained earnings balance of $200,000 first and the remainder of the dividend, $400,000 ($600,000 - $200,000), will come from the company's paid-up capital.

Let's examine the impact of this dividend payment on Sharon. She owns 1,000 shares and would receive a total dividend of $3,000 ($3.00 x 1,000).

The amount of the total dividend representing the regular dividend is:

= $200,000 retained earnings / 200,000 shares

= $1.00 per share

The liquidating dividend of the total dividend is calculated as follows:

= $3.00 total dividend - $1.00 regular dividend

= $2.00 per share

The retained earnings are subtracted from the total dividend balance; and then this amount is divided by the total number of shares to get the regular dividend. After the regular dividend is paid out, whatever is left over is the liquidating dividend balance. Therefore, Sharon receives a regular dividend of $1,000 (1,000 x $1.00) and a liquidating dividend of $2,000 (1,000 x $2.00). Since liquidating dividends represent a return of a shareholder's original investment, they are usually not taxed when received by the shareholder.

Stock Dividend

A stock dividend is a dividend payment made in the form of additional shares rather than a cash payout. Companies may decide to distribute this type of dividend to shareholders of record if the company's availability of liquid cash is in short supply. These distributions are generally acknowledged in the form of fractions paid per existing share, such as if a company issued a stock dividend of 0.05 shares for each single share held by existing shareholders.

Also known as a "scrip dividend," a stock dividend is a distribution of shares to existing shareholders in lieu of a cash dividend. This type of dividend arises when a company wants to reward its investors but either doesn't have the capital to distribute or it wants to hold onto its existing liquidity for other investments. Stock dividends also have a tax advantage in that they aren't taxed until the shares are sold by an investor. This makes them advantageous for shareholders who do not need immediate capital.

The board of a public company, for example, can approve a 5% stock dividend, which gives existing investors an additional share of company stock for every 20 shares they already own. However, this means that the pool of available equities increases by 5%, diluting the value of existing shares. Therefore, in this example, even though an investor who owns 100 shares in a company may receive 5 additional shares, the total market value of those shares remains the same. In this way, a stock dividend is very similar to a stock split.

Small Stock Dividends versus Large Stock Dividends

When issuing a stock dividend, the total value of equity remains the same from both the investor's perspective and the company's perspective. However, all stock dividends require a journal entry on behalf of the company issuing the dividend. This entry transfers the value of the issued stock from the retained earnings account to the paid-in capital account. The amount transferred between the two accounts depends on whether the dividend is a small stock dividend or a large stock dividend.

A stock dividend is considered small if the shares issued are less than 25% of the total value of shares outstanding before the dividend. A small stock dividend journal entry is made that transfers the market value of the issued shares from retained earnings to paid-in capital.

Large stock dividends arise when the new shares issued are more than 25% of the value of the total shares outstanding prior to the dividend. An associated journal entry is made to transfer the par value of the issued shares from retained earnings to paid-in capital.

Dividend Policy

Dividend policy determines the ultimate distribution of the firm's earnings between retention (that is reinvestment) and cash dividend payments of shareholders.

Dividend policy means the practice that management follows in making dividend payout decisions, or in other words, the size and pattern of cash distributions over the time to shareholders.

In other words, dividend policy is the firm's plan of action to be followed when dividend decisions are made. It is the decision about how much of earnings to pay out as dividends versus retaining and reinvesting earnings in the firm.

Dividend policy means policy or guideline followed by the management in declaring of dividend. A dividend policy decides proportion of dividend and retains earnings. Retained earnings are an important source of internal finance for long term growth of the company while dividend reduces the available cash funds of company.

As long as the firm has investment project whose returns exceed its cost of capital, it will use retained earnings to finance these projects.

There is a reciprocal relationship between retained earnings and dividend i.e. larger the retained earnings, lesser the dividend and smaller the retained earnings, larger the dividend.

James E. Walter says "Choice of dividend policy almost effects the value of the enterprise"

"Dividend policy must be evaluated in light of the objective of the firm namely, to choose a policy that will maximize the value of the firm to its shareholders" Financial Management and Policy.

As we know in corporation, owners are shareholders but management is done through Board of directors. It is the Board of Directors to decide whether to pay dividend or retain earnings for future projects. It is a matter of conflict between shareholders and directors. Shareholders expect a quick return on their capital. On the other hand, directors have to consider a number of factors in determining divided policy.

Investors must keep an eye on the company's dividend policy for most companies regular boosts in the face of irregular earnings can be a warning signal. So can the refusal of Management to lower dividends when earning fall or capital requirement rise. Companies with high dividend and rising debt may be borrowing money to pay shareholders. For investors who are seeking stock that will advance on their performance and earning and earning per share, lower dividend may mean high returns. (Adopted from the Quality of earnings.

The dividend policy of a company reflects how prudent its financial management is. The future prospects, expansion, diversification mergers are effected by dividing policies and for a healthy and buoyant capital market, both dividends and retained earnings are important factors.

Most of the company follows some kind of dividend policy. The usual policy of a company is to retain a position of net earnings and distribute the remaining amount to the shareholders. Many factors have to be evaluated before forming a long term dividend policy.

Dividend Policy Theories

Over the time various theories of dividend policy have emerged; some of the main theories are as follows:

The Residual Theory of Dividend Policy

The residual theory of dividend policy holds that the firm will only pay dividend from residual earnings, that is dividends should be paid only if funds remain after the optimum level of capital expenditures is incurred i.e. all suitable investment opportunities have been financed.

With a residual dividend policy, the primary focus of the firm is on investments and hence dividend policy is a passive decision variable. The value of a firm is a direct function of its investment decisions thus making dividend policy irrelevant.

Dividend Irrelevancy Theory

The dividend irrelevancy theory asserts that dividend policy has no effect on either the price of the firm or its cost of capital.

Dividend Irrelevance Arguments

Dividend policy does not affect share price because the value of the firm is a function of its earning power and the risk of its assets. If dividends do affect value, it is only due to:

a) Information effect : The informational content of dividends relative to management's earnings expectations

b) Clientele effect: A clientele effect exists which allows firms to attract shareholders whose dividend preferences match the firm's historical dividend payout patterns.

A study conducted by Aswath Damodaran found that:

a) Older investors were more likely to hold high dividend stocks and

b) Poorer investors tended to hold high dividend stocks

Hence, firms with older investors pay higher dividends and firms with wealthier investors pay lower dividends.

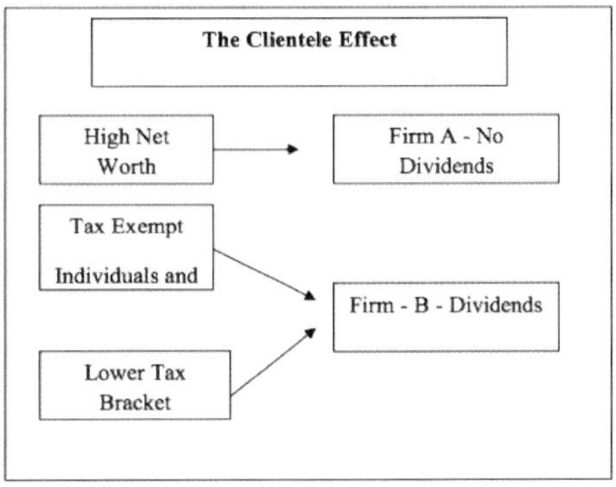

Figure: The Clientele Effect

Signaling effect: Rise in dividend payment is viewed as a positive signal whereas a reduction in dividend payment is viewed as a negative signal about the future earnings prospects of the company, thus leading to an increase or decreases in share prices of the firm. Managers use dividends as signals to transmit information to the capital market. Theoretical models tells us that dividend increases convey good news and dividend decreases convey bad news.

However, this theory is based on the following assumptions:

1. There is an existence of perfect capital markets i.e. No personal or corporate taxes and no transaction costs.
2. The firm's investment policy is independent of its dividend policy.
3. Investors behave rationally and information is freely available to them
4. Risk or uncertainty does not exist.

The above-mentioned assumptions exclude personal and corporate taxes as well as any linkage to capital investment policy as well as other factors that limit its application to real world situations.

The Bird in the Hand Theory

The essence of this theory is not stockholders are risk averse and prefer current dividends due to their lower level of risk as compared to future dividends. Dividend payments reduce investor uncertainty and thereby increase stock value. This theory is based on the logic that ' what is available at present is preferable to what may be available in the future'. Investors would prefer to have a sure dividend now rather than a promised dividend in the future (even if the promised dividend is larger). Hence dividend policy is relevant and does affect the share price of a firm.

The Tax Differential Theory

This theory simply concludes that since dividends are taxed at higher rates than capital gains, investors require higher rates of return as dividend yields increase. This theory suggests that a low dividend payout ratio will maximize firm value.

Percent Payout Theory

Rubner argued that shareholders prefer dividends and directors and managers requiring additional finance would have to convince the investors that proposed new investments would increase their wealth. However to increase their job security and status in the eyes of the shareholders companies can adopt 100 per cent payout. However this policy is not followed in practice.

Percent Retention Theory

Clarkson and Eliot argued that given taxation and transaction costs dividends are a luxury that is not afforded by shareholders as well as by companies and hence a firm can follow a policy of 100 per cent retention. Firms can thus avail of new investment opportunities that would be beneficial to shareholders too.

Agency Cost Theory

Since Jenson and Meckling , many studies have provided arguments that link agency costs with the other financial activities of a firm. It has been argued that firms payout dividends in order to reduce agency costs. Dividend payout keeps firms in the capital market, where monitoring of managers is available at lower cost. If a firm has free cash flows (Jensen (1986), it is better off sharing them with stockholders as dividend payout in order to reduce the possibility of these funds being wasted on unprofitable (negative net present value) projects. This modern view of dividend policy emphasizes the valuable role of dividend policy in helping to resolve agency problem and thus in enhancing shareholder value.

An Overview of Dividend Policy Theories

The dividend policy theories focus on the issue of the relevancy of dividend policy to the value of a firm.

Dividend Irrelevance

- Dividends do not make any difference (M & M theory)
- If there are no taxes disadvantages associated with dividends.

Dividend Relevance

- Dividends are relevant and have positive impact on firm value
- If stockholders like dividends, or dividends operate as a signal of future prospects. (Lintner & Gordon)
- Dividends help to resolve agency problem and thus enhancing shareholder value. (Jenson)
- Dividends are not good (Graham and Dodd)
- If dividends have a tax disadvantage and increasing dividends reduce value.

There are therefore, conflicting viewpoints regarding the impact of dividend decision on value of a firm.

Types of Dividend Policy

In a classic study, Lintner surveyed a number of managers in the 1950's and asked how they set their dividend policy. Most of the respondents said that there were a target proportion of earnings that determined their policy. One firm's policy might be to pay out 40 % of earnings as dividends whereas another company might have a target of 50 %. On the basis of interviews with corporate executives, Lintner concluded that firms select target payout ratios to which they gradually adjust actual dividend payments over time. This would suggest that dividends change with earnings.

However, dividend policies may vary between various firms as every firm sets its own policy for dividend distribution.

Firms may pursue any one of the following dividend policies:

Generous or Liberal Dividend Policy

Firms that follow this policy reward shareholders generously by stepping up dividend over the time.

Stable Dividend Policy

Firms may follow the policy of:

Stable dividend payout ratio: According to this policy, the percentage of earnings paid out of dividends remains constant. The dividends will fluctuate with the earnings of the company.

Stable rupee (inflation adjusted) dividend policy: As per this policy the rupee level of dividends remains stable.

Low Regular Dividend Plus Extra Dividend Policy

As per this policy, a low, regular dividend is maintained and when times are good an extra dividend is paid. Extra dividend is the additional dividend optionally paid by the firm if earnings are higher than normal in a given period. Although the regular portion will be predictable, the total dividend will be unpredictable.

Residual Dividend Policy

Under this policy, dividends are paid out of earnings not needed to finance new acceptable capital projects. The dividends will fluctuate depending on investment opportunities available to the company.

Multiple Dividend Increase Policy

Some firms follow the policy of very frequent and small dividend increases. The objective is to give shareholders an illusion of movement and growth.

Erratic Dividend Policy

Dividends are paid erratically when the management feels it will not strain the resources of the firm. Interests of the shareholders are not taken care of while making the dividend decisions.

It has been observed by various researchers that firms generally prefer to follow a stable or a gradually rising dividend policy.

Uniform Cash Dividend Plus Bonus Policy

Under this policy, the minimum rate of dividend per share is paid in cash plus bonus shares are issued out of accumulated reserves. However bonus shares are not given compulsorily on an annual basis. They may be given over a period of a certain number of years, for example 3-5 years depending on the accumulated reserves of the company that can be utilized for the purpose of issuing bonus.

Stable Dividend Policy: A Policy of Dividend Smoothing

Lintner had observed that managers tend to value stable dividend policies and corporations tend to smooth dividends relative to earnings. That is, dividends are increased gradually and rarely cut, resulting in a much lower variability of dividends as compared to the variability in earnings.

Most Companies adapt a basic policy of maintaining its internal reserves to ensure stable income far into the future, while at the same time seek to distribute a sufficient amount of earnings to shareholders in accordance with business results. with a decrease in EPS, DPS has decreased and with increase in earnings the dividend per share has increased .However increase in dividends is lagging behind increase in earnings in order to 'smoothen' or 'stabilize' dividend payments over the time.

Firm may adapt any of the following stable dividend policies:

- Stable dividend payout ratio
- Stable dividends per share
- A regular plus extra dividend policy

Stable Dividend Payout Ratio

As per this policy the percentage of dividends paid out of earnings remains constant.

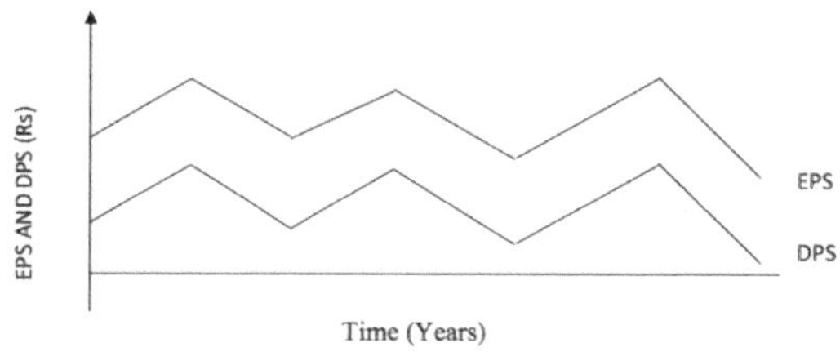

Figure: Stable Payout Ratio Policy

Stable Dividends Per Share

According to this policy, the firm pays a certain fixed amount of dividend per share every year. Annual dividend per share is increased only when the company reaches a new level of earnings and expects to maintain it.

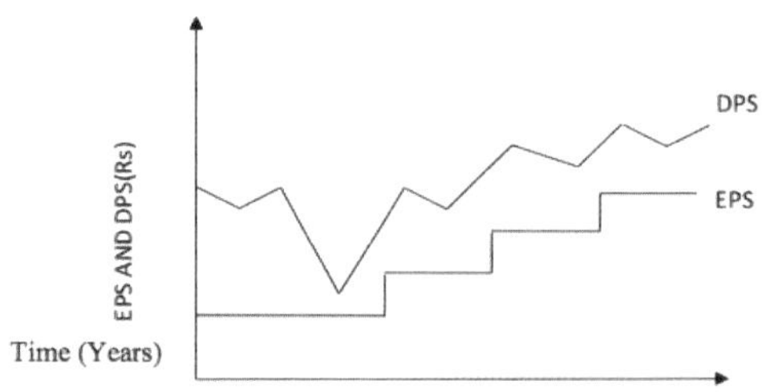

Figure: Stable Dividend per Share Policy

A Regular Plus Extra Dividend Policy

According to this policy a certain fixed percentage or a minimum amount of dividend is paid every year, which is referred to as regular dividend. The firm pays 'additional' or 'extra' dividend if earnings are higher than normal in any year.

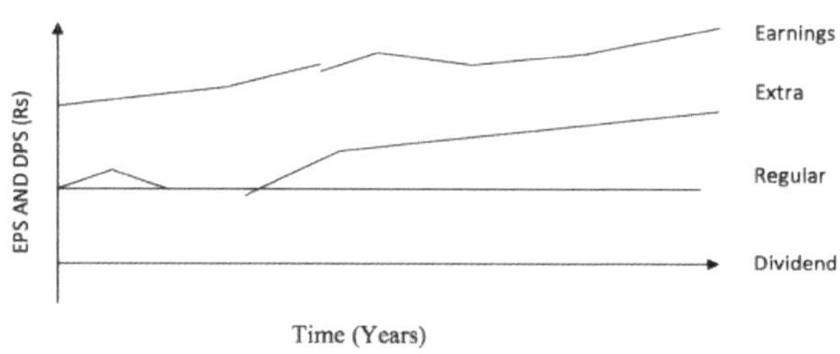

Figure: Regular and Extra Dividend Policy

Rationale for Stable Dividend Policy

Most firms adapt a stable dividend policy. If a firm's earnings are temporarily depressed or if it needs a substantial amount of funds for investment, then it might well maintain its regular dividend using borrowed funds to meet its needs, until things returned to normal. The logic or rationale for stable dividend policy is:

- Stockholders like stable dividends - Many of them depend on dividend income, and if dividends were cut, this might cause serious hardship to them. A stable dividend policy is desirous for many investors such as retired persons, who take dividends as a source to meet their current living expenses.
- A stable dividend policy would reduce investor uncertainty, and reductions in uncertainty are generally associated with lower capital costs and higher stock prices, other things being equal.
- Institutional investors generally prefer to invest in companies having stable dividend records
- Adoption of stable dividends is advantageous for a company interested in raising funds from external sources as shareholders willingly invest in companies having stable dividends as they have more confidence in such companies.

The disadvantage is that such a policy might decrease corporate flexibility. Once a company has adapted a stable dividend policy, any change in such a policy may have adverse effects on the company image and may result in creating serious doubts in the minds of investors about financial standing of the company, which might prove to be very dangerous for the company at a later stage.

Measures of Dividend Policy

Dividend Payout

It measures the percentage of earnings that the company pays in dividends. The Dividend payout ratio of a firm indicates the percentage of earnings that is distributed to the owners in the form of cash; calculated by dividing the firm's cash dividend per share by its earnings per share.

Dividend Payout = Dividends per share/ Earnings per share

Dividend Yield

It measures the return that an investor can make from dividends alone.

Dividend Yield = Dividends / Stock Price

Dividend Cover

It Indicates the vulnerability or margin of safety, of dividend payments to a drop in earnings. The dividend cover ratio is used to assess a company's ability to pay dividends to its ordinary shareholders from its distributable earnings.

Dividend Cover = Earnings per Share / Dividends per share

Dividend Yield

Dividend yield is an easy way to compare the relative attractiveness of various dividend-paying stocks. It tells an investor the yield he/she can expect by purchasing a stock. Dividend yield is the relation between a stock's annual dividend payout and its current stock price. Depending on how much a stock price moves during the day, the dividend yield is constantly changing as the price of the stock changes.

Most solid companies pay a quarterly dividend that is somewhat predictable to investors. These companies typically pay a regular quarterly dividend around the same times every year. Many of these companies raise their dividends once a year – finding themselves on 10-year dividend increasers and Dividend Aristocrat lists.

For a company that has a stock price that is trending upward, it will need to raise its dividend payout in order to maintain its dividend yield. For example. if a stock goes up by 50%, but does not raise its dividend, its yield will drop significantly

Calculating Dividend Yield

To calculate dividend yield, use the dividend yield formula. This can be done by dividing the annual dividend by the current stock price:

$$Dividend\ Yield = \frac{Annual\ Dividend}{Current\ Stock\ Price}$$

For example, if stock XYZ had a share price of $50 and an annualized dividend of $1.00, its yield would be 2%.

$1.00 / $50 = .02

When the 0.02 is put into percentage terms, it would make a 2% yield.

If this share price rose to $60, but the dividend payout was not increased, its yield would fall to 1.66%.

The dividend yield is calculated using the annual yield (every regular payout paid that year). It is not calculated by using quarterly, semi-annual or monthly payouts.

Risks Embedded

An investor desiring to put together a portfolio that generates high dividend income should place great scrutiny on a company's dividend payment history. Only those corporations with a continuous record of steadily increasing dividends over the past 20 years or longer should be considered for inclusion. Furthermore, the investor should be convinced the company can continue to generate the cash flow necessary to make the dividend payments.

If you look at the subprime mortgage mess from 2007-2009, companies were sometimes showing yields in the 10%-20% range, but that was only because the stock price had been hit hard, which resulted in a higher dividend yield. So, be careful when you are excited about jumping into a stock, just because the yield may be high.

When analyzing a high yield dividend stock, it is always important to determine why the stock's yield is so high. There are two reasons why a stock may have an above average yield.

The Stock Price has Taken a Hit

When a stock price declines and the dividend payout remains the same, the dividend yield will increase. For example, if stock XYZ was originally $50 with a $1.00 annual dividend, its dividend yield would be 2%. If that stock's share price fell to $20 and the $1.00 dividend payout was maintained, its new yield would be 5%. While this 5% dividend yield may be attractive to some dividend investors, this is a value trap.

It is always important for investors to understand why a stock's yield is abnormally high. A company that has a stock price that has fallen from $50 to $20 is probably struggling and should not be considered a solid investment.

An example of this situation is the home builder stocks during the 2008-2009 financial crisis. The chart below shows an inflated dividend yield for Lennar (LEN) during the financial crisis. The blue line shows the company's falling stock price while the black line shows its rising dividend yield.

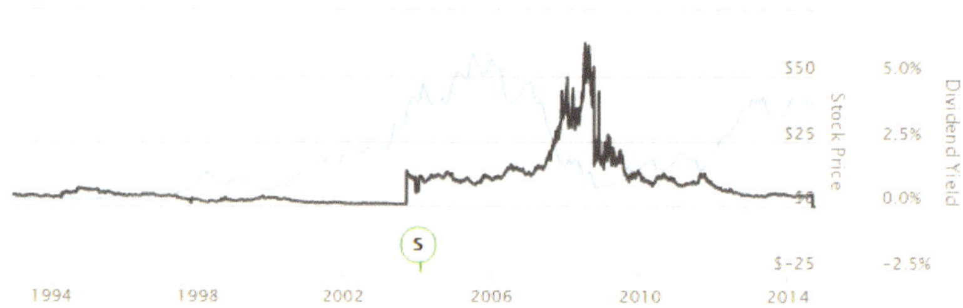

REIT or an MLP

Real Estate Investment Trusts and Master Limited Partnerships are very popular among dividend investors as they tend to offer much higher dividend yields than stocks. These companies tend to offer high dividends since they are required to distribute at least 90% of earnings to shareholders in the form of dividends. These companies do not pay regular income tax on a corporate level, instead the tax burden is passed down to the investor.

Dividend Payout Ratio

The dividend payout ratio measures the percentage of net income that is distributed to shareholders in the form of dividends during the year. In other words, this ratio shows the portion of profits the company decides to keep to fund operations and the portion of profits that is given to its shareholders.

Investors are particularly interested in the dividend payout ratio because they want to know if companies are paying out a reasonable portion of net income to investors. For instance, most start up companies and tech companies rarely give dividends at all. In fact, Apple, a company formed in the 1970s, just gave its first dividend to shareholders in 2012.

Conversely, some companies want to spur investors' interest so much that they are willing to pay out unreasonably high dividend percentages. Inventors can see that these dividend rates can't be sustained very long because the company will eventually need money for its operations.

Formula

The dividend payout formula is calculated by dividing total dividend by the net income of the company.

Dividend Payout Ratio	
Dividend Payout Ratio =	$\frac{\text{Total Dividends}}{\text{Net Income}}$

This calculation will give you the overall dividend ratio. Both the total dividends and the net income of the company will be reported on the financial statements.

You can also calculate the dividend payout ratio on a share basis by dividing the dividends per share by the earnings per share.

Obviously, this calculation requires a little more work because you must figure out the earnings per share as well as divide the dividends by each outstanding share. Both of these formulas will arrive at the same answer however.

Analysis

Since investors want to see a steady stream of sustainable dividends from a company, the dividend payout ratio analysis is important. A consistent trend in this ratio is usually more important than a high or low ratio.

Since it is for companies to declare dividends and increase their ratio for one year, a single high ratio does not mean that much. Investors are mainly concerned with sustainable trends. For instance, investors can assume that a company that has a payout ratio of 20 percent for the last ten years will continue giving 20 percent of its profit to the shareholders.

Conversely, a company that has a downward trend of payouts is alarming to investors. For example, if a company's ratio has fallen a percentage each year for the last five years might indicate that the company can no longer afford to pay such high dividends. This could be an indication of poor operating performance.

Generally, more mature and stable companies tend to have a higher ratio than newer start-up companies.

Example

Joe's Kitchen is a restaurant change that has several shareholders. Joe reported $10,000 of net income on his income statement for the year. Joe's issued $3,000 of dividends to its shareholders during the year. Here is Joe's dividend payout ratio calculation.

Dividend Payout Ratio	
30 % =	$\frac{\$3,000}{\$10,000}$

As you can see, Joe is paying out 30 percent of his net income to his shareholders. Depending on Joe's debt levels and operating expenses, this could be a sustainable rate since the earnings appear to support a 30 percent ratio.

References

- What-is-a-special-dividend, knowledge-center: fool.com, Retrieved 10 June 2018
- Special-dividend-definition-rules-and-impact-on-stock-price-234: simplysafedividends.com, Retrieved 21 May 2018
- Liquidating-dividend-definition-example: study.com, Retrieved 26 March 2018
- Dividend-yield, dividend-investing-101: dividend.com, Retrieved 11 July 2018
- Dividend-payout-ratio, financial-ratios: myaccountingcourse.com, Retrieved 21 April 2018

6

Working Capital Management

The management of a company's working capital for the sustainment of business operations is called working capital management. It involves the management of short-term assets and short-term liabilities. This chapter closely examines the key concepts of working capital management, such as working capital, accounting liquidity, financial ratio, economic value added, debtor finance, etc. for an extensive understanding of the subject.

Working Capital

Working capital is the difference between a company's current assets and current liabilities. It is a financial measure, which calculates whether a company has enough liquid assets to pay its bills that will be due in a year. When a company has excess current assets, that amount can then be used to spend on its day-to-day operations.

Current assets, such as cash and equivalents, inventory, accounts receivable and marketable securities, are resources a company owns that can be used up or converted into cash within a year.

Current liabilities are the amount of money a company owes such as accounts payable, short-term loans and accrued expenses, which are due for payment within a year.

Working Capital Formula

The working capital formula is:

Working capital = current assets – current liabilities

The working capital formula tells us the short-term, liquid assets remaining after short-term liabilities have been paid off. It is a measure of a company's short-term liquidity and important for performing financial analysis, financial modeling, and managing cash flow.

Below is an example balance sheet used to calculate working capital, where "CA" is Current Assets, "CL" is Current Liabilities, and "WC" is Working Capital.

Current Assets:		
Cash	$20,000.00	CA
Accounts Receivable	15,000.00	
Inventories	45,000.00	
	80,000.00	-
Current Liabilities:		
Accounts Payable	$25,000.00	CL
Short-term borrowings	5,000.00	
Accrued liabilities	10,000.00	=
	40,000.00	
Working Capital	**$40,000.00**	WC

Example Calculation with the Working Capital Formula

As an example, a company can increase its working capital by selling more of its products. If the price per unit of the product is $1000 and cost per unit in inventory is $600, the company's working capital will increase by $400 for every unit, because either cash or accounts receivable will increase.

Comparing the working capital of a company against its competitors in the same industry can demonstrate its competitive position. If Company A has working capital of $40,000 while Companies B and C have $15,000 and $10,000, respectively, Company A can spend more money to grow its business faster than its competitors.

Positive vs Negative Working Capital

Having positive working capital can be a good sign of the short-term financial health for a company because it has enough liquid assets remaining to pay off short-term bills and to internally finance the growth of their business. Without additional working capital, a company may have to borrow additional funds from a bank or turn to investment bankers to raise more money.

Negative working capital means assets aren't being used effectively, and a company may a liquidity crisis. Even if a company has lots invested in fixed assets, it will face financial challenges if liabilities come due too soon. This will lead to more borrowing, late payments to creditors and suppliers and, as a result, a lower corporate credit rating for the company.

When Negative Working Capital is ok

Depending on the type of business, companies can have negative working capital and still do well. Examples are grocery stores like Walmart or fast-food chains like McDonald's that can generate cash very quickly due to high inventory turnover rates and by receiving payment from customers in a matter of a few days. These companies need little working capital.

Products that are bought from suppliers are immediately sold to customers before the company even gets a chance to pays the vendor or supplier. In contrast, capital-intensive companies that manufacture heavy equipment and machinery usually can't raise cash quickly, as they sell their products on a long-term payment basis. Since they can't sell fast enough, cash won't be available immediately during tough financial times, so having enough working capital is desirable.

Learn more about a company's Working Capital Cycle, and the timing of when cash comes in and out of the business.

Adjustments to the Working Capital Formula

While the above formula and example are the most standard definition of working capital, there are other more focused definitions.

Examples of alternative formulas:

- Current Assets – Cash – Current Liabilities (excludes cash)
- Accounts Receivable + Inventory – Accounts Payable (this represents only the "core" accounts that make up working capital in day-to-day operations of the business)

Current Asset

Current assets are balance sheet assets that can be converted to cash within one year or less. Accounts that are considered current assets include cash and cash equivalents, marketable securities, accounts receivable, inventory, prepaid expenses, and other liquid assets. These short-term assets are a key component of a company's net working capital and short-term liquidity.

Current Assets Formula

It's easy to calculate the current assets of your company. However, it's important to make sure that all assets classified as "current" are included in the calculation, since there are many. We will show you the formula and discuss each of the components below, including an example calculation.

The current assets formula is:

Current Assets =
(Cash & Cash Equivalents) + (Accounts Receivables) + (Inventory) + (Marketable Securities) + (Prepaid Expenses) + (Other Liquid Assets)

Cash and Cash Equivalents

Cash includes bills, currency notes, coins, checks received but not yet deposited, and petty cash. Cash equivalents typically include money in bank accounts, money market accounts, and short-term investments with a maturity of 90 days or less (like U.S. Treasury bills and commercial paper). Cash and cash equivalents are typically reported on the balance sheet as the first current asset.

Accounts Receivables

Accounts receivables represent the value of a company's outstanding invoices owed by customers for products and/or services delivered. Accounts receivables should ideally be collected within 90 days or less with a 90% collection rate. They are considered current assets because they can be converted to cash when collected and typically have repayment terms between 30-90 days.

Inventory

Inventory refers to any raw materials, in-process products, and/or finished goods that are ready or soon to be ready for sale. Inventory is considered a current asset because it is converted to cash when sold. Ideally, inventory should be sold within one year or less to risk overstocking.

Marketable Securities

Marketable securities represent a company's short-term investments or unrestricted financial instrument available for sale. Marketable securities are considered current assets because their maturities are typically less than one year. They are usually traded on an open market – such as a public stock exchange or public bond exchange – at a set price to readily available buyers.

Prepaid Expenses

Prepaid expenses are expenditures paid for in advance. They are reported on a balance sheet as current assets until the bill actually becomes due. Prepaid expenses are short-term assets because they typically come due within a few months of being recorded. One example of a prepaid expense is prepaid rent.

For example, if your rent is $1,000 per month and you choose to pay for the next 3 months at once, your prepaid rent asset account will increase to $3,000. At the start of each month when rent is due, you'll reduce your prepaid rent account by $1,000 and recognize an equal rent expense of $1,000.

Other Liquid Assets

Other liquid assets include any other assets that can be converted to cash within one year. This can include previous long-term investments that are maturing within a year or a property or piece of equipment that is set to be sold within a year.

Current Assets Example

To calculate current assets, all you have to do is add your short-term balance sheet assets together that can be converted into cash within one year. Let's take a look at the following example for a better understanding.

Let's say that your company's short-term assets include the following on your balance sheet:

- Cash & Cash Equivalents: $90,000
- Accounts Receivable: $30,000
- Marketable Securities: $120,000
- Inventory: $50,000
- Prepaid Expenses: $18,000

Based on the above data, your short-term assets are calculated as follows:

$$\$90{,}000 + \$30{,}000 + \$120{,}000 + \$50{,}000 + \$18{,}000 = \$308{,}000$$

Importance of Current Assets

Current assets are important because they are used to pay for operational expenses and other short-term financial obligations. The value of your short-term assets to your current liabilities gives you insights into your short-term liquidity, also known as your net working capital. Typically, more short-term assets than liabilities is good, while fewer short-term assets than liabilities results in financial insolvency.

However, the ideal ratio of your short-term assets to your current liabilities is between 1.2 to 2. Anything lower than 1 means your short-term assets are not enough to cover your current financial obligations. Although, if your current ratio is higher than 2, it may indicate that your company isn't efficiently using its short-term assets to generate revenue. For more information on short-term liquidity, you can read our guides on the current ratio and the quick ratio.

Calculating Average Current Assets

The average current assets of a company is the average value of a company's short-term assets from one period to another. Average current assets is typically calculated as average annual assets. This gives business owners an idea of the average monthly short-term assets they should expect, which helps them manage, plan, and budget for the future.

For example, to calculate average total assets for the year, add the total current assets from the end of the previous year to the total short-term assets from the end of the present year, and then divide by two. The formula for the average current assets is as follows:

Average Current Assets = (Total current assets for previous period + Total current assets for current period) / 2

For example, if on Dec 31st, 2017, your current assets are $97,000, and then on Dec 31st, 2018, your current assets are $73,00, your average short-term assets for the period would be:

($97,000 + $73,000) / 2 = $85,000

Current assets are key to a company's short-term liquidity. Assets are classified and reported as short-term assets on a company's balance sheet if they can be converted to cash within one year or less. Typically, a company that has more short-term assets than current liabilities is considered financially stable.

Current Liability

Current (or short-term) liabilities are liabilities that a company is required to settle within the next twelve months or which it expects to settle within its normal operating cycle.

Liabilities are financial obligations which require transfer of assets (mainly cash) for settlement. They are classified into current and non-current liabilities based on the urgency of their settlement. Comparison of current liabilities with current assets helps creditors, debt-holders and investors assess a company's liquidity position.

Here is a list of typical current liabilities:

- Accounts payable
- Salaries payable
- Short-term debt payable
- Short-term notes payable
- Current lease liability
- Interest payable

- Current tax payable
- Accrued expenses
- Dividends payable

Accounts payable, salaries payable, accrued expenses and current tax payable are classified as current liabilities because they are expected to be paid off within a normal operating cycle. These liabilities are reported as current even if the company expects them to be paid after 12 months.

Short-term debt payable, short-term notes payable and current lease liability represent that portion of the relevant long-term liability which is due within next 12 months.

Interest payable is normally a current liability because it is due with 12 months.

Dividends payable is a current liability because corporate laws normally require them to be paid within a certain period after declaration date.

Example

Classify the following liabilities of STU, Inc. into current and non-current as at 31 August 2015:

1. Trade payables of $220 million (of which $20 million are due on 15 October 2016)
2. Salaries payable of $45 million
3. Pension liability of $550 million (of which $10 million is payable within next 12 months)
4. Current tax payable of $12 million
5. Net deferred tax liability of $22 million
6. Total lease liability of $25 million (of which $4 million is the current portion of finance lease and $3 million is related to operating lease payable within 12 months)
7. Dividends of $15 million declared on 14 August 2015 to be paid on 14 September 2015.
8. Long-term loan payable to banks of $500 million (of which $120 million is due in next 12 months which the company can't reschedule on its own)
9. Notes payable of $40 million (10 million due within 12 months)

If the company's total assets and non-current assets are $1,910 million and $1,400 million, demonstrate how information about current liabilities help better assess liquidity and solvency of a company.

Solution

All amount are USDs in million.

Item	Total Liabilities	Current Liabilities	Non-Current Liabilities	Explanation
a	220	220	0	Trade payable is a current liability even if payable after 12 months.
b	45	45	0	Salaries are due to be paid in a normal operating cycle
c	550	10	540	Pension payable is a non-current liability except the current portion.
d	12	12	0	Current tax is payable within normal operating cycle
e	22	0	22	Accounting standards such as IFRS always classify deferred tax liability as non-current.
f	25	7	18	Current portion = current portion of finance lease + current operating lease rentals
g	15	15	0	Dividends are expected to be paid within 12 months
h	500	120	380	$120 million is the current portion because it is 'unconditionally' due within 12 months.
i	40	10	30	The amount due with in 12 months is classified as current.
Total	1429	439	990	

STU, Inc. current assets = total assets – non-current assets = $1,910 million – $1,400 = $510 million

Since current liabilities are $439 million against current assets of $510 million, the current ratio is 1.16. It means that the company has enough current assets (i.e. assets that are due to be converted to cash in next 12 months) to pay-off its short-term liabilities.

Solvency is assessed by debt ratio which compares total assets with total liabilities. In case of STU, Inc., debt ratio is 0.75 (= $1,429/$1,910) which shows that 75% of the company's assets are financed by debt and hence total assets are adequate to pay off liabilities in case of a crisis.

Information about timing of cash inflows and cash outflows is very critical particularly in the short-term which is why liabilities and assets are categorized into current and non-current portion to assess the financial position both in the short-term and long-term.

Accounting Liquidity

Liquidity, or accounting liquidity, measures the ability of an individual or company to meet their short-term financial obligations.

A debtor is considered to have a high level of liquidity if they can purchase new assets with ease and pay short-term debts when they are due. Liquidity is usually presented as a ratio or a percentage of current liabilities.

Liquidity is most commonly used to refer to accounting liquidity, which should not be confused with asset liquidity or market liquidity. Liquidity is most commonly used to refer to accounting liquidity, which should not be confused with asset liquidity or market liquidity.

Cash as a Measure of Liquidity

A high level of liquidity is typically indicated by large sums of cash or significant amounts of current assets. Cash is considered as the standard measure of liquidity, as cash can be used to pay off debts or make purchases more quickly and easily than other types of assets.

For example, if a business wants to buy a new computer for £500, they can purchase the computer most quickly if they have enough cash. If the business has a piece of machinery valued at £500, they would either need to trade the two assets – which is extremely unlikely – or sell the machinery then use the cash from the sale to purchase the computer.

Calculating Liquidity

There are several different formulas and ratios to calculate and measure a company's liquidity. Some of the most common ratios are the current ratio, the quick ratio, and the cash ratio.

Calculating Liquidity with the Current Ratio

The current ratio is the easiest way of measuring liquidity, whereby you divide total current assets by total current liabilities. According to the current ratio, the higher the ratio, the higher the liquidity. If a company has a ratio above 1, they are considered to be able to pay their short-term obligations. To calculate a company's current ratio, use the following formula:

$$\text{Current ratio} = \text{current assets} \div \text{current liabilities}$$

Calculating Liquidity with the Quick Ratio

Also known as the acid test, the quick ratio is more conservative than the current ratio as it does not consider current assets such as inventory. The following formula calculates a company's quick ratio:

Quick ratio = (cash equivalents + marketable securities + accounts receivables) ÷ current liabilities

Calculating Liquidity with the Cash Ratio

The cash ratio does not consider accounts receivables or inventory; it therefore measures a company's liquidity as if it were about to go out of business. Whilst this is useful for telling creditors the value of highly liquid assets, this ratio is not commonly used in financial reporting. The cash ratio is as follows:

Cash ratio = (cash + marketable securities) ÷ current liabilities.

Financial Ratio

Financial ratios are useful indicators of a firm's performance and financial situation. Most ratios can be calculated from information provided by the financial statements. Financial ratios can be used to analyze trends and to compare the firm's financials to those of other firms. In some cases, ratio analysis can predict future bankruptcy. Financial ratios can be classified according to the information they provide. The following types of ratios frequently are used:

- Liquidity ratios
- Asset turnover ratios
- Financial leverage ratios
- Profitability ratios
- Dividend policy ratios

Liquidity Ratios

Liquidity ratios provide information about a firm's ability to meet its short-term financial obligations. They are of particular interest to those extending short-term credit to the firm. Two frequently-used liquidity ratios are the current ratio (or working capital ratio) and the quick ratio.

The current ratio is the ratio of current assets to current liabilities:

$$\textit{Current Ratio} = \frac{\textit{Current Assets}}{\textit{Current Liabilities}}$$

Short-term creditors prefer a high current ratio since it reduces their risk. Shareholders may prefer a lower current ratio so that more of the firm's assets are working to grow the business. Typical values for the current ratio vary by firm and industry. For example, firms in cyclical industries may maintain a higher current ratio in order to remain solvent during downturns.

One drawback of the current ratio is that inventory may include many items that are difficult to liquidate quickly and that have uncertain liquidation values. The quick ratio is an alternative measure of liquidity that does not include inventory in the current assets. The quick ratio is defined as follows:

$$\textit{Quick Ratio} = \frac{\textit{Current Assets} - \textit{Inventory}}{\textit{Current Liabilities}}$$

The current assets used in the quick ratio are cash, accounts receivable, and notes receivable. These assets essentially are current assets less inventory. The quick ratio often is referred to as the acid test.

Finally, the cash ratio is the most conservative liquidity ratio. It excludes all current assets except the most liquid: cash and cash equivalents. The cash ratio is defined as follows:

$$\textit{Cash Ratio} = \frac{\textit{Cash} + \textit{Marketable Securities}}{\textit{Current Liabilities}}$$

The cash ratio is an indication of the firm's ability to pay off its current liabilities if for some reason immediate payment were demanded.

Asset Turnover Ratios

Asset turnover ratios indicate of how efficiently the firm utilizes its assets. They sometimes are referred to as efficiency ratios, asset utilization ratios, or asset management ratios. Two commonly used asset turnover ratios are receivables turnover and inventory turnover.

Receivables turnover is an indication of how quickly the firm collects its accounts receivables and is defined as follows:

$$\textit{Receivables Turnover} = \frac{\textit{Annual Credit Sales}}{\textit{Accounts Receivable}}$$

The receivables turnover often is reported in terms of the number of days that credit sales remain in accounts receivable before they are collected. This number is known as the collection period. It is the accounts receivable balance divided by the average daily credit sales, calculated as follows:

$$Average\ Collection\ Period = \frac{Accounts\ Receivable}{Annual\ Credit\ Sales / 365}$$

The collection period also can be written as:

$$Average\ Collection\ Period = \frac{365}{Receivables\ Turnover}$$

Another major asset turnover ratio is inventory turnover. It is the cost of goods sold in a time period divided by the average inventory level during that period:

$$Inventory\ Turnover = \frac{Cost\ of\ Goods\ Sold}{Average\ Inventory}$$

The inventory turnover often is reported as the inventory period, which is the number of days worth of inventory on hand, calculated by dividing the inventory by the average daily cost of goods sold:

$$Inventory\ Period = \frac{Average\ Inventory}{Annual\ Cost\ of\ Goods\ Sold / 365}$$

The inventory period also can be written as:

$$Inventory\ Period = \frac{365}{Inventory\ Turnover}$$

Other asset turnover ratios include fixed asset turnover and total asset turnover.

Financial Leverage Ratios

Financial leverage ratios provide an indication of the long-term solvency of the firm. Unlike liquidity ratios that are concerned with short-term assets and liabilities, financial leverage ratios measure the extent to which the firm is using long term debt.

The debt ratio is defined as total debt divided by total assets:

$$Debt\ Ratio = \frac{Total\ Debt}{Total\ Assets}$$

The debt-to-equity ratio is total debt divided by total equity:

$$Debt-to-Equity\ Ratio = \frac{Total\ Debt}{Total\ Equity}$$

Debt ratios depend on the classification of long-term leases and on the classification of some items as long-term debt or equity.

The times interest earned ratio indicates how well the firm's earnings can cover the interest payments on its debt. This ratio also is known as the interest coverage and is calculated as follows:

$$Interest\ Coverage = \frac{EBIT}{Interest\ Charges}$$

where EBIT = Earnings Before Interest and Taxes

Profitability Ratios

Profitability ratios offer several different measures of the success of the firm at generating profits.

The gross profit margin is a measure of the gross profit earned on sales. The gross profit margin considers the firm's cost of goods sold, but does not include other costs. It is defined as follows:

$$Gross\ Profit\ Margin = \frac{Sales\ -\ Cost\ of\ Goods\ Sold}{Sales}$$

Return on assets is a measure of how effectively the firm's assets are being used to generate profits. It is defined as:

$$Return\ on\ Assets = \frac{Net\ Income}{Total\ Assets}$$

Return on equity is the bottom line measure for the shareholders, measuring the profits earned for each dollar invested in the firm's stock. Return on equity is defined as follows:

$$Return\ on\ Equity = \frac{Net\ Income}{Shareholder\ Equity}$$

Dividend Policy Ratios

Dividend policy ratios provide insight into the dividend policy of the firm and the prospects for future growth. Two commonly used ratios are the dividend yield and payout ratio.

The dividend yield is defined as follows:

$$Dividend\ Yield = \frac{Dividends\ Per\ Share}{Share\ Price}$$

A high dividend yield does not necessarily translate into a high future rate of return. It is important to consider the prospects for continuing and increasing the dividend in the future. The dividend payout ratio is helpful in this regard, and is defined as follows:

$$Payout\ Ratio = \frac{Dividends\ Per\ Share}{Earnings\ Per\ Share}$$

Use and Limitations of Financial Ratios

Attention should be given to the following issues when using financial ratios:

- A reference point is needed. To to be meaningful, most ratios must be compared to historical values of the same firm, the firm's forecasts, or ratios of similar firms.
- Most ratios by themselves are not highly meaningful. They should be viewed as indicators, with several of them combined to paint a picture of the firm's situation.
- Year-end values may not be representative. Certain account balances that are used to calculate ratios may increase or decrease at the end of the accounting period because of seasonal factors. Such changes may distort the value of the ratio. Average values should be used when they are available.
- Ratios are subject to the limitations of accounting methods. Different accounting choices may result in significantly different ratio values.

Current Ratio

Current ratio (also known as working capital ratio) is a popular tool to evaluate short-term solvency position of a business. Short-term solvency refers to the ability of a business to pay its short-term obligations when they become due. Short term obligations (also known as current liabilities) are the liabilities payable within a short period of time, usually one year.

A higher current ratio indicates strong solvency position and is therefore considered better.

Formula

Current ratio is computed by dividing total current assets by total current liabilities of the business. This relationship can be expressed in the form of following formula or equation:

$$Current\ ratio = \frac{Current\ assets}{Current\ liabilities}$$

Above formula comprises of two components i.e., current assets and current liabilities. Both the components are available from the balance sheet of the company. Some examples of current assets and current liabilities are given below:

Examples of current assets:

- Cash
- Marketable securities
- Accounts receivables / debtors
- Inventories / stock
- Prepaid expenses

Examples of current liabilities:

- Accounts payable / creditors
- Accrued payable
- Short term bonds payable

Example

On December 31, 2016, the balance sheet of Marshal company shows the total current assets of $1,100,000 and the total current liabilities of $400,000. Your are required to compute current ratio of the company.

Solution

Current ratio = Current assets/Current liabilities

= $1,100,000/$400,000

= 2.75 times

The current ratio is 2.75 which means the company's currents assets are 2.75 times more than its current liabilities.

Significance and Interpretation

Current ratio is a useful test of the short-term-debt paying ability of any business. A ratio of 2:1 or higher is considered satisfactory for most of the companies but analyst should be very careful while interpreting it. Simply computing the ratio does not disclose the true liquidity of the business because a high current ratio may not always be a green signal. It requires a deep analysis of the nature of individual current assets and current liabilities. A company with high current ratio may not always be able to pay its current liabilities as they become due if a large portion of its current assets consists of slow moving or obsolete inventories. On the other hand, a company with low current ratio may be able to pay its current obligations as they become due if a large portion of its current assets consists of highly liquid assets i.e., cash, bank balance, marketable securities and fast moving inventories. Consider the following example to understand how the composition and nature of individual current assets can differentiate the liquidity position of two companies having same current ratio figure.

Limitations of Current Ratio

Current ratio suffers from a number of limitations. Some are given below:

1. Different ratio in different parts of the year: Some businesses have different trading activities in different seasons. Such businesses may show low current ratio in some months of the year and high in others.
2. Change in inventory valuation method: To compare the ratio of two companies it is necessary that both the companies use same inventory valuation method. For example, comparing current ratio of two companies would be like comparing apples with oranges if one uses FIFO cost flow assumption and the other uses LIFO cost flow assumption for the valuation of inventories. The analyst would, therefore, not be able to compare the ratio of two companies even in the same industry.
3. Current ratio is a test of quantity, not quality: It is not an exact science to test liquidity of a company because the quality of each individual asset is not taken into account while computing this ratio.
4. Possibility of manipulation: Current ratio can be easily manipulated by equal increase or equal decrease in current assets and current liabilities. For example, if current assets of a company are $10,000 and current liabilities are $5,000, the current ratio would be 2:1 as computed below:$10,000 : $5,000 2:1

   If both current assets and current liabilities are reduced by $1,000, the ratio would be increased to 2.25:1 as computed below: $9,000 : $4,000 2.25:1

To reduce the effect of above limitations current ratio is usually used in conjunction with other ratios like inventory turnover ratio, debt to equity ratio and quick ratio etc. These ratios can test the quality of current assets and together with current ratio provide a better idea of solvency.

Debt Ratio

Debt ratio is a solvency ratio that measures a firm's total liabilities as a percentage of its total assets. In a sense, the debt ratio shows a company's ability to pay off its liabilities with its assets. In other words, this shows how many assets the company must sell in order to pay off all of its liabilities.

This ratio measures the financial leverage of a company. Companies with higher levels of liabilities compared with assets are considered highly leveraged and more risky for lenders.

This helps investors and creditors analysis the overall debt burden on the company as well as the firm's ability to pay off the debt in future, uncertain economic times.

Formula

The debt ratio is calculated by dividing total liabilities by total assets. Both of these numbers can easily be found the balance sheet. Here is the calculation:

Debt Ratio

$$\text{Debt Ratio} = \frac{\text{Total Liabilities}}{\text{Total Assets}}$$

Make sure you use the total liabilities and the total assets in your calculation. The debt ratio shows the overall debt burden of the company—not just the current debt.

Analysis

The debt ratio is shown in decimal format because it calculates total liabilities as a percentage of total assets. As with many solvency ratios, a lower ratios is more favorable than a higher ratio.

A lower debt ratio usually implies a more stable business with the potential of longevity because a company with lower ratio also has lower overall debt. Each industry has its own benchmarks for debt, but .5 is reasonable ratio.

A debt ratio of .5 is often considered to be less risky. This means that the company has twice as many assets as liabilities. Or said a different way, this company's liabilities are only 50 percent of its total assets. Essentially, only its creditors own half of the company's assets and the shareholders own the remainder of the assets.

A ratio of 1 means that total liabilities equals total assets. In other words, the company would have to sell off all of its assets in order to pay off its liabilities. Obviously, this is a highly leverage firm. Once its assets are sold off, the business no longer can operate.

The debt ratio is a fundamental solvency ratio because creditors are always concerned about being repaid. When companies borrow more money, their ratio increases creditors will no longer loan them money. Companies with higher debt ratios are better off looking to equity financing to grow their operations.

Example

Dave's Guitar Shop is thinking about building an addition onto the back of its existing building for more storage. Dave consults with his banker about applying for a new loan.

The bank asks for Dave's balance to examine his overall debt levels.

The banker discovers that Dave has total assets of $100,000 and total liabilities of $25,000. Dave's debt ratio would be calculated like this:

Debt Ratio	
.25 =	$\frac{\$25{,}000}{\$100{,}000}$

As you can see, Dave only has a debt ratio of .25. In other words, Dave has 4 times as many assets as he has liabilities. This is a relatively low ratio and implies that Dave will be able to pay back his loan. Dave shouldn't have a problem getting approved for his loan.

Quick Ratio

Quick Ratio, also known as Acid Test Ratio, shows the ratio of cash and other liquid resources of an organization in comparison to its current liabilities.

Formula

$$Quick = \frac{Cash\ in\ hand + Cash\ at\ Bank + Receivables + Marketable\ Securities}{Current\ Liabilities}$$

Explanation

Quick ratio shows the extent of cash and other current assets that are readily convertible into cash in comparison to the short term obligations of an organization. A quick ratio of 0.5 would suggest that a company is able to settle half of its current liabilities instantaneously.

Quick ratio differs from current ratio in that those current assets that are not readily convertible into cash are excluded from the calculation such as inventory and deferred tax credits since conversion of such assets into cash may take considerable time.

Quick ratio may therefore alternatively be calculated as follows:

$$Quick\ Ratio = \frac{Current\ Assets - Inventory - Advances - Prepayments}{Current\ Liabilities}$$

Advances to suppliers and prepayments may be excluded from the calculation as they do not result in inflow of cash resources in the future that may be used to settle liabilities.

Example

ABC PLC has the following assets and liabilities as at 31st December 2012:

	$m	$m
Non Current Assets		
Goodwill	75	
Fixed Assets	75	**150**
Current Assets		
Cash in hand	25	
Cash in bank	50	
Short term investments (Note 1)	75	
Inventory	25	
Receivable	100	**275**
Current Liabilities		
Trade payables	100	
Income tax payables	60	**160**
Non Current Liabilities		
Bank Loan	50	
Deferred tax payable	25	**75**

Note: Short term investments include treasury bills amounting $45 million and investment in unlisted shares amounting $30 million.

Quick ratio will be calculated as follows:

$$\text{Quick Ratio} = \frac{\text{Cash in hand + Cash at Bank + Receivables + Marketable Securities}}{\text{Current Liabilities}}$$

$$= \frac{25+50+45+100}{160} = 1.375$$

Variations

In industries which typically have long receivables recovery duration such as in the construction sector, it may be appropriate to calculate the quick ratio by excluding receivables from the numerator to give a more suitable evaluation of the company's liquidity.

Interpretation and Analysis

Quick ratio is an indicator of solvency of an entity and must be analyzed over a period of time and also in the context of the industry the company operates in.

Generally, companies should aim to maintain a quick ratio that provides sufficient leverage against liquidity risk given the level of predictability and volatility in a specific business sector among other considerations. The more uncertain the business environment, the more likely that companies would maintain higher quick ratios. Conversely, where cash flows are stable and predictable, companies would seek to keep quick ratio at relatively lower levels. In any case, companies must achieve the right balance between liquidity risk arising from a low quick ratio and the risk of loss resulting from a high quick ratio.

A quick ratio that is greater than industry average may suggest that the company is investing too many resources in the working capital of the business which may more profitably be used elsewhere. If a company has too much spare cash, it may consider investing the surplus funds in new ventures and in case company is out of investment options it may be prudent to return the excess funds to shareholders in the form of increased dividend payments.

Acid test ratio which is lower than the industry average may suggest that the company is taking too much risk by not maintaining an appropriate buffer of liquid resources. Alternatively, a company may have a lower quick ratio due to better credit terms with suppliers than the competitors.

When analyzing the quick ratio over several periods, it is important to take into account seasonal variations in some industries which may cause the ratio to be traditionally higher or lower at certain times of the year as seasonal businesses experience irregular bursts of activities leading to varying levels current assets and liabilities over time.

Industry Standards

Acid test ratio must be assessed in the context of the specific industry of an organization.

Certain business sectors traditionally have a very low quick ratio such as the retail sector. Companies leading the retail sector are able to negotiate very favorable credit terms with suppliers due to their dominance in the market leading to relatively high current liabilities in comparison to their liquid assets. The business environment is also relatively stable in the retail sector and the expansion of operations is incremental which allow such companies to maintain lower acid test ratios without taking too much risk.

As per 2011 annual reports, quick ratios of Wal-Mart Stores, Inc and Tesco PLC were 0.2 and 0.29 respectively.

Conversely, industries which expand at a very fast pace require higher levels of liquid resources at their disposal to satisfy their investment needs. Examples of companies operating in such industries include the fast food giants such as McDonald's and Burger King. Such companies require high levels of liquid assets to finance the growth in operations achieved through collaboration with franchisees.

As per 2011 annual reports, quick ratios of McDonald's Corporation and Burger King Holdings, Inc. were 1.05 and 1.30 respectively.

Importance

Quick ratio is a measure of a company's ability to settle its current liabilities on a very short notice. Current ratio may provide a misleading indication of a company's liquidity position when a considerable portion of its current assets is illiquid. Quick ratio is therefore a more reliable measure of liquidity for manufacturing companies and construction firms that have relatively high levels of inventory, work in progress and receivables.

Return on Capital

Return on capital is a profitability ratio. It measures the return that an investment generates for capital contributors, i.e. bondholders and stockholders. Return on capital indicates how effective a company is at turning capital into profits.

Formula

The general equation for return on capital is: (Net income - Dividends) / (Debt + Equity)

Return on capital is also known as "return on invested capital (ROIC)" or "return on total capital."

For example, Manufacturing Company MM has $100,000 in net income, $500,000 in total debt and $100,000 in shareholder equity. Its operations are simple -- MM makes and sells widgets.

We can calculate MM's return on capital using the above equation:

(Net income - Dividends)/(Debt + Equity) = (100,000 - 0)/(500,000 + 100,000) = 16.7%

Note that for some companies, net income may not be the best profitability measure to use. You want to make sure that the profit metric you put in the numerator provides a genuine measure of profitability.

Return on capital is most useful when you're using it to calculate the returns generated exclusively by the business operation itself, not the short-lived results from one-time events. Gains/losses from foreign currency fluctuations and other one-time events contribute to the net income listed on the bottom line, but they're not results from business operations. Try to think of what your business "does" and only consider income related to those core business operations.

For example, Conglomerate CC lists $100,000 as net income, $500,000 in total debt and $100,000 in shareholder equity. But when you look at CC's income statement, you notice a lot of extra line-items, like "gains from foreign currency transactions" and "gains from one-time transactions."

In the case of CC, if you use the net income number, you are not being very specific as to where the returns are being generated. Were they from strong business results? Were they from fluctuations in the foreign currency markets? Did CC sell a subsidiary?

For CC, it makes more sense to use an income measure called net operating profits after tax (NOPAT) as the numerator. It's not found on the income statement, but you can calculate it yourself using the following equation:

NOPAT = Earnings before Interest & Taxes * (1 - Tax Rate)

Using NOPAT in the equation will tell you the return the company generated with its core business operations for both its bondholders and stockholders.

Importance

A firm's return on capital can be an excellent indicator of the size and strength of its moat. If a company is able to generate returns of 15-20% year after year, it has a great system for transforming investor capital into profits.

Return on capital is especially useful for companies that invest a large amount of capital, like oil and gas firms, computer hardware companies, and even big box stores. As an investor, it's imperative to know that if a company uses your money, you'll get a respectable return on your investment.

Economic Value Added

Economic value added is a measure of surplus value created on a given investment. When a person is investing his funds, he does this only because he expects to earn a profit from the investment. Let us say, gold seems to be a good instrument to invest with a high profit margin.

- Total investment (i.e. price at which gold is purchased) = $ 1000
- Brokerage paid to the dealer for purchase of gold = $ 15

In a year, I would like to sell off the gold on account of liquidity crunch.

- Selling price of gold = $ 1200
- Brokerage paid to the dealer on sale of gold = $ 10

In the above Economic Value Added example,

- Economic Value Added = Selling price – Expenses associated with selling the asset – Purchase price – Expenses associated with buying the asset
- Economic Value Added = \$ 1200 – \$ 10 – \$ 1000 – \$ 15 = \$ 175

If we just see the profit, then the profit on selling gold was \$ 1200 – \$ 1000 i.e. \$ 200. But the actual creation of wealth is only \$ 175 on account of expenses incurred. This is a very crude example of Economic Value Added (EVA).

Economic Value Added (Eva) Concept

Economic value added (EVA) is the economic profit by the company in a given period. It measures the company's financial performance based on the residual wealth calculated by deducting its cost of capital from its operating profit, adjusted for taxes on a cash basis.

It helps to capture the true economic profit of a company like we calculated the Economic Value Added of investing gold in the above. Economic Value Added example was developed and trademarked by Stern Stewart and Co. as an internal financial performance measure.

Economic Value Added Formula

The three main components of Economic Value Added (EVA) are:

1. Net Operating Profit After Tax
2. Capital Invested
3. WACC i.e. the Weighted Average Cost of Capital

Economic Value Added can be calculated with the help of the following formula:

Economic Value Added EVA formula= Net Operating Profit After Tax – (Capital Invested x WACC)

Here, Capital Invested x WACC stands for the cost of capital. This cost is deducted from the Net Operating Profit After Tax to arrive at the economic profit or the residual wealth created by the organization.

Economic Value Added Example (Basic)

Eva Formula – Net Operating Profit After Tax (Nopat)

This represents how much will be the company's potential cash earnings without its capital cost. It is important to deduct tax from the Operating Profit to arrive at the true operating inflow that a company will earn.

NOPAT = Operating Income x (1 – Tax Rate).

EVA Example for calculating Net Operating Income After Tax is as follows:

ABC Company		
Abstract of the Revenue Statement		
Particulars	Year	
	2016	2015
Revenue:		
Project Advisory Fees	$ 2,00,000	$ 1,86,000
Total Revenue (A)	$ 2,00,000	$ 1,86,000
Expenses:		
Direct Expenses	$ 1,00,000	$ 95,000
Total Operating Expenses (B)	$ 1,00,000	$ 95,000
Operating Income (C = A minus B)	$ 1,00,000	$ 91,000
Tax Rate	30%	30%
Tax on operating income (D = C * Tax Rate)	$ 30,000	$ 27,300
Net Operating Income After Tax (C minus D)	$ 70,000	$ 63,700

Eva Formula – Capital Invested

This represents the total capital invested through equity or debt in a given company.

Continuing with the above EVA example of ABC Company, let us say the company has a total invested capital of $ 30,000. Of this $ 20,000 is through equity funding and the rest ($ 10,000) is by means of long term debt.

Eva Formula – WACC

Weighted Average Cost of Capital is the cost the company incurs for sourcing its funds. The importance of deducting the cost of capital from the Net Operating Profit is to deduct the opportunity cost of the capital invested. Formula to calculate the same is as follows:

$$WACC = RD (1- Tc)*(D / V) + RE *(E / V)$$

The formula looks complicated scary but if understood, it is fairly simple. It is much more easier if the formula is put in words as follows:

Weighted Average Cost of Capital = (Cost of Debt) * (1 – Tax Rate) * (Proportion of debt) + (Cost of Equity) * (Proportion of equity)

This makes the formula easier to understand and also self-explanatory.

Now, understanding the notations of the formula:

- RD = Cost of Debt
- Tc = Tax Rate
- D = Capital invested in the organization through Debt
- V = Total Value of the firm simply calculated as Debt + Equity
- RE = Cost of Equity
- E = Capital invested in the organization through Equity

An important point to note about this formula is that that Cost of Debt is multiplied by (1 – Tax Rate) as there is tax saving on interest paid on debt. On the other hand, there is no tax saving on the cost of equity and hence the tax rate is not taken into account.

Let us now look at how WACC is calculated.

ABC Company		
Balance Sheet of the Company		
Particulars	Year	
	2016	2015
Equity	$ 20,000	$ 17,000
Debt	$ 10,000	$ 7,000
Sources of Funds (A)	$ 30,000	$ 24,000
Fixed Assets	$ 20,000	$ 18,000
Current Assets	$ 20,000	$ 16,000
Less: Current Liabilities	$ 10,000	$ 10,000
Uses of Funds (B)	$ 30,000	$ 24,000
Cost of Debt	8%	8%
Cost of Equity	10%	12%

WACC for the year 2016

= 8% * (1- 30%) * ($ 10,000 / $ 30,000) + 10% * ($ 20,000 / $ 30,000)

= (8% * 70% * 1/3) + (10% * 2/3) = 1.867% + 6.667% = = 8.53%

WACC for the year 2015

= 8% * (1- 30%) * ($ 7,000 / $ 24,000) + 12% * ($ 17,000 / $ 24,000)

= (8% * 70% * 7/24) + (10% * 17/24) = 1.63% + 8.50% = 10.13%

Economic Value Added Eva Calculation

From the above, we have all three factors ready for Economic Value Added calculation for the year 2016 and 2015.

Economic Value Added (EVA) for the year 2016 = Net Operating Profit After Tax – (Capital Invested * WACC)

- = $ 70,000 – ($ 30,000 * 8.53%)
- = $ 70,000 – $ 2,559 = = $ 67,441

Economic Value Added (EVA) for the year 2015 = Net Operating Profit After Tax – (Capital Invested * WACC)

- = $ 63,700 – ($ 24,000 * 10.13%)
- = $ 63,700 – $ 2,432 = = $ 61,268

Accounting Adjustments for Economic Value Added Calculation

Now since we have understood the basics of EVA calculation, let us go a bit further to understand what can be some of the real-life accounting adjustments involved especially at the Operating Profit level:

Sr. No.	Adjustment	Explanation	Changes to Net Operating Profit	Changes to Capital Employed
1	Long-term expenses	There are certain expenses which can be classified as long-term expenses such as research and development, branding of a new product, re-branding of old products. These expenses may be incurred in a given period of time but generally have an effect over and above a given year. These expenses should be capitalized while EVA calculation as they generate wealth over a period of time and not just reduce profit in a given year.	Add to Net Operating Profit	Add to Capital Employed. Also, check out Return on Capital Employed
2	Depreciation	Let us categorize depreciation as accounting depreciation and economic depreciation for purpose of understanding. Accounting depreciation is one which is calculated as per Accounting policies and procedures. Whereas economic depreciation is one which takes into account the true wear and tear of the assets and should be calculated as per the usage of assets rather than a fixed useful life.	Add accounting depreciation Reduce economic depreciation	Difference in the value of accounting depreciation and economic depreciation should be adjusted from the capital employed

3	Non-cash expenses	These are expenses which do not affect the cash flow of a given period. EVA Example: Foreign exchange contracts are reported at fair value as on the reporting date. Any loss incurred is charged to the Income Statement. This loss does not lead to any cash outflow and should be added back to the Net Operating Profit.	Add to Net Operating Profit	Add to capital employed by adding it to Retained Earnings
4	Non-cash incomes	Similar to non-cash expenses, there are non-cash incomes which do not affect the cash flow of a given period. These should be subtracted from the Net Operating Profit.	Subtract from Net Operating Profit	Subtract from capital employed by subtracting it from Retained Earnings
5	Provisions	To arrive at accounting profits, numerous provisions are created such as deferred tax provisions, provision for doubtful debts, provision for expenses, allowance for obsolete inventory, etc. These are provisional figures and do not actually affect the economic profit. In fact, these provisions are generally reversed on the first day of the next reporting period.	Add to Net Operating Profit	Add to capital employed
6	Taxes	Tax should also be calculated on actual cash outflow rather than the mercantile system where all accruals are taken into account and only then tax is deducted.	Tax is supposed to be deducted after calculating Net Operating Profit. So it directly deducted and no other adjustments are required.	
7	Long-term expenses	There are certain expenses which can be classified as long-term expenses such as research and development, branding of a new product, re-branding of old products. These expenses may be incurred in a given period of time but generally have an effect over and above a given year. These expenses should be capitalized while EVA calculation as they generate wealth over a period of time and not just reduce profit in a given year.	Add to Net Operating Profit	Add to Capital Employed. Also, check out Return on Capital Employed
8	Depreciation	Let us categorize depreciation as accounting depreciation and economic depreciation for purpose of understanding. Accounting depreciation is one which is calculated as per Accounting policies and procedures. Whereas economic depreciation is one which takes into account the true wear and tear of the assets and should be calculated as per the usage of assets rather than a fixed useful life.	Add accounting depreciation Reduce economic depreciation	Difference in the value of accounting depreciation and economic depreciation should be adjusted from the capital employed

9	Non-cash expenses	These are expenses which do not affect the cash flow of a given period. EVA Example: Foreign exchange contracts are reported at fair value as on the reporting date. Any loss incurred is charged to the Income Statement. This loss does not lead to any cash outflow and should be added back to the Net Operating Profit.	Add to Net Operating Profit	Add to capital employed by adding it to Retained Earnings
10	Non-cash incomes	Similar to non-cash expenses, there are non-cash incomes which do not affect the cash flow of a given period. These should be subtracted from the Net Operating Profit.	Subtract from Net Operating Profit	Subtract from capital employed by subtracting it from Retained Earnings
11	Provisions	To arrive at accounting profits, numerous provisions are created such as deferred tax provisions, provision for doubtful debts, provision for expenses, allowance for obsolete inventory, etc. These are provisional figures and do not actually affect the economic profit. In fact, these provisions are generally reversed on the first day of the next reporting period.	Add to Net Operating Profit	Add to capital employed
12	Taxes	Tax should also be calculated on actual cash outflow rather than the mercantile system where all accruals are taken into account and only then tax is deducted.	Tax is supposed to be deducted after calculating Net Operating Profit. So it directly deducted and no other adjustments are required.	

Colgate Economic Value Added Example Eva

Calculating Colgate's Nopat

Let us have a look at the Income Statement of Colgate.

COLGATE-PALMOLIVE COMPANY
Consolidated Statements of Income
For the years ended December 31,
(Dollars in Millions Except Per Share Amounts)

	2016	2015	2014
Net sales	$ 15,195	$ 16,034	$ 17,277
Cost of sales	6,072	6,635	7,168
Gross profit	9,123	9,399	10,109
Selling, general and administrative expenses	5,249	5,464	5,982
Other (income) expense, net	37	62	570
Charge for Venezuela accounting change	—	1,084	—
Operating profit	3,837	2,789	3,557
Interest (income) expense, net	99	26	24
Income before income taxes	3,738	2,763	3,533
Provision for income taxes	1,152	1,215	1,194

- Operating Profit of Colgate in 2016 is $3,837 million

The operating profit above does contain noncash items like Depreciation and Amortization, Restructuring costs etc.

In our EVA example, we assume that the book depreciation and economic depreciation are same for Colgate and hence, no adjustment is needed when we calculated NOPAT.

However, restructuring cost needs to be adjusted for. Below is the snapshot of Colgate's restructuring costs from its 10K filings.

	2016	2015	2014
Cost of sales	$ 46	$ 20	$ 29
Selling, general and administrative expenses	77	64	62
Other (income) expense, net	105	170	195
Total 2012 Restructuring Program charges, pretax	$ 228	$ 254	$ 286
Total 2012 Restructuring Program charges, aftertax	$ 168	$ 183	$ 208

- Colgate's restructuring charges in 2016 = $228 million

Adjusted Operating Profit = Operating Profit + Restrucutring Expenses

- Adjusted Operating Profit (2016) = $3,837 million + $228 million = $4,065 million

For calculating NOPAT we required the tax rates.

We can calculate the effecitve tax rates from income statement as per below.

	2016	2015	2014
Net sales	$ 15,195	$ 16,034	$ 17,277
Cost of sales	6,072	6,635	7,168
Gross profit	9,123	9,399	10,109
Selling, general and administrative expenses	5,249	5,464	5,982
Other (income) expense, net	37	62	570
Charge for Venezuela accounting change	—	1,084	—
Operating profit	3,837	2,789	3,557
Interest (income) expense, net	99	26	24
Income before income taxes	3,738	2,763	3,533
Provision for income taxes	1,152	1,215	1,194
Net income including noncontrolling interests	2,586	1,548	2,339

Effective Tax rate = Provision for Income Taxes / Income Before income taxes

- Effective tax rate (2016) = $1,152/$3,738 = 30.82%

NOPAT = Adjusted Operating Profit x (1-tax rate)

- NOPAT (2016) = $4,065 million x (1-0.3082) = $2,812 million

Colgate's Invested Capital

Let us now calculate the second item required for calculating Economic Value Added i.e. Invested Capital.

Liabilities and Shareholders' Equity		
Current Liabilities		
Notes and loans payable	$ 13	$ 4
Current portion of long-term debt	—	298
Accounts payable	1,124	1,110
Accrued income taxes	441	277
Other accruals	1,727	1,845
Total current liabilities	3,305	3,534
Long-term debt	6,520	6,246
Deferred income taxes	246	233
Other liabilities	2,035	1,966
Total liabilities	12,106	11,979
Commitments and contingent liabilities	—	—
Shareholders' Equity		
Common stock, $1 par value (2,000,000,000 shares authorized, 1,465,706,360 shares issued)	1,466	1,466
Additional paid-in capital	1,691	1,438
Retained earnings	19,922	18,861
Accumulated other comprehensive income (loss)	(4,180)	(3,950)
Unearned compensation	(7)	(12)
Treasury stock, at cost	(19,135)	(18,102)
Total Colgate-Palmolive Company shareholders' equity	(243)	(299)
Noncontrolling interests	260	255
Total equity	17	(44)
Total liabilities and equity	$ 12,123	$ 11,935

Invested capital represents the actual debt and equity invested in the company.

Total Debt = Notes and Loan Payable + Current Portion of Long-Term Debt + Long Term Debt

- Total Debt (2016) = $13 + $0 + $6,520 = $6,533 million

	2016	2015
Deferred tax liabilities:		
Goodwill and intangible assets	$ (451)	$ (458)
Property, plant and equipment	(380)	(380)
Other	(202)	(150)
	(1,033)	(988)
Deferred tax assets:		
Pension and other retiree benefits	599	541
Tax loss and tax credit carryforwards	34	30
Accrued liabilities	246	235
Stock-based compensation	127	123
Other	82	151
	1,088	1,080
Net deferred income taxes	$ 55	$ 92

Adjusted Equity = Colgate Shareholders Equity + Net Deferred tax + Non Controlling Interest + Accumulated Other comprehensive (income) loss

- Adjusted Equity (2016) = -$243 + $55 + $260 + $4,180 = $4,252 million

Colgate's Invested Capital (2016) = Debt (2016) + Adjusted Equity (2016)

- Colgate's Invested Capital (2016) = $6,533 million + $4,252 million = $10,785 million

Find WACC of Colgate

Indicate by check mark whether the registrant is a shell company (as defined in Rule 12b-2 of the Exchange Act). Yes ☐ No ☒

The aggregate market value of Colgate-Palmolive Company's Common Stock held by non-affiliates as of June 30, 2016 (the last business day of its most recently completed second quarter) was ap[illegible] billion.

There were 882,856,721 shares of Colgate-Palmolive Company Common Stock outstanding as of January 31, 2017.

We note from above that Colgate's number of shares = 882.85 million

Current Market Price of Colgate = $72.48 (as of closing 15th September, 2017)

Market value of equity of Colgate = 72.48 x 882.85 = $63,989 million

Liabilities and Shareholders' Equity		
Current Liabilities		
Notes and loans payable	$ 13	$ 4
Current portion of long-term debt	—	298
Accounts payable	1,124	1,110
Accrued income taxes	441	277
Other accruals	1,727	1,845
Total current liabilities	3,305	3,534
Long-term debt	6,520	6,246
Deferred income taxes	246	233

As we have earlier noted,

Total Debt = Notes and Loan Payable + Current Portion of Long-Term Debt + Long Term Debt

- Total Debt (2016) = $13 + $0 + $6,520 = $6,533 million

Let us now find the cost of equity of Colgate using CAPM model

- Ke = Rf + (Rm – Rf) x Beta

We note from below that the risk-free rate is 2.17%

Ten-Year Treasury Constant Maturity

By Bankrate.com

Treasury securities — Updated 9/13/2017

	This week	Month ago	Year ago
Ten-Year Treasury Constant Maturity	2.17	2.27	1.59

For the United States, Equity Risk Premium is 6.25%.

Uganda	Africa	B1	5.05%	13.32%
Ukraine	Eastern Europe & Russia	Caa3	11.21%	21.94%
United Arab Emirates	Middle East	Aa2	0.56%	7.03%
United Kingdom	Western Europe	Aa1	0.45%	6.88%
United States of America	North America	Aaa	0.00%	6.25%
Uruguay	Central and South America	Baa2	2.13%	9.23%
Venezuela	Central and South America	Caa3	11.21%	21.94%
Vietnam	Asia	B1	5.05%	13.32%
Zambia	Africa	B3	7.29%	16.46%

Let us look at the Beta of Colgate. We note that Colgate's Beta has increased over the years. It is currently 0.805

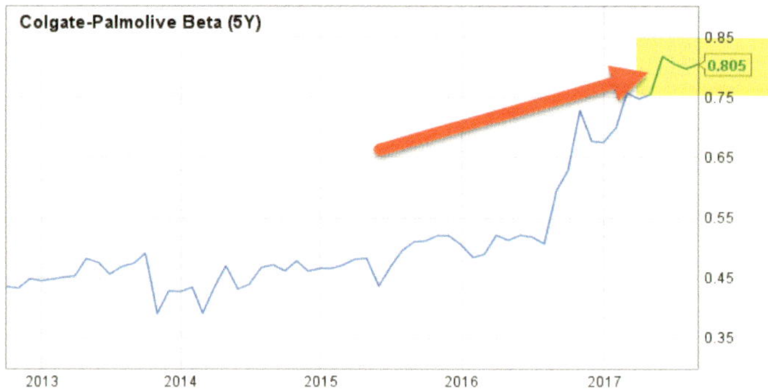

- Cost of Equity = 2.17% + 6.25% x 0.805
- Cost of Equity of Colgate = 7.2%

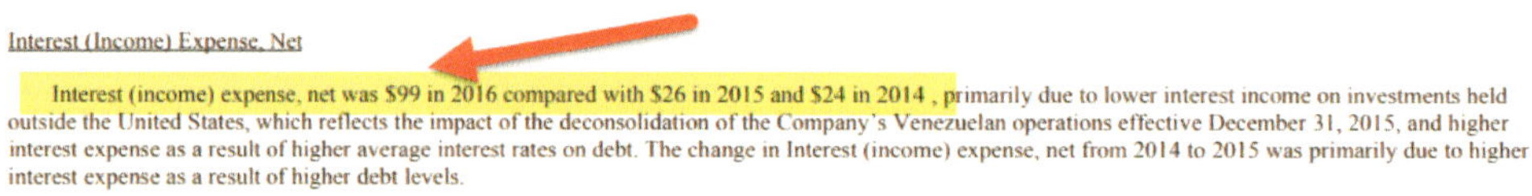
Interest (Income) Expense, Net

Interest (income) expense, net was $99 in 2016 compared with $26 in 2015 and $24 in 2014 , primarily due to lower interest income on investments held outside the United States, which reflects the impact of the deconsolidation of the Company's Venezuelan operations effective December 31, 2015, and higher interest expense as a result of higher average interest rates on debt. The change in Interest (income) expense, net from 2014 to 2015 was primarily due to higher interest expense as a result of higher debt levels.

- Interest Expense (2016) = $99
- Total Debt (2016) = $13 + $0 + $6,520 = $6,533 million
- Effective Interest Rate (2016) = $99/6533 = 1.52%

Let us now calculate WACC

- Market Value of Equity = $63,989 million
- Value of Debt = $6,533 million
- Cost of Equity = 7.20%
- Cost of Debt = 1.52%
- Tax rate = 30.82%

WACC = E/V * Ke + D/V * Kd * (1 – Tax Rate)

WACC = (63,989/(63,989+6,533)) x 7.20% + (6,533 /(63,989+6,533)) x 1.52% x (1-0.3082)

WACC = 6.63%

Colgate's Economic Value Added Eva Calculation

Economic Value Added formula= Net Operating Profit After Tax – (Capital Invested x WACC):

- Colgate's NOPAT (2016) = $4,065 million x (1-0.3082) = $2,812 million

- Colgate's Invested Capital (2016) = $6,533 million + $4,252 million = $10,785 million
- Economic Value Added (Colgate) = $2,812 million – $10,785 million x 6.63%
- Economic value added = $2097 million

Importance of Economic Value Added

The very basic objective of every business is to maximize the shareholder value. The investor is the key stakeholder around which all business activities are focused.

The key factors which are important while maximizing shareholder value are:

- Wealth maximization is more important as compared to profit maximization. There is a difference between the two. Wealth maximization aims to accelerate the worth of the organization as a whole. Maximizing profit can be said to be a subset of maximizing wealth. EVA focuses on wealth creation.
- Economic Value Added (EVA) takes into account the Weighted Average Cost of Capital. It goes with the logic that it is important to cover the cost of equity and not the just the interest portion of debt.
- Organizations tend to focus on profits and ignore the cash flow. This often leads to a liquidity crunch and can also lead to bankruptcy. Economic Value Added (EVA) focuses on cash flows more than profits.
- By taking the Weighted Average Cost of Capital, it takes into account both short-term as well as long-term perspectives.

Advantages and Disadvantages of using Economic Value Added (Eva)

Like any other financial ratio/indicator, even Economic Value Added (EVA) has its own sets of advantages and disadvantages. Let us have a look at the basic pointers for the same.

Advantages of using Economic Value Added (Eva)

- As discussed above, it helps to give a clear picture about wealth creation as compared to other financial measures used for analysis. It takes into account all costs including the opportunity cost of equity and it does not stick to accounting profits.
- It is comparatively simple to understand.
- EVA can also be calculated for different divisions, projects, etc. and the appropriate investment decisions can be taken for the same

- It also helps to develop a relationship between the use of capital and Net Operating Profit. This can be analyzed to make the most out of opportunities and also make appropriate improvements, wherever necessary.

Disadvantages of using Economic Value Added (Eva)

1. There are a lot of assumptions involved in calculating the Weighted Average Cost of Capital. It is not easy to calculate the cost of equity which is a key aspect of WACC. On account of this, there are chances that EVA itself can be perceived to be different for the same organization and for the same period as well. In the above Economic Value Added example, the cost of equity has changed from the year 2015 to the year 2016. This can be one of the major factors due to a decrease in EVA.
2. Apart from the WACC, there are other adjustments also which are required to the Net Operating Profit After Tax. All non-cash expenses need to be adjusted for. This becomes difficult in case of an organization with multiple business units and subsidiaries.
3. Comparative analysis is difficult with Economic Value Added (EVA) on account of the underlying assumptions of WACC.
4. EVA is calculated on historical data and future predictions are difficult.

Debtor Finance

Debtor financing is an umbrella term used that encompasses a number of products that finance invoices.

The most common debtor finance solutions are invoice factoring and invoice discounting.

Invoice factoring and discounting are used by companies that offer 30- to 60-day terms to customers but have problems waiting for payments. Debtor finance works by funding slow-paying invoices, which improves your cash flow and provides funds to pay for business expenses.

Most small businesses that sell products and services to large businesses have to offer net 30- to 60-day payment terms to their clients. In most cases, you must offer these terms to retain clients. Otherwise, clients could decide to work with a competitor who is willing to provide the payment terms they request.

However, offering payment terms has credit risks. It can also create cash flow problems, especially for small and mid-sized companies who don't have a cash reserve and can't afford to wait 30 to 60 days to get paid. In some cases, cash flow problems can be serious and prevent the small business from meeting obligations, such as paying suppliers or employee wages.

Debtor Financing Improves Cash Flow

Debtor finance is designed to fix cash flow problems created by slow-paying clients. By financing slow-paying invoices, debtor financing accelerates your revenues – improving your working capital and providing your company with funds to pay suppliers, wages or other expenses.

Working of Debtor Financing

Debtor financing works by financing your invoices – usually a company's strongest asset. The transaction structure varies based on the specific type of debtor finance solution that you decide to use.

Invoice Factoring

Invoice factoring finances invoices individually. The factoring company advances 80% – 85% of the invoice's value as soon as the invoice is submitted for financing. The factoring company advances the remaining 15% – 20%, less fees, once the customer pays the invoice in full. As part of their services, the factoring company also helps manage credit and collections.

Generally, invoice factoring works best for small companies who don't have established credit and collections departments. You can learn more by reading.

Invoice Discounting

Invoice discounting lines operate like revolving lines of financing. Instead of managing individual invoices, the client finances a batch of invoices. The client receives 80% – 85% of the total value of the invoices as available funds. The line is adjusted regularly as your customers pay their invoices and as your company raises new invoices.

Since the invoice discount company does not manage detailed invoice information, they do not handle credit and collections tasks. Instead, these tasks are managed by the client.

Generally, invoice discounting lines are better suited for larger companies that have established credit controls and collections procedures.

Benefits of Debtor Financing

A well-implemented financing programme can provide a number of benefits for small business owners. The most important benefit is that your cash flow improves, often quickly. This improvement provides financial stability, which is important for any business.

Your company will be able to extend payment terms to clients without worrying about potential cash flow problems. This capability can be important if you were not able (or willing) to extend terms in the past due to low cash reserves.

Lastly, the financing facility is flexible and is tied to your sales. The facility can increase as your sales grow. Debtor financing can be an ideal source of funding for small companies that are growing quickly.

Qualification

One advantage of using debtor financing is that it has simple qualification requirements, especially when compared to overdrafts, business loans and other products. Generally, your business must be well organized, have good customers and be free of major legal and tax problems.

Small businesses can usually qualify for this programme.

Costs

The cost of using the programme is determined by the size of the financing facility, the credit quality of the invoices, the industry of the client and general risk characteristics of the account. Rates vary, so you should consult a representative directly.

Days Sales Outstanding

Days sales outstanding (DSO) is a measure of the average number of days that it takes a company to collect payment after a sale has been made. DSO is often determined on a monthly, quarterly or annual basis, and can be calculated by dividing the amount of accounts receivable during a given period by the total value of credit sales during the same period, and multiplying the result by the number of days in the period measured.

The formula for calculating days sales outstanding can be represented with the following formula:

$$= \frac{\text{Accounts Receivable}}{\text{Total Credit Sales}} \times \text{Number of Days}$$

OR

$$= \left[\frac{\text{Accounts Receivable}}{\left(\frac{\text{Total Credit Sales}}{\text{Number of Days}} \right)} \right]$$

Days sales outstanding is an element of the cash conversion cycle, and is often referred to as days receivables or average collection period.

Due to the high importance of cash in running a business, it is in a company's best interest to collect on its outstanding account receivables as quickly as possible. While companies can most often expect with relative certainty that they will in fact receive outstanding receivables, because of the time value of money principle, money that a company spends time waiting to receive is money lost. By quickly turning sales into cash, a company has a chance to put the cash to use again more quickly.

A high DSO number shows that a company is selling its product to customers on credit and taking longer to collect money. This may lead to cash flow problems because of the long duration between the time of a sale and the time the company receives payment. A low DSO value means that it takes a company fewer days to collect its accounts receivable. In effect, the ability to determine the average length of time that a company's outstanding balances are carried in receivables can in some cases tell a great deal about the nature of the company's cash flow.

For example, suppose that during the month of July, Company A made a total of $500,000 in credit sales and had $350,000 in accounts receivable. There are 31 days in July, so Company A's DSO for July can be calculated as:

($350,000 / $500,000) x 31 = 0.7 x 31 = 21.7

With a DSO of 21.7, Company has a short average turnaround in converting its receivables into cash. Generally speaking, a DSO under 45 is considered low; however, what qualifies as a high or low DSO may often vary depending on business type and structure. For example, a DSO of 40 may still cause cash flow problems for a small or new business that has little available capital. Because of the lower earnings that often accompany small or new businesses, such businesses often seek to retrieve their accounts receivable quickly in order to cover startup costs, wages, overhead, and other expenses. On the other hand, a DSO of 60 may cause few issues for a large and well-established corporation with high available capital. Though the company could likely improve its earnings by reducing its DSO and, thereby, maximize its potential to reinvest earnings, it is unlikely that the company will need to trim salaries or cut other costs in order to make ends meet.

Generally, a high DSO can suggest a few things, including that the company's customer base has credit issues or that the company is deficient in its collection processes. Conversely, a very low DSO ratio may suggest that the company is too strict with regard to its credit policy, which could alienate customers and thus hurt sales as well.

It is important to remember that the formula for calculating DSO only accounts for credit sales. While cash sales may be considered to have a DSO of 0, they are not factored into DSO calculations because they represent no time between a sale and the company's receipt of payment. If they were factored into the calculation, they would decrease the DSO, and companies with a high proportion of cash sales would have lower DSOs than those with a high proportion of credit sales.

Uses of 'Days Sales Outstanding - DSO'

Days sales outstanding has a wide variety of applications. It can indicate the amount of sales a company has made during a specific time period; how quickly customers are paying; if the company's collections department is working well; if the company is maintaining customer satisfaction; or if credit is being given to customers that are not creditworthy.

While looking at an individual DSO value for a company can provide a good benchmark for quickly assessing a company's cash flow, trends in DSO are much more useful than an individual DSO value. If a company's DSO is increasing, it may indicate a few things. It may be that customers are taking more time to pay their expenses, suggesting either that customer satisfaction is declining, that salespeople within the company are offering longer terms of payment to drive increased sales, or that the company is allowing customers with poor credit to make purchases on credit. Additionally, too sharp of an increase in DSO can cause a company serious cash flow problems. If a company is accustomed to paying its expenses at a certain rate on the basis of consistent payments on its accounts receivable, a sharp rise in DSO can disrupt this flow and force the company to make drastic changes.

Generally, when looking at a given company's cash flow, it is helpful to track that company's DSO over time to determine if its DSO is trending in any particular direction or if there are any patterns in the company's cash flow history. DSO may often vary on a monthly basis, particularly if the company is affected by seasonality. If a company has a volatile DSO, this may be cause for concern, but if a company's DSO dips during a particular season each year, this is often less of a reason to worry.

Limitations of 'Days Sales Outstanding - DSO'

Like any metric attempting to gauge the efficiency of a business, days sales outstanding comes with a set of limitations that are important for any investor to consider before using it.

Most simply, when using DSO to compare the cash flows of multiple companies, one should compare companies within the same industry, ideally when they have similar business models and revenue numbers as well. As mentioned above, companies of different size often have very different capital structures, which can greatly influence DSO calculations, and the same is often true of companies in different industries.

DSO is not particularly useful in comparing companies with significant differences in the proportion of sales that are credit, as determining the DSO of a company with a low proportion of credit sales does not indicate much about that company's cash flow. Comparing such companies with those that have a high proportion of credit sales also does not usually indicate much of importance.

Furthermore, DSO is not a perfect indicator of a company's accounts receivable efficiency, as fluctuating sales volumes can affect DSO, with increase sales frequently lowering the DSO value. Delinquent Days Sales Outstanding (DDSO) is a good alternative for credit collection assessment for use alongside DSO. Like any metric measuring a company's performance, DSO should not be considered alone, but instead should be used with other metrics as well.

Day's Payable Outstanding

The days payable outstanding (DPO) is a financial ratio that calculates the average time it takes a company to pay its bills and invoices to other company and vendors by comparing accounts payable, cost of sales, and number of days bills remain unpaid.

In other words, DPO means the average number of days a company takes to pay invoices from suppliers and vendors. Typically, this ratio is measured on a quarterly or annual basis to judge how well the company's cash flow balances are being managed. For instance, a company that takes longer to pay its bills has access to its cash for a longer period and is able to do more things with it during that period.

For example, let's assume Company A purchases raw material, utilities, and services from its vendors on credit to manufacture a product. This credit or accounts payable isn't due for 30 days. This means that the company can use the resources from its vendor and keep its cash for 30 days. This cash could be used for other operations or an emergency during the 30-day payment period. DPO takes the average of all payables owed at a point in time and compares them with the average number of days they will need to be paid.

The importance of DPO becomes obvious. A company with a high DPO can deploy its cash for productive measures such as managing operations, producing more goods, or earning interest instead of paying its invoices upfront.

Let's take a look at the equation and how to calculate DPO.

Formula

The days payable outstanding formula is calculated by dividing the accounts payable by the derivation of cost of sales and the average number of days outstanding. Here's what the equation looks like:

Days Payable Outstanding (DPO)		
Days Payable Outstanding	=	Accounts Payable / (Cost of Sales / Number of days)

Days Payable Outstanding = [Accounts Payable / (Cost of Sales / Number of days)]

The DPO calculation consists of two three different terms.

Accounts Payable – this is the amount of money that a company owes a vendor or supplier for a purchase that was made on credit. This total number can be found on the balance sheet.

Cost of Sales – this is the total cost incurred by the company in manufacturing the product or bringing the product to a level at which it can be sold to the customer. It includes all direct costs such as raw material, utilities, transportation cost, and rent directly applicable to manufacturing. This can be found on the income statement of a company.

Number of days – this is the actual number of days that the account payable and cost of sales in based (for example 365 days).

Let's take a look at a DPO example.

Example

Ted owns a clothing manufacturer that purchases materials from several vendors. At the end of the year, his accounts payable on the balance sheet was $1,000,000. On average, he paid $15,000 ($5,475,000 / 365 days) of invoices each day. Ted would calculate his DPO like this:

Days Payable Outstanding (DPO)		
67 Days	=	$1,000,000 / ($5,475,000 / 365 Days)

This means that Ted pays his invoices 67 days after receiving them on average.

Now let's make the example a little more complicated and include money that Ted will collect from customers. Here are some terms from his latest purchases from vendors and sales to customers.

- Accounts Payable: $100
- Due date of A/P: 10 days
- Accounts receivable from sales to customers: $100

- Due date of A/R: 5 days

In the above, over simplified example, we are assuming that Ted has to pay $100 in 10 days to his vendors and he will receive $100 from his customers in 5 days. So the net impact of these transactions will be that the company can hold on to $100 for 5 days. Hypothetically, if the interest rate is 1 percent, then in 5 days the company can earn $1 (1% of $100 in 5 days) without even charging a margin to its customers (remember the company bought goods for $100 and sold the finished product for the same price).

There are several factors at play which define the level of DPO, primary among them are:

1) Type of industry
2) Competitive positioning of a company – A market leader with significant purchasing power can negotiate favorable terms with its supplier so as to have a very high DPO.
3) Competitiveness – if there are many suppliers with little differentiation than they will have to offer longer payment cycle to gain business from a client.

Ultimately, the DPO may depend on the contract between the vendor and the company. The vendor might offer discounts for early payment. In that case, the company will have to weigh the option of holding on the cash versus availing the discount.

Let's look at a Real World Example

Consider the case of Wal-Mart and Tesco. These retail giants have significant market clout, which allows them to negotiate better deals with their suppliers and pay as late as possible. In the case of Wal-Mart the DPO has hovered around 38- 39 days for last 3-4 years, implying that Wal-Mart might be typically paying its suppliers after more than a month of sourcing the products from them. On the other hand, Tesco has a DPO of ~60 days, implying two month lag in payment to suppliers. Days Payable Outstanding (unit – number of days)

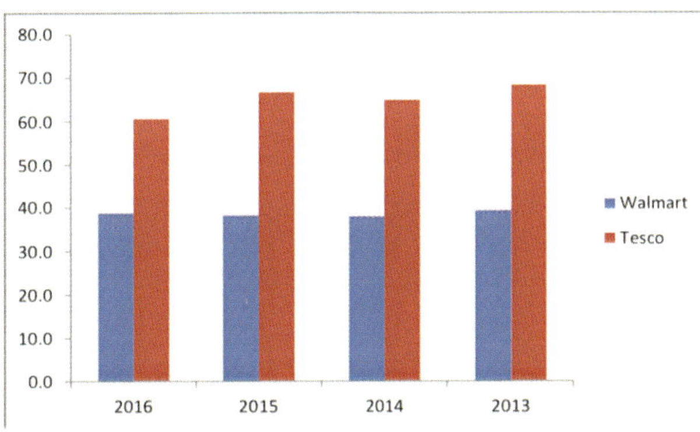

Analysis and Interpretation

DPO is an important financial ratio that investors look at to gauge the operational efficiency of a company. A higher DPO means that the company is taking longer to pay its vendors and suppliers than a company with a smaller DPO. Companies with high DPOs have advantages because they are more liquid than companies with smaller DPOs and can use their cash for short-term investments.

A high ratio also has disadvantages. Vendors and suppliers might get mad that they aren't being paid early and refuse to do business with the company or refuse to give discounts. Days payable outstanding walks the line between improving company cash flow and keeping vendors happy.

It's important to always compare a company's DPO to other companies in the same industry to see if that company is paying its invoices too quickly or too slowly. If a company is paying invoices in 20 days and the industry is paying them in 45 days, the company is at a disadvantage because it's not able to use its cash as long as the other companies in its industry. It may want to lengthen its payment periods to improve its cash flow as long as this doesn't mean losing an early payment discount or hurting a vendor relationship.

Talking about Wal-Mart, it has a DPO of 39 days, while the industry average is for example 30 days. This might imply that Wal-Mart has been able to negotiate better terms with the suppliers compared to the broader industry. We need to be careful while selecting the peers for comparison. DPO can be impacted by product mix (for example Amazon might have very high DPO because of its historical business of books which tend to have longer payment cycle).

Investors also compare the current DPO with the company's own historical range. A consistent decline in DPO might signal towards changing product mix, increased competition, or reduction in purchasing power of a company. For example, Wal-Mart has historically had DPO as high as 44-46 days, but with the increase in competition (especially from the online retails) it has been forced to ease the terms with its suppliers.

Usage Explanations and Cautions

A company has to maintain the delicate balance of improving DPO and not pushing its supplier too much to spoil the relationship completely. A company can employ several techniques to improve DPO, few of them are

1) Identify products with shortest DPO and formulating ways to improve the DPO of that product either by re-negotiating with the supplier or changing suppliers

2) Change product mix

3) Internal restructuring of the operations team to improve the efficiency of payable processing.

In conclusion, Days Payable Outstanding (DPO) is a key metric to analyze the operational efficiency of a company and can act as an important source of generating extra returns for the investors, but it should always be viewed relative to the industry and product mix. For example, just because one company has a higher ratio than another company doesn't mean that company is running more efficiently. The lower company might be getting more favorable early pay discounts than the other company and thus they always pay their bills early.

It's important to keep all of these things in mind when analyzing the days outstanding payable ratio.

References

- Working-capital-formula, modeling, knowledge: corporatefinanceinstitute.com, Retrieved 19 June 2018
- What-are-current-assets-formula: fitsmallbusiness.com, Retrieved 25 April 2018
- Current-liabilities, financial: accountingexplained.com, Retrieved 27 March 2018
- What-is-debtor-financing: au.comcapfactoring.com, Retrieved 20 March 2018
- Days-payable-outstanding-dpo, financial-ratios: myaccountingcourse.com, Retrieved 17 April 2018

Permissions

All chapters in this book are published with permission under the Creative Commons Attribution Share Alike License or equivalent. Every chapter published in this book has been scrutinized by our experts. Their significance has been extensively debated. The topics covered herein carry significant information for a comprehensive understanding. They may even be implemented as practical applications or may be referred to as a beginning point for further studies.

We would like to thank the editorial team for lending their expertise to make the book truly unique. They have played a crucial role in the development of this book. Without their invaluable contributions this book wouldn't have been possible. They have made vital efforts to compile up to date information on the varied aspects of this subject to make this book a valuable addition to the collection of many professionals and students.

This book was conceptualized with the vision of imparting up-to-date and integrated information in this field. To ensure the same, a matchless editorial board was set up. Every individual on the board went through rigorous rounds of assessment to prove their worth. After which they invested a large part of their time researching and compiling the most relevant data for our readers.

The editorial board has been involved in producing this book since its inception. They have spent rigorous hours researching and exploring the diverse topics which have resulted in the successful publishing of this book. They have passed on their knowledge of decades through this book. To expedite this challenging task, the publisher supported the team at every step. A small team of assistant editors was also appointed to further simplify the editing procedure and attain best results for the readers.

Apart from the editorial board, the designing team has also invested a significant amount of their time in understanding the subject and creating the most relevant covers. They scrutinized every image to scout for the most suitable representation of the subject and create an appropriate cover for the book.

The publishing team has been an ardent support to the editorial, designing and production team. Their endless efforts to recruit the best for this project, has resulted in the accomplishment of this book. They are a veteran in the field of academics and their pool of knowledge is as vast as their experience in printing. Their expertise and guidance has proved useful at every step. Their uncompromising quality standards have made this book an exceptional effort. Their encouragement from time to time has been an inspiration for everyone.

The publisher and the editorial board hope that this book will prove to be a valuable piece of knowledge for students, practitioners and scholars across the globe.

Index